A CONSTITUTIONAL HISTORY OF INDIA

A CONSTITUTIONAL HISTORY OF INDIA

Dr. Archna Chaturvedi

Commonwealth

A Constitutional History of India

Edition : 2018

ISBN 81-7169-978-2

Published by :

COMMONWEALTH PUBLISHERS
4831/24, Prahlad Street,
Ansari Road, Darya Ganj,
New Delhi - 110002
Ph. : 23275511, 23257835
e-mail : commonwealthbooks@gmail.com

Typesetting by :

Rishu Computers
Delhi - 110051

Printed at :
Roshan Offset Printers
Delhi

PREFACE

This book gives you the story of constitution of India in an interesting and highly thought provoking manner. It has for you letters, treaties, private correspondence, administrative reports and speeches of the authorities who made the constitutional history of India, covering the period from 1600 to 1950. Detailed notes and references of the documents provide scope and material for micro studies on various aspects of political history of India and south Asia.

We take this opportunity to record our acknowledgements to the authorities on the subject.

Librarian and their staff members have rendered us all possible co-operation and help. We are grateful to them all.

Co-operation and encouragement of my publisher and his staffmembers and their hardwork deserves the love and patronage of my readers.

Dr. Archna Chaturvedi

Contents

1

The Rule under the Company

The East India Company

The origins of the Constitution of the Indian Republic are rooted in the history of India under the British. That history began with the incorporation in England of the East India Company in 1600, although the British did not become a ruling power of India until the second half of the eighteenth century. The story of the Company, from a commercial concern to the establishment of a vast empire, reads more like romance than history. Its beginning was marked by the acquisition of territories, erection of forts and employment of troops for defensive purposes. Then came the downfall by the end of the seventeenth century of the Mughal Empire, which had been the major unifying force in the country, and the consequent disintegration of a centralized administration and the rise of innumerable local rulers fighting among themselves. Here was the opportunity for the Company to enter the political arena of India. The victory of the Company's forces in the battle of Plassey in 1757 against Siraj-ud-Doula, the Nawab of Bengal, laid the foundation of the vast British Indian Empire.

The transformation of the Company from a commercial concern into a territorial power had important consequences.[1] It disclosed the inherent incapacity of a trading body to assume the responsibility for the administration of a vast country.[2] Cornewall Lewis a member of the House of Commons, declared in the debate held in Parliament on the Bill that finally transferred the Government of India from the Company to the Crown, that no civilized government existed on this earth which was more corrupt, more perfidious and more rapacious than the Government of the East India Company from 1765—84.

The British Parliament passed the Regulating Act, 1773, the first major measure calculated to remove the evils inherent in the constitution of the Company in England and to improve the tone of its administration in India through Parliamentary control.

The Regulating Act, 1773

In England the two institutions which determined and looked after the entire operation of the Company were the Court of Proprietors and the Court of Directors. Any shareholder who held shares worth five hundred pounds was entitled to have a vote in the former body while one who held shares worth a hundred pounds was eligible to be elected to the latter body. There were twenty-four Directors on the Court. Although the salary of a Director was only three hundred pounds a year, the post had great attractions on account of the opportunity that it provided for nepotism. Many Director's easily found lucrative jobs in India for their sons and relations. Hence there was a scramble to purchase enough shares to get oneself elected to the Court of Directors. Votes in the Court of Proprietors were manipulated so as to shield the evil deeds of servants of the Company in India. It became the ambition of many servants when they returned home to get into the Court of Directors by making use of the ill-gotten gains they had acquired in India. Hence there arose the evil of 'trafficking in votes'. The Regulating Act tried to mitigate this evil by raising the qualification for Proprietor to one thousand pounds and a Director to two thousand pounds. It also extended the period for which the Directors were elected. Further, it provided that instead of the whole body being re-elected at one time, one-fourth of the membership of the Court of Directors should be renewed annually.

Besides, to deal specifically with evils of the Company's administration in India, the Act provided the following five remedial measures :

(a) A new executive for the Government of the Presidency of Bengal.

(b) A new relationship between the Presidency of Bengal and those of Madras and Bombay.

(c) Reforms for the Civil Service.

(d) Setting up of a Supreme Court at Calcutta.

(e) A new procedure for the making of Regulations.

The most serious defect in the Government of Bengal was the inability of its executive to check and correct the actions of the servants of the Company. The Act sought to remedy this by vesting in a Governor-General and four Councillors the civil and military government of Bengal, Bihar and Orissa. They were to hold office for five years and were not removable in the meantime except by the King on the representation of the Court of Directors. The importance of this provision lay in the fact that Parliament sought to control the actions of the Governors by imposing upon them Councils consisting of men specially sent out from England and who were not servants of the Company. The Council was to take all its decisions by a majority. The Governor-General had a casting vote in case of an equality of votes. The decision of the Council was binding upon him.

One of the anomalies in the working of the Company's administration in India prior to 1773 was that the three Presidencies, Bengal, Bombay and Madras, were independent of each other. Each was responsible only to the Court of Directors in England. As a result, there was no effective co-ordination of the activities of the three Presidencies. In fact, their policies at times even collided with each other. The Act attempted to remedy this by establishing the supremacy of the Bengal Presidency over the other two by authorizing it exclusively to deal with matters of war and peace.

Prior to the Act, the salaries of the Company's servants, the civil and military alike, were almost nominal. Naturally, few resisted the temptation of enhancing their incomes through illegal and immoral means such as bribes, presents, private trade and usurious money-lending practices. The Act prohibited these evil practices and imposed on offenders such penalties as fine, imprisonment or deportation to England for trial. Further, it provided for the payment of liberal salaries for the higher classes of the Company's servants.

The only important Court that existed in Calcutta before 1773 was the Mayor's Court. Appeals against this Court lay first to the

President and Council at Calcutta and finally in the King-in-Council in England. The basic defect of this system was that there was no separate and independent judicial check over the actions of the executive. To remedy this unwholesome situation, the Act sought to establish by a Royal Charter an independent judicial tribunal, the Supreme Court, with a Chief Judge and three Puisne Judges. The Court was to exercise civil, criminal, admiralty and ecclesiastical jurisdiction. An appeal against the Court's decision was to be to the King-in Council in England.

The last of the important measures contemplated by the Act was the provision for the making of Regulations. According to this, the Governor-General in Council was to have the power to make Regulations for the good order and civil government of the possessions of the Company. The Regulations so framed were required to be registered the published in the Supreme Court with the assent of the Court. They could be set aside only by the King-in-Council.

The foregoing analysis will indicate that the objective of the Regulating Act was to remove from the Company the political power that it had in India and transfer it to Parliament—although this was not fully achieved by the Act—leaving to the Court of Directors only the external pageant of a large establishment. In its effect the Act has been compared, in its relation to the Act of 1858 which finally brought about the complete transfer of power from the Company to the Crown, with the earliest traction engine in its relation to the latest model of a locomotive. A close study of the Act will show that it relied considerably on the theory of separation of powers which was so popular in Europe at that time. Thus, the regulations made by the Governor-General in Council were required to be registered in the independent Supreme Court, which in its turn was to be a check upon the servants of the Company. Unfortunately, this system of checks and balances when put into effect did not work properly, thus proving the inherent defects of the Act itself.

The Act in operation showed three main defects. First, the working of the Governor-General in Council was most inefficient. The rule of making decisions by a majority in the Council was found to operate against the will of the Governor-General as three of the four members were usually united against him. As a result, during the first two years of his Governor-Generalship, Warren Hastings was rendered absolutely powerless. Only when death removed one of the rival members from the scene could he establish his authority by getting a majority of the Council on his side. Thus the Governor-General's position was very weak both in Bengal and in regard to the control he was expected to exercise over the other two Presidencies.

Secondly, the Act was vague about the extent of the control to be exercised by the Governor-General over the subordinate Presidencies and, by any interpretation, the control envisaged was not extensive. This was proved by later events, notably by the Maratha and the Mysore wars initiated by the Bombay and Madras authorities respectively and to which Hastings was opposed.

Thirdly, the Act had not defined the relationship between the Supreme Court and the courts of the Company, the civil and criminal courts in the Districts over which the Governor-General in Council had appellate powers. The Supreme Court claimed as a right its jurisdiction to hear appeals from the Governor-General in Council on the ground that it was constituted by a Royal Charter. The Court also claimed jurisdiction upon the entire native population and not merely on the 'British subjects' of the Company. Naturally, conflict between the Court and the Governor-General in Council was inevitable and this proved to be the worst defect of the Act. Moreover, the Supreme Court was not popular with the native population. The English lawyers struck the greatest fear among the local people and the rule of the Supreme Court, in the words of Macaulay, proved a reign of terror. The Court was charged with stopping the wheels of Government by technicalities of English law and of effecting a total dissolution of the social order.

The disastrous working of the Regulating Act, in effect, convinced the British Parliament that the endeavour to subject the Company's Government in India to direct parliamentary control was a complete failure. Nevertheless, the Regulating Act marks an important stage, by fixing the location of the administrative centre of gravity definitely at Calcutta with the Governor-General as its acknowledged head and deriving his authority from an Act of the British Parliament. From the point of view of the people of India, the most important provision of the Act was that which required every officer to submit to the Board of Directors on his return to England, a list of properties acquired by him, with an explanation of how they were acquired. It was a commendable attempt to secure purity of administration. But in reality, it failed to achieve the desired result.

Pitt's India Act, 1784

The measures introduced by the Regulating Act were not working satisfactorily. Reports of the many misdeeds of the Company's Government in India reached England and the matter was raised in Parliament and heated debates ensued. Prompt enquiry was demanded and, as a result, Parliament appointed two committees, one of which was presided over by Edmund Burke. The findings of the committees went against the Governor-General and the Chief Justice and their recall was recommended. But the Court of Proprietors refused to recall Warren Hastings who, in their opinion, was doing a wonderful job in India. This indeed amounted to a constitutional crisis, for it demonstrated the unreality of parliamentary control over the Company's political affairs.

To remedy this unwholesome situation, the coalition cabinet of Lord North and Charles Fox, which was then in power, brought forth a Bill with far-reaching provisions. It sought to distinguish sharply between the commercial and political functions of the Company, and to place the latter under the complete control of the Crown. The Bill was passed by the House of Lords but, as the House of Commons did not accept it, the Ministry itself had to resign.

Pitt the Younger who formed the next Cabinet introduced a new Bill which was carefully drafted in order not to antagonize the Court of Directors. The Bill was passed and received royal assent in 1784 and became known as Pitt's India Act. According to the Act, the Court of Directors were allowed to manage the commercial affairs of the Company as they liked. But with respect to its political affairs, a Board of six Commissioners, popularly known as the Board of Control, was appointed to control such affairs. The Board had on it the Chancellor of the Exchequer, a Secretary of State and four Privy Councillors. They were all appointed by the King and were to hold office during his pleasure.

The Board, as its composition itself would indicate, was a powerful body and had full powers of 'superintendence, direction and control' of all operations of the civil and military government of the British territorial possessions in the East Indies.

The Act had reduced the powers of the Court of Proprietors to the receipt of dividends and the election of Directors who, however, retained their right to make appointments in India. But the Crown had the power to recall any of the Company's servants.

The changes which the Act brought about in India were few and comparatively unimportant. The membership of the Councils of the Governor-General and the Governors was reduced to three and the Commander-in-Chief was made a member. The power of the Governor-General in Council over the subordinate Presidencies was extended to include the application of the revenues of the Presidencies. Finally, the Act enunciated a new principle in the Company's relations with the Indian Princes, namely, a policy of non-intervention so as to avoid all wars and conquests.

Territorial Expansion

The principle of non-intervention, however, was a short-lived one Lord Cornwallis, who succeeded Hastings as Governor-General indeed did make an attempt to practise it. But he could not succeed. The territorial ambitions of Tipu Sultan of Mysore compelled Cornwallis to enter into a Triple Alliance of the English, the Nizam and the Marathas, wage a war with Tipu, defeat him and force him to part with half of his dominions. As a result, the Company extended its sway over Malabar, Coorg, Dindigual, Baramahal and the command of the passes through which the Sultan of Mysore used to descend upon Madras.

Cornwallis was succeeded by Lord Wellesley who was convinced that if the English were to stay in India, it could not be on the basis of their being one among the many Indian powers contending for supremacy, but of their being the paramount power in India. As a result of the pursuit of this new policy, the British Empire in India was, under Wellesley's direction, transformed into the British Empire of India. The device that he employed for this purpose was a system of subsidiary alliances with Indian rulers. According to this, a Prince who came under the system had to *(i)* leave all his disputes with his neighbours to the arbitration of the English, *(ii)* stop all dealings with other European powers, *(iii)* allow for his security, the stationing within his territory of a British subsidiary force, and *(iv)* cede territory to the Company to cover the maintenance of the subsidiary force, or in the alternative, pay a specified amount annually for the same purpose. The Nizam of Hyderabad was one of the first to come under the system. Others followed suit. Those who did not come in voluntarily were forced to. Wellesley had already exterminated Tipu. He next turned to the Marathas who were not willing to accept the Subsidiary Alliance System. In a series of battles he defeated the divided Maratha rulers and brought them under his control. Wellesley's significant contribution to the British Indian Empire has been summed up by Sir Alfred Lyall in the following words:

By occupying the Imperial cities of Delhi and Agra with the contiguous tracts on both sides of the Jamuna, and by annexing the whole country between the Ganges and the Jamuna rivers, he carried forward British territory from Bengal north-westward to the mountains with a frontier resting upon the upper course of the Jamuna; and by his acquisitions of the Cuttack Province he secured the continuity of the British territory southeastward along the sea-coasts, joined the two Presidencies of Bengal and Madras and established sure communications between them.[3]

Wellesley's costly wars, however, alarmed the Court of Directors of the Company who recalled him and appointed in his place, once again, Lord Cornwallis. But Cornwallis died soon after his arrival in India. Sir George Barlow was his successor. Neither he nor his successor Lord Minto followed an expansionist policy. But Lord Hastings who succeeded Minto proved to be a follower of Wellesley. He proceeded upon the principle that the British power had become the suzerain power in India. On the basis of this principle the foreign relations of the Indian Princes came under the surveillance of the paramount power which also made itself responsible for their military protection. Further, there was considerable extension of the territory that was under the Company's direct rule.[4]

Lord William Bentick who succeeded Hastings was a person imbued with pacific motives. Nevertheless, he could not avoid reaping the fruits of Wellesley's Subsidiary System. The Nizam of Hyderabad, on account of arrears in the payment for the subsidiary force, had to cede Berar to the English. Mysore and Coorg were taken over to avoid 'maladministration and internal strife'. Thus a number of Native States, big and small, were brought under the direct rule of the Company during Bentick's Governor-Generalship.

The process of expansion continued in the periods of Lord Minto and Lord Auckland.[5] As a result, the scope of Anglo-Indian diplomacy was extended even beyond the western frontiers of India and embraced all West Asia. Lord Dalhousie enacted the grand finale of this fascinating drama of territorial expansion by annexing the whole of the Punjab and Lower Burma through conquest, and a number of native States in central and northern India through the application of the Doctrine of Lapse.[6] In addition to annexation by conquest and lapse, Dalhousie added Oudh to British India in 1856 on the ground that protracted misgovernment prevailed in the State. Thus, the transformation of the East India Company from a commercial concern to a territorial power, which began with Clive in 1757 and extended over a period of a century, culminated under Canning, the successor of Dalhousie, in the establishment of a mighty British Empire, unrivalled in authority and unparalleled in history, embracing the entire Indian subcontinent.[7]

Side by side with the territorial expansion of the Company's possessions in India there was also increasing parliamentary control over its affairs. The periodic renewal of the Company's Charter gave Parliament the opportunity to hold enquiries into its affairs. These provided the basis for altering, modifying, or even abrogating its privileges. There are at least five such important occasions when Parliament expressed its will through definite enactments extending its control over the Company. The first of these was in 1786.

The Act of 1786

The Act was very short and yet very significant. It was passed chiefly at the instance of Lord Cornwallis who succeeded Warren Hastings. According to it, the Governor-General was empowered to override the majority of his Council on his own responsibility. It thus removed a serious defect of the Regulating Act and made the Governor-General's position more authoritative.

Charter Act of 1793

The Act made no important change to the position then existing. It affirmed that the territorial possessions and the exclusive privileges of trade enjoyed by the Company would continue for a further period of twenty years. It also provided for the payment of the salaries of the members and staff of the Board of Control out of Indian revenues.

The Charter Act of 1813

This Act was preceded by a searching enquiry conducted by a Committee of the House of Commons into the financial affairs of the Company. The Report of the Committee, in the words of Ilbert, was a standard authority on Indian land tenures, and the best authority on the judicial and police arrangement of the time.[8] Although the Act renewed the Charter for a further period of twenty years, it took away the exclusive privilege of the Company to trade in India. The Indian trade was thrown open to all British subjects except in tea in which the Company was allowed to retain a monopoly. The Act also provided for the maintenance of separate accounts for commercial and political activities by the Company. It confirmed the patronage of the Court of Directors subject to the approval of the Crown in the case of higher appointments and of the Board of Control in the case of certain others. It also limited the number of British troops the Company was allowed to maintain in India at its own expense. Finally, it allowed British subjects to go out to India either as traders or as missionaries and also to settle down there under a system of licences.

The Charter Act of 1833

Of all the Acts passed by the British Parliament to regulate the affairs of the East India Company, the Charter Act of 1833 stands out as the most comprehensive and far-reaching in effect. According to Lord Morley, it was 'certainly the most extensive measure of Indian Government between Mr. Pitt's famous Act of 1784 and Queen Victoria's assumption of the Government of India.'

There were circumstances both in India and England which necessitated the passing of the Act. In India, the policy of intervention and territorial aggrandizement pursued by Wellesley and Hastings added enormously to the territories of the Company and to consequent difficulties in administration. In England, parliamentary reforms had brought into being a reformed House of Commons where liberalism was on the ascendancy. Further, there was a clamour for freedom of trade with India, unrestricted immigration of Europeans into India, reform of Indian laws and improvement in the state of education prevailing in India. It is also important to mention the influence, among others, of two liberals who were intimately associated with the Company's headquarters in England at the time. These were Macaulay and James Mill. The former who was then in Parliament was Secretary to the Board of Control, and the latter was Examiner of India Correspondence at India House.

As a result of the Act, the last traces of the commercial monopoly which the Company enjoyed were abolished and all restrictions to European immigration into India were removed. The unhindered flow of Europeans into India made the reform of Indian law imperative. But the powers exercised by the Governor-General in Council were not sufficient to meet the situation. The Council's Regulations could have no jurisdiction over the Supreme Court. The only remedy was, therefore, to increase and extend the Council's powers. Accordingly, the Governor-General in Council was empowered by the Act 'to make laws and regulations for all persons and for all Courts' in British India. Such laws were not to be registered with the Supreme Court, but automatically became Acts of the Governor-General in Council. Further, a Law Commission was appointed on the recommendation of Macaulay, for 'the codification of the laws' which were already in existence. The three great principles which were to govern such codification, according to Macaulay, were 'Uniformity where you can have it, diversity where you must have it, but in all cases certainty'. To facilitate the law-making functions of the Governor-General in Council, a Law Member, an English Barrister, was added to the Council. It was also provided that the Council's powers of law-making would override the authority of the Governors of Madras and Bombay who were at the same time deprived of their independent powers of law-making. Macaulay was the first Law Member under the Act and was also appointed the President of the Law Commission. Finally, under the Act, a new presidency was created, the Presidency of Agra.

While the Regulating Act had initiated a process of centralization by creating the office of the Governor-General, the Act of 1833 marked the culmination of that process by establishing the complete mastery of the Governor-General in Council over the entire British Indian administration. From 1833 to 1861 when the Indian Councils Act was passed, British India was in the grip of this highly centralized system of administration which had its impact on the character of the British Government in India until its disappearance in 1947. The salient features of this system of government will be discussed in some detail latter. We may here continue the general survey of parliamentary enactments.

The Charter Act of 1853

The most significant provision of the Act of 1853 was that it did not renew the Charter for a specified period. Instead, it said that the Indian territories would remain under the government of the Company, 'in trust for the Crown, until Parliament should otherwise direct.' The Act reduced the number of Directors to eighteen from twenty-four and provided that six of them should be appointed by the Crown. It authorized the appointment of a Lieutenant-Governor for Bengal. It also provided for the enlargement of the Executive Council of the Governor-General to cope with its extended functions in law-making. Finally, it took away the patronage of appointments from the Court of Directors, and the Civil Service of India was thrown open to competition. A year later, by a new enactment, the Act of 1854, Parliament provided for the appointment of Chief Commissioners to head minor provinces in India.

The Act of 1858

The Indian Revolution of 1857, the first attempt to overthrow British rule in India after it was firmly established, gave the death blow to the old system. The Revolution touched off a new discussion on India in the House of Commons resulting in the adoption of certain Resolutions embodying the principles which should form the basis of a new policy. A Bill was introduced on this basis which finally became 'The Act for the Good Government of India' of 1858.

The Act in no substantial way altered the system of government that prevailed in India but confined itself to the improvement of the machinery by which the Indian Government was to be superintended and controlled in England.

The Act abolished the Court of Directors and the Board of Control altogether. It transferred the government, territories and revenues of India from the Company to the Crown. Further, it declared that India was to be governed by and in the name of the English Sovereign and authorized the appointment of an additional principal Secretary of State (for India) and created the Council of India.

Queen Victoria's proclamation of 1858 which brought the East India Company's century-old rule to an end said among other things:

1. Now, therefore, we. . . have taken upon ourselves the said Government.
2. We appoint him, Viscount Canning, to be our First Viceroy and Governor-General in and over our said territories, and to administer the government thereof in our name, and generally to act in our name and on our behalf, subject to such orders and regulations as he shall, from time to time, receive through one of our Principal Secretaries of State.
3. We hereby announce to the native princes of India, that all treaties and engagement made with them by or under the authority of the East India Company are by us accepted and will be scrupulously maintained, and we look for the like observance on their part.
4. We desire no extension of our present territorial possessions; and while we will permit no aggression upon our dominions or our rights to be attempted with impunity, we shall sanction no encroachment of those of others.
5. We shall respect the rights, dignity and honour of native princes as our own; and we desire that they, as well as our subjects, should enjoy that prosperity and that social advancement which can only be secured by internal peace and good government.
6. We hold ourselves bound to the natives of our Indian

territories by the same obligations of duty which bind us to all our other subjects, and those obligations, by the blessing of Almighty God, we shall faithfully and conscientiously fill.

7. We disclaim alike the right and the desire to impose our convictions (religious) on any of our subjects. We declare it to be our royal will and pleasure that none be in anywise favoured, none molested or disquieted by reason of their religious faith or observances, but that all shall alike enjoy the equal and impartial protection of the law and we do strictly charge and enjoin all those who may be in authority under us that they abstain from all interference with the religious belief or worship of any of our subjects on pain of our highest displeasure.

8. And it is our further will that, so far as may be, our subjects, of whatever race of creed, be freely and impartially admitted to office in our service, the duties of which they may be qualified by their education, ability and integrity duly to discharge.

9. We know and respect the feelings of attachment with which the natives of India regard the lands inherited by them from their ancestors and we desire to protect them in all rights connected therewith, subject to the equitable demands of the State; and we will that generally, in framing and administering the law, due regard be paid to the ancient rights and customs of India.

10. When, by the blessing of Providence, internal tranquility shall be restored, it is our earnest desire to stimulate the peaceful industry of India, to promote works of public utility and improvement, and to administer the Government for the benefit of all our subjects resident therein. *In their prosperity will be our strength, in their contentment our security, and in their gratitude our best reward. . .*[9]

NOTES

1. A comprehensive survey of the Company's government in India may be seen in D.N. Banerjee, *Early Administrative System of the East India Company in Bengal, 1943.*

2. There seemed a danger not only that misgovernment in India might tarnish the name of Great Britain as an Imperial State, but that the Indian interests in England, supported by huge revenues and corrupt Parliamentary influence, might gain a preponderating and improper power in home affairs.' *The Cambridge History of India*, vol. v, p. 183. See also Thompson and Garratt, *British Rule in India*, pp. 128-31.

3. Sir Alfred Lyall, Expansion of British Dominion in India, p. 231.

4. For example, as a result of the war with Nepal, 'all the hilly country that overhangs Rohilkhand, Agra and Oudh was annexed and the British frontier pushed northward till it touched Tibet, Ibid. p. 263.

5. Napoleon's treaty of friendship with the Czar of Russia in 1807 revised his plans to conquer India by leading an army through West Asia against India. This made Lord Minto send special missions to the rulers of West Asian States like Persia and Afghanistan.

6. Dalhousie himself defined the doctrine as follows:

   'I take occasion of recording my strong and deliberate opinion that in the exercise of wise and sound policy, the British Government is bound not to put aside or neglect such rightful opportunities of acquiring territory or revenue, as may from time to time present themselves, whether they arise from the lapse of subordinate States, by the failure of all the heirs natural, where the succession can be sustained only by the sanction of the Government being given to the ceremony of adoption according to Hindu Law.' The States that fell victim to this policy were Satara, Sambalpur, Jhansi and Nagpur.

7. Writing about the relationship of the British with the Indian States, Sir William Lee-Warner marks out three distinctly different periods: *(i)* the period of 'ring-fence' extending to 1813 when the Company refused to afford protection to native States lying beyond a certain limit; *(ii)* that of 'subordinate isolation' which, lasted till 1857 when Lord Hastings broke down the 'ring-fence' and filled the map of India with 'protected' States; and *(iii)* of 'subordinate union' from 1858 under which the Queen of England guaranteed to the then existing States protection under the Crown as well as territorial integrity. See B. G. Sapre, *The Growth of Indian Constitution and Administration, 1929*, p. 73.

8. Sir L. C. Ilbert, *The Government of India*, p. 73.

9. Emphasis ours.

2

Growth of the London Company

The English desire to trade with India and the Far East was due to the necessity of getting spices which made their food-stuffs palatable. Formerly, the English used to get those spices from the Dutch, but the latter started charging abnormally high rates. Consequently, on 22nd September, 1599, a resolution was passed under the chairmanship of Lord Mayor to form an English association to trade directly with India. On 31st December, 1600, Queen Elizabeth granted a Charter to the Governor and Company of merchants of London trading into the East Indies.

The Charter authorised the London Company to traffic and trade freely "into and from the East Indies, in the countries, and parts of Asia and Africa, and into and from all Islands, ports, havens, cities, creeks, towns and places of Asia and Africa and America, or any of them beyond the Cape of Bona Esperanza to the Streigts of Magellan." The Charter was given for 15 years and could be ended by giving a notice of two years. However, in 1609, James I renewed the Company's Charter "for ever", though with a proviso that it might be revoked by giving a notice of three years if it was proved that the monopoly given to the Company was injurious to the interest of the realm.

Constitution of the Company

A regards the constitution of the London Company, to begin with it was a regulated company and not a joint-stock company. According to Ilbert, "the members of such a company were subject to certain common regulations and were entitled to certain common privileges, but each of them traded on his separate capital, and there was no joint-stock" (Government of India, Historical Survey, p.7). The London Company functioned as a syndicate with concessions for the Indian trade. Whenever a new expedition was to be sent to India, merchants collected together and subscribed funds for the same. When the goods arrived, those were disposed of and the profits were distributed among those who had contributed towards its funds. One voyage had nothing to do with the other. Experience showed that the natives from whom the English merchants bought their goods raised their prices at the sight of the English ships. In order to avoid that hardship, it was considered desirable to station British agents at important places. Those agents kept on buying the goods when their prices were low. It was the force of circumstances that linked up the accounts of one voyage with that of another. After 1612, the subscribers threw their contributions into a joint stock, but that arrangement was not on a permanent basis. That was done in 1657 in the time of Cromwell.

Only those persons were the members of the London Company who purchased shares in the first voyage or in the subsequent voyages. The amount contributed by members varied from time to time. The sons of the members could also claim to be the members of the Company on attaining the age of 21. A person could also become a member through service or apprenticeship or on the payment of a small amount at the time of admission. Generally, a person could become a member by paying £100. In certain cases, even those persons were made the members of the London Company who could be expected to help it in any way.

The constitution of the Company was democratic. Its members elected every year a Governor and 54 Committees. These committees came to be known as Directors later on. The Governor and the committees were given the power to direct the voyages of the Company, provision of shipping and merchandises, sale of merchandise and the management of other things relating to the Company. In addition to the Governor and the committees, other officers such as a Deputy Governor, Secretary and Treasurer were appointed. As a rule, the Governor and the committees managed the work of the London Company, but on certain occasions, a general meeting of all the members of the company was held.

The Company was given certain legislative powers. It was authorised "to make, ordain, and constitute such and so many reasonable laws, constitutions, orders, and ordinances, as to them or the greater part of them being then and there present shall seem necessary and convenient for the good government of the said company, and of all factor, master, mariners and other officers, employed or to be employed in any of their voyages and for the better advancement and continuance of the said trade and traffic. "The Company was also authorised to impose such pains, punishments and penalties as might be considered necessary or convenient for the enforcement of its laws and ordinances. However, the laws and the punishments to be prescribed by the Company were to be reasonable and not contrary or repugnant to the laws, statutes or customs of the realm of England. It is to be noted that the legislative powers of the London Company were much more limited and circumscribed than those given to the companies for New England. For example, the Governor and the Company of Massachusetts Bay were given the power "to make laws and ordinances for the good and welfare of the said company and for the government and ordering of the said Lands and plantations and the People inhabiting and to inhabit the same." A comparison of the two brings one to the conclusion that the Massachusetts company was given definite powers to make laws and govern the territory, but that was not so in the case of the London Company.

Growth of the Company

In 1615, the Company was authorised to issue commissions to its captains. But it was specifically laid down that in capital cases a verdict must be found by a jury. Its object was to maintain discipline on the ships.

In 1623, the Company was authorised to grant commissions to its President and chief officers for the punishment of offences committed by the servants of the Company on land. In capital cases, the trial was to be by jury. It will be seen that the Company came to have the power to control its servants both on the high seas and in India.

The London Company had to face a lot of difficulty at the hands of the interlopers and rivals. In this connection, reference may be made to the Assada Company. This company is also known as the Courteen Association after name of Sir William Courteen, its founder. Sir William got a license to trade with the East Indies in 1635. The company founded a settlement at Assada in Madagascar and carried on trade vigorously. It inflicted great losses on the London Company. As a result of a compromise, the Assada Company was merged into the London Company.

The London Company also got a set-back on account of the Civil War in England. The Company, however, gained much at the hands of Cromwell. The treaty of Westminster of 1654 gave the London Company £85,000 as compensation for the Massacre of Amboyna in 1623 and for its illegal exclusion from the trade with the Spice Islands. The Charter of 19th October, 1657 required the Company to have "one continuous joint-stock", with the result that it "was transformed from a feeble relic of the medieval trade guild into a vigorous forerunner of the Modern Joint Stock Company." Under the Charter of 1657, any one could become a member of the Company by paying an entrance fee of £5 and by subscribing at least £100 to the stock of the Company. A member could vote in the general meeting only if he had stock worth £500. Those who held stock worth £1,000 or more could be elected as members of the committees. The term of office of the Governor and the Deputy Governor was reduced to two years.

Charter of 1661

A new Charter was issued in 1661 by Charles II. It was recognised that the company had effective authority in India. The Company had not merely trading factories but also fortresses. It was authorised to send ships of war, men and ammunition for the security of its factories. It could also erect forts. It could choose commanders and officers and give them commissions under its seal. It could exercise power and command over its fortresses. It appointed governors and other officers.

The Governor and his Council were given general judicial authority "to judge all persons belonging to the said Governor and Company or that shall live under them, in all cases, whether civil or criminal according to the laws of this kingdom and to execute judgement accordingly." Where there was no Governor, the Chief factor and council were empowered to send offenders for punishment either to a place where there was a Governor and a Council or to England.

Charles II had got the Island of Bombay from Portugal by the Marriage Treaty of 1661. By the Charter of 1668, he transferred the Island to the London Company on an annual payment of £10. The Company was authorised to make laws, orders, and ordinances for the good government of the port, and island of Bombay. The Company was given judicial authority. It was also given military powers. The Charter of 1676 gave the Company the power of coining money at Bombay.

The Charter of 1683 gave the Company full power to declare and make peace and war with any other Power. The Company was also given power to raise, arm, train and muster a sufficiently strong army. The Charter also provided for the establishment of a Court consisting of one person learned in civil law and two assistants to be appointed by the Company.

The Charter of 1686 authorised the Company to appoint admirals and other sea officers. The Company was given a general power to coin any species of money.

The Charter of 1693 added £744,000 to the capital of the Company. No individual member was to be allowed to subscribe more than £10,000. For every one thousand pounds, the subscriber was given one vote, but no one could exercise more than 10 votes. The salaries of the Governors and Deputy Governor were fixed. The Charter of 1694 made the principle of rotation of offices compulsory. Neither the Governor nor the Deputy Governor could remain in office for more than two years. Eight committees out of twenty-four were to be elected every year.

In 1611, Hawkins failed to get any permission for regular trade. Sir Thomas Roe was England's ambassador to the Mughal Court between 1615 and 1619. He did not succeed in getting permission to settle in Bengal or Sind. The first settlements were at Surat, Agra, Ahmedabad and Broach.

In 1611, the London Company started a factory at Massaulipatam which was the chief port of Golconda. In 1626, another settlement was made at Armagaon. In 1639, the London Company got power to build a fortress, mint money and govern Madras. In 1641, Fort St. George was founded. In 1690, the English established a settlement at Sutanati which was to be the site of future Calcutta. In 1696, the factory was fortified. In 1698, the neighbouring villages were bought. The factory was named Fort William and it became the seat of a Presidency in 1700.

It is desirable to mention the case of *East India Company* v. *Sandys*. In this case, the Company brought an action against one Mr. Sandys on the ground that he had traded in the East Indies without a license. The case ended in favour of the Company. The Company also detained *the Redbridge* which was lying in the Thames, but was believed to e bound for the East Indies. The action of the Company was challenged. It was contended that the Company had no such right to detain a ship. On 19th January, 1694, the House of Commons passed a resolution that "all the subjects of England have equal right to trade to the East Indies unless prohibited by Act of Parliament." Although a resolution of parliament had not the force of law, yet it undoubtedly had the effect of encouraging interlopers. As the Company was determined to stop them, there was bound to be trouble.

At this time, Mr. Montagu was the Chancellor of the Exchequer. He was in need of money for the State, and was finding out ways and means for the same. The monopoly in trade was virtually put up for auction among all those who could give the Government £2,000,000 at 8% p.a. The London Company offered £700,000 which was insufficient. But a new Company was willing to subscribe the whole amount needed. The result was that a Bill was passed in 1698 by the British Parliament. The Act provided for a subscription of £2,000,000 Sterling as a loan to the State which in return was to grant "General Society" the exclusive right of trading to the East Indies. The London Company was to be given a notice of three years (expiring in 1701) to wind up its business.

In order to strengthen its position, the old company bought shares worth £315,000 in the new company. There was ruinous competition between the two companies for some time. The result was that the new company began to lose heavily. Ultimately, a compromise was arrived at in 1702. According to that compromise, "the Old Company was to maintain its separate existence for seven years, but the trade of the two companies was to be carried on jointly, in the name of the English Company, but for the common benefit of both under the direction of twenty-four managers, twelve to be selected by each company. At the end of the seven years, the old Company was to surrender its Charters." The new Company was to carry on its trade in the name of "The United Company of Merchants of England trading to the East Indies." In March 1709, the London Company surrendered its Charters to Queen Anne.

The Constitution of the new Company was essentially similar to that of the old Company. However, more modern terminology was used in the Constitution of the new Company. "The Company consisted of all persons holding a share into the capital stock, then amounting to £2,000,000. Every individual, whether male or female, possessing £500, either in his or her own right or otherwise, was entitled to vote and to take part in discussions in the meeting of Proprietors, who when assembled were termed by the Charter a 'General Court of Proprietors'. The Proprietors were to select out of their body, every year, twenty-four members each possessing £2,000 stock, to be Directors of the Company. Thirteen members formed a quorum and when assembled for business were termed as "Court of Directors." By the Charter, four General Courts were to be held in the year each quarterly. A committee was to be chosen to frame by laws for the government of the Company, which laws had the same force as those famed by parliament when not opposed to any existing Act."

The new East India Company came into existence practically at the same time when the Mughal Empire began to disintegrate after the death of Aurangzeb in 1707. On account of the lack of an effective sovereign power in the country, the East India Company had to struggle very hard against her rivals. At the beginning, the Company had to struggle for its very existence. But in the long run, it succeeded in establishing its supremacy all over India. In 1858, the Company itself was abolished, and the vast Empire established by it in India was taken over by the Crown. The next chapter is concerned with the story of the growth of the English East India Company up to 1858.

3

The English East India Company (1709–1858)

Historical Survey

It is true that after 1709 the English East India Company had not to face any rivals at home, but it was called upon to meet many difficulties on the subcontinent of India. The Portuguese and the Dutch were not serious rivals. The English East India Company could simply ignore them with contempt. But it met serious opposition at the hands of the French East India Company and the Indian Princes.

As regards the French East India Company, it had been started in 1664 in the time of Louis XIV under the patronage of Colbert. The Company did not make much progress upto 1720. In 1725, it acquired Mahe in Malabar. In 1739, it got Karikal on the Coromandal coast. In 1735, Dumas was appointed the Governor of Pondicherry. In 1741, he was succeeded by Dupleix as the Governor.

Dupleix was a great dreamer and he dreamt the dream of founding the French Empire in India on the ruins of the Mughal Empire. The disunity prevailing in the country was helpful in the accomplishment of his aim. He could easily play one Indian Prince against the other. Moreover, the military system of the West was superior to that of the Indians.

While Dupleix was dreaming and planning to found a French Empire in India, there was going on a struggle for supremacy between the English and the French both in Europe and North

America. In the war of Austrian Succession, the English backed Maria Theresa and the French supported Frederick, the Great, of Prussia. This opportunity was availed of by the French and English Companies in India to match their strength with each other. In 1744, the English besieged Pondicherry and would have taken it if Anwar-ud-Din, the Nawab of Carnatic, had not intervened on behalf of the French. The English were made to raise the siege. In 1746, the French besieged Madras. When the British requested the Nawab of Carnatic to intervene on their behalf, the latter was won over by the French by a promise that Madras will be handed over to him after its fall. However, the French refused to hand over Madras to the Nawab after capturing it. This led to a conflict between the French and the Nawab, but the latter was defeated in the battle of St. Thomas in 1746. The French had to return Madras to the English in 1748 according to the terms of the treaty of Aix la Chapelle. This is known as the First Carnatic War.

During the Second Carnatic War, Dupleix supported Muzaffar Jung against Nasir Jung for the Deccan throne. Nasir Jung was defeated, but when Muzaffar Jung was killed, he put Salabat Jung on the Deccan throne in 1751 and sent Bussy to safeguard the French interests. Dupleix also put forward Chanda Sahib as a candidate to the Carnatic throne in opposition to Anwar-ud-Din. Anwar-ud-Din was killed in 1749 in the battle of Ambur and Chanda Sahib was put on the Carnatic throne. However, that success was short-lived on account of the emergence of Clive on the scene. It was the capture of Arcot in 1751 by Clive that forced Chanda Sahib to raise the siege of Trichnopoly where Mohammed Ali, the son of Anwar-ud-Din, was taking refuge. Chanda Sahib was himself defeated and lost his life. Thus, the English came to have their hold over the Carnatic. Dupleix was called back because he could not recover his lost position. The treaty of Pondicherry of 1755 ended the Second Carnatic War.

The Third Carnatic War coincided with the Seven Years' War in Europe and North America. Count Lally could not accomplish anything substantial. He was defeated in the battle of Wandiwash in 1761. According to Malleson, this defeat "shattered to the ground the mighty fabric which Martin, Dumas and Dupleix had contributed to erect; it dissipated all the hopes of Lally; it sealed the fate of Pondicherry." It is true that the French got back

Pondicherry, Chandarnagar and Mahe by the Treaty of Paris in 1763, but they were never in a position later on to challenge the position of the English East India Company in India.

When the English were establishing their hold in the south, they were simultaneously penetrating into Bengal. After the break-up of the Mughal Empire, Ali Vardi Khan had established himself in Bengal. He died in 1754 and was succeeded by Siraj-ud-Daula. The so-called Blackhole tragedy led to a conflict between the English and the Nawab. However, the latter was defeated in the Battle of Plassey in 1757 by Clive. Instead of taking over the administration of Bengal in their own hands, the English put on the Bengal throne Mir Jaffar. In 1765, Clive established what is known as the Dual Government in Bengal. The English shared with the Nawab of Bengal the administration of the Province of Bengal. As the system did not work satisfactorily, the same was abolished in 1772 and the whole of the administration of Bengal was taken over by the English. But it seems desirable to give a detailed account of the system of Dual Government in Bengal.

Daul Government of Bengal (1765—72)

The system of Daul Government of Bengal which was set up by the Clive is not so easy to explain as it might appear at first sight. It was not the simple division of control over the administration of Bengal between the English East India Company and the Nawab of Bengal. The position was somewhat as follows:—

The Nawab or Subedar of Bengal as Viceroy of the Mughal Emperor, exercised two functions : *(1)* the Diwani, *i.e.*, revenue and civil justice, and *(2)* the Nizamat, *i.e.*, military power and criminal justice. As Sir James Stephen points out, the Nawab granted practically the Nizamat to the Company in February 1765. In August 1765, Emperor Shah Alam granted the Diwani to the Company. The Company thus got the Diwani form the Emperor and the Nizamat from the Subedar. So far the position was clear. But the difficulty was created by the fact that the servants of the East India Company did not undertake their duties as Diwani or Nazim in their own person. The nominal head of the administration was a Deputy Naib or Nawab whom the Nawab bound himself to appoint with their sanction. A similar Deputy was appointed for Bihar. But the whole administration was carried on for many years through the agency of the native servants. However, in 1769 English supervisors (afterwards called Collectors) were appointed to control the native revenue officers. But instead of improving matters, they only made confusion worse confounded and corruption more corrupt.

Such was the dual system of Government set up in Bengal by Clive. It might be asked as to why it was that Clive hesitated to take over the administration of the province when he could have done that so easily. The Nawab was merely a puppet in the hands of the British. As a matter of fact, all power was in the hands of the British. He was their creature and depended upon them for his existence. Clive would have rendered a great service by abolishing his office and assuming the control of the government directly, rather than agree to play the role of the wire-puller from behind the scene. As pointed out by Dodwell in Cambridge History of India, the great disadvantage of the scheme was that it separated power from responsibility. The English were given control over the province but they did not feel any responsibility for its administration and could not be held responsible for anything done badly. This was made clear when in 1770, a severe famine broke out in Bengal. The servants of the Company did not feel any duty towards the people who were left to die in thousands. That appalling distress can be attributed to the system of dual government set up by Clive. P.E. Roberts criticises the system in these words : "The unfortunate divorce of power from responsibility soon cause a recrudescence of the old abuses."

But as Dodwell points out, the system set up in 1765 had certain immediate advantages. It was suited to the exigencies of the time. It secured that control over the Nawab which was regarded as the most pressing need of the time. It also secured protection against the complaints of the foreign powers and demands of the home government. Clive still remembered how the ostensible assumption of power contributed to produce the unyielding opposition of the English to the schemes of Dupleix. The writs of the Emperor or Parvanas of the Nawab, though valueless without the support of the English power, could not be fully discounted at Paris or the Hague without a serious breach of diplomatic etiquette. It was thought that something less than the assumption of full dominion would be less likely to excite legal difficulties in England or provoke the interference of Parliament. "In short the grant of the Diwani was designed to secure the full control of Bengal affairs so far as the company's interests went without incurring the inconvenience of formal dominion." (Dodwell).

Roberts says that even Clive would not have denied the charge that the system set up by him was not perfect. But he maintains that "Clive could not afford to indulge in counsels of perfection; he had to deal with actualities. He admitted that the Nawab had only 'the name or shadow of authority', yet 'this name—this shadow it is indispensably necessary that we should venerate." Verelst tells us that it was impossible to take over the full government of the province. In the first place, the number of servants of the company required for the task of administration was very limited. Secondly, they were quite ignorant of the task of administration, for they were merely writers in the Company's service.

From 1765 to 1772, the actual administration was in the hands of two Indian officials known as Naib Diwans, the Company itself being the actual Diwan. Mohammad Raza Khan was in Bengal and Raja Shitab Rai was in Bihar. In 1769 were appointed British Supervisors who were given "a controlling though not an immediate, power over the Collectors." The evil of the system was that while the Company itself was in serious financial straits, its servants were returning to England with big fortunes.

Becher, Resident at Murshidabad, wrote thus in 1769 : "It must give pain as an Englishman to have reason to think, that since the accession of the company to the Diwani, the condition of the people of this country has been worse than it was before and yet I am afraid the fact is undoubted. This fine country which flourished under the most despotic and arbitrary government, is verging towards its ruin, while the English have really so great a share in the administration."

Moreover, the Directors strongly suspected that the Naib Diwans were intercepting a large part of the revenue which would have filled the Company's treasury. Hastings was appointed in 1772 definitely with a view to end the Dual system. The court of Directors had decided to "stand forth as Diwan." He was in fact selected to take the place of the three supervisors. "We now arm you with our full powers." Wrote the Directors of the Company, "to make a complete reformation." Although he was given definite instructions on most points, it is to a certain extent true, as Lord Thinlow says, that he was ordered "to destroy the whole fabric of the double government—he was to form a system for the government of Bengal, under instructions so general, that I may fairly say the whole plan was left to his judgement and discretion."

Formally, the abolition of the Dual government did no more than that the company was henceforth to collect the revenues through the agency of its own servants. But in reality, it meant becoming responsible for the whole civil administration. Hastings hardly exaggerated it when he described it as "implanting the authority of the company, and the sovereignty of Great Britain, in the constitution of this country." The first step was the abolition of the offices of Naib Diwans of Bengal and Bihar, and the prosecution of Mohd. Raza Khan and Raja Shitab Rai for peculation. After undergoing a long trial and being kept in custody for rather more than a year, they were both acquitted. The trial was merely a formal affair designed indirectly to remove them. Although Warren Hastings was opposed to it, it served the purpose. "The retrospections and examinations are death to my views," said Hastings.

Thus it was that the Dual System which was set up by Clive, was abolished by Warren Hastings. It was not intended to last for ever. It was a stop-gap. It was a make-shift arrangement which aimed at tiding over the difficulties confronting the English in 1765. It was the creation of the genius of the Englishmen who believe in bit-by-bit advance. It was the policy of muddling through, which, though often misunderstood, serves its purpose in the long run.

From 1772 to 1857.

During the Governor-Generalship of Warren Hastings, the English had to fight the Second Mysore War and the First Maratha War (1778—82). The English had to meet a formidable foe in the person of Haider Ali in the Second Mysore War, but that war ended by the treaty of Mangalore in 1784. Both parties agreed to return their gains to each other. The First Maratha War ended with the treaty of Salbai in 1782 and the English got the Island of Salsette.

The Third Mysore War was fought in the time of Cornwallis from 1790—1792. By the treaty of Seringapatam of 1792, Sultan Tipu had to surrender to the English one-half of his territory. He was also required to pay a huge war-indemnity.

In the time of Lord Wellesley, the Nizam of Hyderabad entered into a subsidiary alliance with the English Company. During the Fourth Mysore War, Tipu was killed and Mysore fell into the hands of the English in 1799. The latter, however, restored the Hindu Raja to the throne of Mysore. The Second Maratha War also took place in the time of Wellesley. The Peshwa entered into the treaty of Bassein (1802) with the English. That was not liked by the other Maratha Chiefs such as Bhonsla, Scindhia and a Holkar and led to a war between the Marathas and the English. Bhonsla was defeated and had to sign the treaty of Deogaon in 1803. Scindhia was defeated and had to sign the treaty of Surji Arjan Gaon in 1803. Holkar also took up arms against the English, but before he could be subdued, Wellesley was recalled the Lord Cornwallis entered into a treaty with him in 1805. It was in the time of Lord Hastings that the Marathas were crushed in 1817-18. As a result of that war, the power of the Marathas was completely shattered and the office of the Peshwa was abolished. They became so weak that they could not challenge the English later on.

It was Lord Minto who checked the growing power of Maharaja Ranjit Singh by entering into the Treaty of Amritsar in 1809. The Cis-Sutlej States were taken under their protection by the English and the river Sutlej was made the boundary line between the English and Maharaja Ranjit Singh. The English did not interfere in the affairs of the Punjab till 1839 when Maharaja Ranjit Singh died. But the anarchy that prevailed in the Punjab after the death of the Maharaja gave the English an opportunity to interfere. The First Sikh War was fought in the time of Lord Hardinge. The Sikhs were defeated and had to sign the treaty of Lahore (1846). They gave up the Jullundur Doab and also agreed to pay a war indemnity. Their army was reduced. The Second Sikh War was fought in the time of Lord Dalhousie. After the Battle of Chillian Wala and Gujarat, the Punjab was annexed in

March 1849.

The English had their eyes on Sindh from the very beginning. They had not allowed Maharaja Ranjit Singh to interfere into Sindh. The First Afghan War gave them an excuse to pass through Sindh and make it their military base. After the Afghan War, the English decided to stay on in Singh. The Amirs of Sindh were encouraged to revolt, and when they did so, they were defeated by Napier in the Battle of Miani. Sindh was annexed in 1843. According to Napier, the conquest of Sindh was a very "advantageous, useful and humane piece of rascality." According to Marshman, "The rascality is more apparent than the advantage, except to the captors, to whom it brought a rich draught of prize money, of which seven lacs fell the share of the General-in-Chief."

The English had to fight against the Gorkhas in the time of Lord Hastings. The Gorkha War lasted from 1814 to 1816. After initial reverses, the English defeated the Gorkhas. The war was ended by the treaty of Sagauli in 1816. The Gorkhas surrendered Garhwal and Kumaon to the west of the river Kali to the British. They acknowledged the independence of the Raja of Sikkim. They agreed to have a British Resident at Kathmandu.

The first Burmese War was fought in the time of Lord Amherst. The war continued from 1826 to 1828. It was ended by the treaty of Yandboo in 1828. The English got Assam, Arakan and the coast of Tenasserim. The Burmese recognised the independence of Manipur State. They were to accept a British Resident at their capital. They agreed to pay war-indemnity. The second Burmese War took place in the time of Lord Dalhousie from 1852 to 1853. As a result of that war, Rangoon and Prome were occupied and Pegu was captured. As the King of Burma refused to enter into a treaty, Dalhousie annexed Lower Burma and Pegu by a proclamation in 1853. The third Burmese War was fought from 1885 to 1886 in the time of Lord Dufferin. As a result of that war, Upper Burma was annexed in 1886. Thus, the English came to have the whole of Burma in 1886.

It is well-known that Lord Dalhousie did his utmost to annex as many Indian States as he could. Some of them he annexed after conquest. Some he annexed on the ground of mis-government. Oudh was annexed on that ground in 1856. He also annexed states by the application of the doctrine of lapse. Thus it was that Dalhousie annexed Satara (1849), Sambalpur, Jhansi (1853), and Nagpur (1853). It was the policy of the wholesale annexation of the Indian states that was partly responsible for the Mutiny of 1857. Profiting from that experience, Queen Victoria declared in 1858 that the policy of the British Government in India would be one of non-annexation of the Indian States. The Indian States were subordinate to the British Government, but otherwise their territorial integrity was not to be touched.

Having discussed briefly the political history of India upto the ending of the Company's rule in 1858, it is desirable to discuss the constitutional history of India from 1773 onwards.

4

The Government under the Crown (1858 to 1919)

The Nature of the Indian Administration under the Crown

The most important office that came into being with the assumption of direct responsibility for the Government of India by the Crown was that of the Secretary of State for India. As a result, all powers, legislative, administrative and financial, came to be centralized in the Secretary of State for India in Council on behalf of the Crown. In India, the administration was headed by the Governor-General in Council who exercised a rigid control over the local government in the Provinces which were headed by Governors, Lieutenant-Governors or Chief Commissioners on the basis of the area or importance of the Province concerned. These Governments had no independent powers but were the agents of the Governor-General in Council. The Provinces were divided into Districts each of which was headed by a Collector-Magistrate or the Deputy Commissioner. This four-tier system of administration can best be described as a 'Centralized Bureaucracy'. It is characterized by a hierarchy or gradation of officers, the lower ones being the agents of, and, therefore, entirely responsible to, those above them.

At the apex of this bureaucratic hierarchy stood the Secretary of State for India and his Council responsible to the British Parliament. Below him was the Viceroy and the Governor-General of India in Council, who was the 'man on the spot' to head the administration. Then came the Governors, Lieutenant-Governors, and Chief Commissioners, and finally the Collectors or Deputy Commissioners. The whole system from top to bottom was well-knit, highly centralized and behaved like an unbreakable steel frame with all the characteristics of a full-fledged autocracy. It may be appropriate here to deal in some detail with the role of each important office in this complex system.

The Secretary of State in Council

By the Act of 1858, the Secretary of State was charged with the 'superintendence, direction and control of all the acts, operations and concerns which in anywise relate to the Government or revenues of India.' In this task he was assisted by a Council composed of men who had expert knowledge and experience of India. Although originally the Council was intended to be a check on the Secretary of State, in course of time, his position became one of overwhelming authority. The only authority that could effectively control the Secretary of State was Parliament. In theory, its authority over the Indian Government was supreme.[1] But in practice, it left everything to the Secretary of State as its agent.[2]

The indifference of Parliament and the impotency of the Council left the Secretary of State master of the field. He came to exercise complete control over the entire range of Indian administration. This control was based upon the above-mentioned theory that the supremacy of Parliament over the affairs of India was absolute. It might seem odd that a Secretary of State sitting at a distance of over 6,000 miles from India should be expected to exercise effective control over the multifarious activities of a gigantic administrative organization in India. Yet such was the fact; and the ingenious methods adopted by successive Secretaries in this regard, involved the systematic interference even in comparatively small matters affecting the working of the Government of India. Governor-Generals who protested were told of the great principle that underlay the whole system, namely, that 'the final control and direction of the affairs of India rest with the Home Government, and not with the authorities appointed and established by the Crown, under Parliamentary enactment, in India itself.'[3]

Thus, the control exercised by the Secretary of State was not only absolute but also embraced every field of activity of the

Indian Government, legislative, administrative and financial. How bitter almost every Governor-General was over this extreme interference can be seen from the following extract from a private letter written by Lord Minto:

> I used to imagine that the Secretary of State aimed only at directing great principles of Indian policy, and that the administration of the country rested with the Government of India, but there has been interference in everything. It only results in intense worry to the Viceroy, for, do what he will, the Secretary of the State cannot administer India.[4]

The Governor-General in Council

We have already seen how with the implementation of the Regulating Act a central authority was created in India in the office of the Governor-General of Bengal which controlled the Presidencies of Madras and Bombay in certain matters. The process continued steadily over a period of sixty years and by the passage of the Act of 1833, it had reached its consummation. It was indeed difficult at that time to draw a line of demarcation between the functions of the Central and the Provincial Governments. The Central Government was fully competent to deal with any matter which was under the immediate management of the Provincial Government. To what extent it was actually exercising its power calls for some detailed consideration.

In the financial field, the control of the Governor-General in Council over the provincial administration was absolute. This was the result of a specific provisicn in the Act of 1858 by which the entire revenues of the country were vested in the Governor-General in Council; the provincial governments could not raise or spend even a rupee on their own account. Although a real attempt was made by Lord Mayo (1870) and his successors to establish a system of Provincial Settlements by which each Province could expect to have adequate funds to maintain a certain standard of administration, its tutelage to the Government of India was still unqualified. There were four main ways by which this financial control was exercised:

(*a*) Careful scrutiny of all provincial budget which required sanction from the Centre.

(*b*) Control of expenditure by a series of financial codes of instructions.

(*c*) Restrictions on the imposition of new provincial taxes which always required central sanction.

(*d*) Prohibition to borrow money either in India or England for capital expenditure. Whenever the Provinces proposed borrowing, the Government of India advanced money to them.

The control by the Centre over provincial legislation was a corollary to the dependence of the Government of India on the Secretary of State. There was no line of demarcation between the respective legislative authority of the Centre and the Provinces. The result was the complete mastery of the Governor-General in Council over the entire legislative field. The Provinces were allowed to enter the field only with prior sanction from the Central Government and the Secretary of State. Further, no Provincial Bill could become an Act without the assent of the Governor-General.

In the administrative field too the control was very extensive. On the one hand, it was the direct result of the financial control. On the other, it was a consequence of the policy of maintaining a uniform administrative system all over the country. The Public Services who were in charge of the administration were recruited by the Secretary of State and their conditions of service were determined by him. Finally, it was the duty of the Government of India to lay down policies of reform and progress of the administrative system, in the form of Resolutions. The Provinces only acted as agents of the Centre in implementing these resolutions.[5]

The foregoing analysis will show that the Government of the country was one. The Provinces, despite their enjoying considerable powers, were in reality the 'agents' of the Central Government. The extent of provincial powers and the nature of control by the Centre, were not the product of a constitutional demarcation of central and local powers as obtains in a federal system but were the result of gradual administrative evolution. The system as a whole was over-centralized and had all the evils of such a system. It sapped the initiative of the local governments, made them subservient to the various departments of the Central Government and stood in the way of the interests of the people and their participation in the Government even at lower levels. The most radical of these evils may be specifically listed as follows:

(*a*) The decadence of the indigenous institution of self-government—the village *panchayat*.

(*b*) Grouping of provinces without regard to wholesome principles such as racial, cultural or linguistic affinities.

(*c*) Enormous growth in public taxation and expenditure, particularly the growth of military expenditure.

(*d*) Insufficient attention given to nation-building activities such as education, public health, irrigation, co-operation, etc.

(*e*) Neglect of indigenous industry and agriculture, resulting in extreme poverty often culminating in epidemics and famines.

(*f*) Excessive curb on the political activities of the people by imposing restrictions upon the freedom of the press, speech and movement.

Gokhale described the inevitable failure of the British bureaucracy in India thus:

> The efficiency attained by a foreign bureaucracy uncontrolled by public opinion, whose members again reside only temporarily in the land in which they exercise official power, is bound to be of a strictly limited character, and it can never compare with that higher and true efficiency which is possible only under a well-regulated system of self-government. The present form of government of India is a strongly centralised bureaucracy in which the men at the Centre hold office for five years only. They then leave the country, carrying away with them all the knowledge and experience of administrative matters acquired at the expense of the country, and their places are taken by new men, who, in their turn retire similarly after five years. As things are, there is no one ever in the Government who is permanently interested in the country as only its own people can be interested. One result is that the true well-being of the people is systematically subordinated to militarism and the service interests of the English mercantile classes; and though under such a system peace and order may be maintained, and even a certain amount of efficient

administration secured, the type of efficiency is bound to remain a low one always. Moreover, it is clear that even such efficiency of administration as has been attained in the past by the existing system, is bound to suffer more and more, owing to the growing antagonism of the governed to that system. No man, for instance ever laboured more strenuously for more efficiency than Lord Curzon, and yet, never was discontent more deeper and more widespread than when he left India, and no Viceroy of recent times has had to succeed to a greater legacy of difficulties than Lord Minto.[6]

The failure of the highly centralized British bureaucracy in India and its evil effects had already created considerable criticism both in India and in Britain. Certain portions of the Queen's Proclamation of 1858 reveal the awareness of these by the British Government and even its eagerness to remedy them. It was also evident that the remedies lay in the adoption of a new policy embodying two principles, decentralization and democratization in administration. Unfortunately, however, the process was too slow and the degree of change was too little to produce any dramatic result in the desired direction. We may now turn our attention to these measures which began with the passing of the Indian Councils Act, 1861.

The Indian Councils Act, 1861

The Regulating Act had initiated the process of centralization; the Act of 1861 inaugurated the process of decentralization. It was the primary charter of the Indian legislatures of the twentieth century. The Act restored to the Councils of Bombay and Madras the legislative power they had lost earlier in favour of the Central Government, and new Councils with similar powers were allowed to be established in other Provinces. Thus the first step was taken in the direction of legislative decentralization. There were, however, rigid restrictions placed upon the powers of the Councils. Earlier, the laws enacted by the Provincial Councils had come into operation automatically. From 1861 the prior sanction of the Governor-General was made necessary for legislation by Provincial Councils in certain matters, and in all cases, for the validity of the law, not only was the assent of the Governor but also that of the Governor-General made necessary. The Governor-

General thus became the head of all legislative authority in British India.

Hitherto, the Provincial Councils had had the power to interfere in the acts of the Executive Government. This had been criticized as highly undesirable. The Act of 1861 removed this defect by strictly confining the functions of the new Councils to legislation.

The terrible events of the so-called Sepoy Mutiny had brought home to the British Government the dangers arising from the exclusion of Indians from association with legislation. At least a beginning was made to remove this defect by including, for the first time, some Indians in the Central Council. The Act provided for the appointment of additional members, not less than six and not more than twelve for two years, of whom not less than half were to be *non-officials*. The latter part of this provision was intended to accommodate some Indians in the Governor-General's Council. Although such inclusion of Indians in the Council was not based upon the principles of democratic representation, and almost invariably those who were nominated were Indian Princes, their Dewans or big land-holders, the significance of such a measure cannot be belittled. It was indeed the result of a recognition of the principle of Indian representation in the Government and marked the beginning of a new trend.

The Indian Councils Act, 1892

The Councils established under the Act of 1861, before long, proved inadequate. The demand to expand the Indian representation on it increased. The newly established Universities of Calcutta, Madras and Bombay had considerably contributed to this demand by giving an impetus to higher education in India and thereby increasing the number of Indians qualified by education and experience for public affairs. The inauguration of the Indian National Congress in 1885 created a new platform for pressing the demand and impressing it upon the authorities. Reform of the Councils, therefore, engaged the attention of the Government. The Indian Councils Act of 1892 was the result. The object of the Act was explained by Lord Curzon who was then the Under-Secretary of State for India, as 'to widen the basis and expand the functions of Government of India, and to give further opportunities to the non-official and native elements in Indian society to take part in the work of the Government, and in that way, to lend official recognition to that remarkable development both of political interest and political capacity that had been visible among the higher classes of Indian society since the Government of India was taken over by the Crown in 1858.'

The Act provided for the increase of the membership of the Councils. But there was controversy over the method of selection of members. The Conservatives thought that election at that stage was totally unwise. The Liberals, on the contrary, thought that the principle of election should be introduced. Finally, a compromise was worked out by which the Government was obliged to consult, prior to nomination, certain representative bodies or institutions such as Municipalities, District Boards, Universities, Chambers of Commerce, Land-holders, etc. These bodies could only make recommendations. It was within the power of the Government with the approval of the Secretary of State, to accept or reject them.

The Act also provided for enlarging the functions of the Councils. As a result, in addition to their legislative function, the Councils were empowered to hold a discussion on the annual financial statement and also ask questions under prescribed conditions and restrictions.

Minto-Morley Reforms, 1909

The advent of Lord Minto and Lord Morley, the former as Governor-General and the latter as the Secretary of State, into the scene of the British Indian Government marked the dawn of a new era. They were representatives of the Liberal Party which had come into power in England. The failure of Lord Curzon's Governor-Generalship (Curzon was Minto's immediate predecessor) was indeed the best proof of the failure of bureaucratic government. A totally different approach, it was felt on all sides, was necessary to make the administration a success. Speaking in the House of Lords, Morley himself made it clear:

> There are two rival schools of thought, one of which believes that better Government of India depends on efficiency, and that efficiency is in fact the end of British rule in India. The other school, while not neglecting efficiency, looks also to what is called political concessions.

As a preliminary to the grant of political concessions, a Royal Commission was appointed to enquire into the causes of and suggest remedies for centralization. This was known as the Royal Commission on Decentralization. The Commission had very limited terms of reference. It was not allowed to go into the relationship between the Secretary of State and the Government of India, or into questions of a purely political nature or questions of general policy. Its enquiry was confined to the relations between the Government of India and the Provinces, and how they could be simplified and improved by decentralization; 'how the system of government could be better adapted both to meet the requirements and promote the welfare of the different Provinces, and without impairing its strength or unity to bring the executive power into closer touch with local conditions.'

It is clear from the nature of the task entrusted to the Commission that the area with which it was concerned was administrative and not constitutional, administrative decentralization and not political autonomy. Yet, its report had a considerable impact on the political and constitutional set-up. The Commission recommended changes on the basis of the following four considerations:

(*a*) The difficulties of administering a vast sub-continent from a single headquarter.

(*b*) The fact that the various Provinces contained diverse nationalities with different languages, traditions and interests.

(*c*) The desirability of creating a large sense of responsibility in provincial and local authorities.

(*d*) The importance of strengthening the administration and educating the people by interesting the latter more largely in public affairs.

On the basis of the recommendations of the Commission, a Bill was introduced in Parliament in 1908 and was passed and became an Act in May 1909, popularly known as the Minto-Morley Reforms.

The chief merit of the Act lay in its provisions to further enlarge the Councils and make them more representative and effective, These may be analysed under two main heads, Constitutional and Functional.

Constitutionally, the Councils were modified in three respects: *(i)* Numbers, *(ii)* Proportion of official and non-official members, and (iii) Methods of appointment or selection. We may examine these in some detail.

Numbers

Under the Act of 1909 the numbers were doubled or more than doubled. For example, under the Act of 1892, the maximum number of additional members authorized was only sixteen for the Government of India. But under the Act of 1909, this was raised to sixty. In the same manner, the maximum number of additional members for the Presidencies of Madras, Bombay and Bengal was raised from twenty to fifty.

Table 1
Comparative Strength of the Legislative Councils under the Act of 1892 and 1909

	Maximum number of additional members under the Act of 1892	*Maximum number of additional members under the Act of 1909*	*Total strength under the Regulations of 1912*
India	16	60	68
Madras	20	50	48
Bombay	20	50	48
Bengal	20	50	53
Bihar and Orissa	..	50	44
U.P.	15	50	49
Punjab	15	30	26
Burma	15	30	17
Assam	20	30	25

Note: There was no Bihar and Orissa Province before 1912.

During the period of 1905—12 Assam was joined to East Bengal, both being called Eastern Bengal and Assam.

The proportion of official and non-official members

Until 1909 the Legislative Councils had a majority of officials. But the Act of 1909 made a significant departure in this respect. According to this, the Governor-General's Legislative Council was still to be dominated by an official majority, but the proportion of non-officials increased substantially. In the Provinces, for the first time, a non-official majority was established. This was definitely a move in the direction of democratization in an otherwise wholly bureaucratic set-up. It must be pointed out, however, that an unofficial majority in the Provincial Councils was impotent to translate its will into action because of the overriding powers of the central majority.

Methods of selection

Nomination was the practice until 1909. But the Minto-Morley Reforms, for the first time in British Indian administration, recognized the principle of indirect election. The Act enabled certain recognized bodies and associations to recommend candidates who, though there was no obligation to accept them, were rarely rejected in practice. Further, it also provided for some members to be elected in accordance with regulations made under the Act with regard to the principle of representation. The Government accepted the position that *(i)* election by the wishes of the people is the ultimate end to be secured, whatever may be the actual machinery adopted for giving effect to it, and *(ii)* that in the circumstances of India, representation by classes and interests was the only practicable method of embodying the principle in the constitution of the Legislative Councils.

The acceptance of the latter principle marks the beginning of communal (religious) electorates in India. Sir Charles Atchison, a member of the Executive Council in 1892, had already expressed the idea that 'the division of the people into creeds and castes and sects with varying and conflicting interests rendered representation in the European sense an obvious impossibility.' This idea took practical shape under the Act of 1909 by the creation of separate electorates such as Muslims, Land-holders, Chambers of Commerce, etc. Although the evil potentialities of this provision did not unfold themselves clearly in those days, it was to become the greatest menace to national unity in later years.

Changes in the Functions of the Councils

The Act of 1861 had strictly limited the functions of the Councils to the field of legislation. The Act of 1892 gave members the power to discuss the budget but not to move resolutions about it or to divide the Council. The Act of 1909 enlarged the scope of the functions of the Councils in three ways:

1. (*a*) To discuss the budget at length before it was finally settled;

   (*b*) To propose resolutions upon it; and

   (*c*) To divide upon those resolutions.

2. The extended powers of the Councils went even beyond discussions on the budget and embraced almost all matters of public importance through resolutions and divisions taken. These resolutions, however, were not binding on the Executive Government but only had the effect of recommendations.

3. The right to ask questions by members was enlarged and supplementaries were also allowed.

On the whole, the Minto-Morley Reforms were a great improvement upon the Act of 1892. Nevertheless, they failed to satisfy the aspirations of the people. First, the Councils were not truly representative of the people as a whole. Narrow franchise and indirect elections failed to instill in the members a sense of responsibility to the people. Secondly, the Councils had no real power in the fields of legislation and finance. They were only debating bodies which aired certain criticisms. Thirdly, neither the subordination of the Provincial Governments to the Government of India nor that of the latter to the Secretary of State was relaxed. Finally, the Act had no answer to the demand for responsible government. In fact, Lord Morley was frank in this respect by openly declaring that he would have nothing to do with the Reforms if they were construed as a step towards the establishment of a parliamentary system of government in India.

What then was the purpose of the Reforms? They were an attempt to graft the principle of constitutionalism upon the existing autocracy of British rule. They were at best the outcome of the old conception which made the Government of India a benevolent despotism which might, as it saw fit for purposes of enlightenment, consult the wishes of its subjects. This was incapable of satisfying the Indian people and naturally, they were disillusioned.

Table 2
Composition of the Provincial Councils under the Regulations of 1912

Name of the Council	Additional												
	Nominated			Elected									
	Ex-officio	Official	Non-Official	Corpora-ti on	Mun. & Dist. Boards	University	Land-holders	Planting Community	Mohom-medans	Ch. of Com.	Indian Commerce	Miscel-laneous	Total
Madras	4	16	5	1	9	1	5	1	2	1	1	..	48
Bombay	4	14	7	1	8	1	3	..	4	2	2	..	48
Bengal	3	16	4	1	10	1	4	1	5	2	1	3	53
Bihar and Orissa	3	15	4	..	10	..	5	1	4	..	..	1	44
U.P.	..	20	6	..	13	1	2	..	4	1	..	..	49
Punjab	..	10	6	..	6	1	..	..	..	1	..	..	15
Burma	..	6	8	..	..	..	..	..	..	1	..	..	17
Assam	..	9	4	..	4	..	2	3	2	..	..	..	25
C.P.	..	10	7	..	4	..	2	..	..	..	..	..	25

NOTES

1. *Montague-Chemsfor Report*, para 33.
2. Ramsay Macdonald once said : 'Parliament has not been a just or watchful steward. It holds no great debates on Indian questions; it looks after its own responsibilities with far less care than it looked after those of the Company; its seats are empty when it has its annual saunter through the Indian budget.'
3. Cf. Lord Mayo's protest in 1870 against the Contract Act and the Evidence Act and the reply of the Secretary of State; also the controversy, between Lord Northbrook and the Secretary of State in Disraeli's Cabinet over financial policy (1784). 'The Government of India was merely an agent of the Secretary of State'.
4. Sir Malcolm Seton, *India Office*, p. 81.
5. *Report of the Royal Commission on Decentralisation*, Chapter II.
6. G.K. Gokhale, *Speeches and Writings*, p. 989.

5

The Government of India Act

Historical Introduction

Twofold Origin of British Authority in India

British Authority in India may be traced, historically, to a twofold source. It is derived partly from the British Crown and Parliament, partly from the Great Mogul and other native rulers of India.

In England, the powers and privileges granted by royal charter to the East India Company were confirmed, supplemented, regulated, and curtailed by successive Acts of Parliament, and were finally transferred to the Crown.

In India, concessions granted by, or wrested from, native rulers gradually established the Company and the Crown as territorial sovereigns, in rivalry with other country powers; and finally left the British Crown exercising undivided sovereignty throughout British India, and paramount authority over the subordinate native States.

It is with the development of this power in England that we are at present concerned. The history of that development may be roughly divided into three, or possibly four, periods.

Periods in History of Constitutional Development

During the first, or trading, period, which began with the charter of Elizabeth in 1600, the East India Company were primarily traders. They enjoyed important mercantile privileges, and for the purposes of their trade held sundry factories, mostly on or near the coast, but they had not yet assumed the responsibilities of territorial sovereignty. The cession of Burdwan, Midnapur, and Chittagong in 1760 made them masters of a large tract of territory, but the first period may perhaps be most fitly terminated by the grant of the *diwani* in 1765, when the Company became practically sovereigns of Bengal, Bihar and Orissa.

During the second period, from 1765 to 1858, the Company were territorial sovereigns, sharing their sovereignty in diminishing proportions with the Crown, and gradually losing their mercantile privileges and functions. This period may, with referenced to its greater portion, be described as the period of double government, using the phrase in the sense in which it was commonly applied to the system abolished by the Act of 1858. The first direct interference of Parliament with the government of India was in 1773, and the Board of Control was established in 1784.

The third period, under which India was governed by the Crown, began with 1858, when, as an immediate consequence of the Mutiny of 1857, the remaining powers of the East India Company were transferred to the Crown.

Perhaps a fourth period should now be added, and might be called the period of constitutional experiments.

In each of these periods a few dates may be selected as convenient landmarks.

Land Marks of First Period

The first period is the period of charters. The charter of 1600 was continued and supplemented by other charters, of which the most important were James I's charter of 1609, Charles II's charter of 1661, James II's charter of 1686, and William III's charters of 1693 and 1698.

The rivalry between the Old or 'London' Company and the New or 'English' Company was terminated by the fusion of the two Companies under Godolphin's Award of 1708.

The wars with the French in Southern India between 1745 and 1761 and the battles of Plassey (1757) and Baxar (1764) in Northern India indicate the transition to the second period.

Land Marks of Second Period

The main stages of the second period are marked by Acts of Parliament, occurring with one exception at regular intervals of twenty years.

North's Regulating Act of 1773 (13 Geo. III, c. 63) was followed by the Charter Acts of 1793, 1813, 1833, and 1853. The exceptional Act is Pitt's Act of 1784.

The Regulating Act organized the government of the Bengal Presidency and established the Supreme Court at Calcutta.

The Act of 1784 (24 Geo. III, sess. 2, c. 25) established the Board of Control.

The Charter Act of 1793 (33 Geo. III, c. 52) made no material change in the constitution of the Indian Government, but happened to be contemporaneous with the permanent settlement of Bengal.

The Charter Act of 1813 (53 Geo. III, c. 155) threw open the trade to India, whilst reserving to the Company the monopoly of the China trade.

The Charter Act of 1833 (3 & 4 Will. IV, c. 85) terminated altogether the trading functions of the Company.

The Charter Act of 1853 (16 & 17 Vict. c. 95) took away from the Court of Directors the patronage of posts in their service, and threw open the covenanted civil service to general competition.

Land Marks of Third Period

The third period was ushered in by the Government of India Act, 1858 (21 and 22 Vict. c. 106), which declared that India was to be governed by and in the name of Her Majesty. The change was announced in India by the Queen's Proclamation of November 1, 1858. Two Acts of 1861 (24 & 25 Vict. cc. 67, 104) added the law member to the Governor General's executive council, remodelled the legislative councils, and provided for the establishment of the Indian High Courts. From that time until the twentieth century Parliamentary legislation for India was confined mainly to matters of detail. The East India Company was not formally dissolved until 1874.

Charter of Elizabeth

The first charter of the East India Company was granted on December 31, 1600. The circumstances in which the grant of this charter arose have been well described by Sir A. Lyall.[1] The customary trade-routes from Europe to the East had been closed by the Turkish Sultan. Another route had been opened by the discovery of the Cape of Good Hope. Thus the trade with the East had been transferred from the cities and states on the Mediterranean to the states on the Atlantic seaboard. Among these latter Portugal took the lead in developing the Indian trade, and when Pope Alexander VI (Roderic Borgia) issued his Bull of May, 1493, dividing the whole undiscovered non-Christian world between Spain and Portugal, it was to Portugal that he awarded India. But since 1580 Portugal had been subject to the Spanish Crown; Holland was at war with Spain, and was endeavouring to wrest from her the monopoly of Eastern trade which had come to her as sovereign of Portugal. During the closing years of the sixteenth century, associations of Dutch merchants had fitted out two great expeditions to Java by the Cape (1595-6 and 1598-9), and were shortly (1602) to be combined into the powerful Dutch East India Company. Protestant England was the political ally of Holland but her commercial rival, and English merchants were not prepared to see the Indian trade pass wholly into her hands. It was in these circumstances that on September 24, 1599, the merchants of London held a meeting at Founders' Hall, under the Lord Mayor, and resolved to form an association for the purpose of establishing direct trade with India. But negotiations for peace were then in progress at Boulogne, and Queen Elizabeth was unwilling to take a step which would give umbrage to Spain. Hence she delayed for fifteen months to grant the charter for which the London merchants had petitioned. The charter incorporated George, Earl of Cumberland, and 215 knights, aldermen, and burgesses, by the name of the 'Governor and Company of Merchants of London trading with the East Indies'. The Company were to elect annually one governor and twenty-four committees, who were to have the direction of the Company's voyages, the provision of shipping and merchandises, the sale of merchandises returned, and the managing of all other things belonging to the Company. Thomas Smith, Alderman of London, and Governor of the Levant Company, was to be the first governor.

The Company might for fifteen years 'freely traffic and use the trade of merchandise by sea in and by such ways and passages already found out or which hereafter shall be found out and discovered . . . into and from the East Indies, in the countries and parts of Asia and Africa, and into and from all the islands, ports, havens, cities, creeks towns and places of Asia and Africa, and America, or any of them, beyond the Cape of Bona Esperanza to the Streights of Magellan'.

During these fifteen years the Company might assemble themselves in any convenient place, 'within our dominions or elsewhere,' and there 'hold court' for the Company and the affairs thereof, and, being so assembled, might 'make, ordain, and constitute such and so many reasonable laws, constitutions, orders, and ordinances, as to them or the greater part of them being then and there present, shall seem necessary and convenient for the good government of the same Company, and of all factors, masters, mariners, and other officers, employed or to be employed in any of their voyages, and for the better advancement and continuance of the said trade and traffick'. They might also impose such pains, punishments, and penalties by imprisonment of body, or by fines and amerciaments, as might seem necessary of convenient for observation of these laws and ordinances. But their laws and punishments were to be reasonable, and not contrary or repugnant to the laws, statutes, or customs of the English realm.

The charter was to last for fifteen years, subject to a power of determination on two years' warning, if the trade did not appear to be profitable to the realm. If otherwise, it might be renewed for a further term of fifteen years.

The Company's right of trading, during the term and within the limits of the charter, was to be exclusive, but they might grant licences to trade. Unauthorized traders were to be liable to forfeiture of their goods, ships, and tackle, and to 'imprisonment and such other punishment as to us, our heirs and successors, for so high a contempt, shall seem meet and convenient'.

The Company might admit into their body all such apprentices of any member of the Company, and all such servants or factors of the Company, 'and all such other' as to the majority present at a court might be thought fit. If any member, having promised to contribute towards an adventure of the Company, failed to pay his contribution, he might be removed, disenfranchised, and displaced.

Points of Constitutional Interest in Charter of Elizabeth

The points of constitutional interest in the charter of Elizabeth are the constitution of the Company, its privileges, and its legislative powers.

Constitution of Company

The twenty-four committees to whom, with the governor, was entrusted the direction of the Company's business, were individuals, not bodies, and were the predecessors of the later directors. Their assembly was in subsequent charters called the court of committees, as distinguished from the court general or general court, which answers to the 'general meeting' of modern companies.

The most noticeable difference between the charter and modern instruments of association of a similar character, is the absence of any reference to the capital of the Company and the corresponding qualification and voting powers of members. It appears from the charter that the adventures had undertaken to contribute towards the first voyage certain sums of money, which were 'set down and written in a book for that purpose', and failure to pay their contributions to the treasurer within a specified date was to involve 'removal and disenfranchisement' of the defaulters. But the charter did not specify the amount of the several contributions,[2] and for all that appears to the contrary each adventurer was to be equally eligible to the office of committee, and to have equal voting power in the general court. The explanation is that the Company belonged at the outset to the simpler and looser form of association to which the City Companies then belonged, and still belong, and which used to be known by the name of 'regulated companies'. The members of such a company were subject to certain common regulations, and were entitled to certain common privileges, but each of them traded on his own separate capital, and there was no joint stock. The trading privileges of the East India Company were reserved to the members, their sons at twenty-one, and their apprentices, factors, and servants. The normal mode of admission to full membership of the Company was through the avenue of apprenticeship or service. But there was power to admit 'others', doubtless on the terms of their offering suitable contributions to the adventure of the Company.

When an association of this kind had obtained valuable concessions and privileges, its natural tendency was to become an extremely close corporation, and to shut its doors to outsiders except on prohibitory terms, and the efforts of those who suffered from the monopoly thus created were directed towards reduction of these terms. Thus by a statute of 1497 the powerful Merchant Adventurers trading with Flanders had been required to reduce to 10 marks (£6 13s. 4d.) the fine payable on admission to their body. By similar enactments in the seventeenth century the Russia Company and Levant Company were compelled to grant privileges of membership on such easy terms as to render them of merely nominal value, and thus to entitle the companies to what, according to Adam Smith, is the highest eulogium which can be justly be stowed on a regulated company, that of being merely useless. The charter of Elizabeth contains nothing specific as to the terms on which admission to the privileges of the Company might be obtained by an outsider. It had not yet been ascertained how far those privileges would be valuable to members of the Company, and oppressive to its rivals.

Privileges of Company

The chief privilege of the Company was the exclusive right of trading between geographical limits which were practically the Cape of Hope on the one hand and the Straits of Magellan on the other, and which afterwards became widely famous as the limits of the Company's charter. The only restriction imposed on the right of trading within this vast and indefinite area was that the Company were not to 'undertake or address any trade into any country, port, island, haven, city, creek, towns, or places being already in the lawful and actual possession of any such Christian Prince or State as at this present or at any time hereafter shall be in league or amity with us, our heirs and successors, and which doth not or will not accept of such trade'. Subject to this restriction the trade of the older continent was allotted to the adventurers with the same lavish grandeur as that with which the Pope had granted rights of sovereignty over the new continent, and with which in our own day the continent of Africa was parceled out among rival chartered companies. The limits of the English charter of 1600 were identical with the limits of the Dutch charter of 1602, and the two charters may be regarded as the Protestant counter-claims to the monopoly claimed under Pope Alexander's Bull. During the first few years of their existence the two Companies carried on their undertakings in co-operation with each other; but they soon began to quarrel, and in 1611 we find the London merchants praying for protection against their Dutch competitors. Projects for amalgamation of the English and Dutch Companies fell through, and during the greater part of the seventeenth century Holland was the most formidable rival and opponent of English trade in the East.

'By virtue of our Prerogative Royal, which we will not in that behalf have argued or brought in question,' the Queen straightly charges and commands her subjects not to infringe the privileges granted by her to the Company, upon pain of forfeitures and other penalties. Nearly a century was to elapse before the Parliament of 1693 formally declared the exercise of this unquestionable prerogative to be illegal as transcending the powers of the Crown. But neither at the beginning nor at the end of the seventeenth century was any doubt entertained about the expediency, as apart from the constitutionality, of granting a trade monopoly of this description. Such monopolies were in strict accordance with the ideas and were justified by the circumstances, of the time.

In the seventeenth century the conditions under which private trade is now carried on with the East did not exist. Beyond certain narrow territorial limits international law did not run, diplomatic relations had no existence.[3] Out side those limits force alone ruled, and trade competition meant war. At the present day territories are annexed for the sake of developing and securing trade. The annexations of the sixteenth century were annexations not of territory, but of trading-grounds. The pressure was the same, the objects were the same, the methods were different. For the successful prosecution of Eastern trade it was necessary to have an association powerful enough to negotiate with native princes, to enforce discipline among its agents and servants, and to drive off European rivals with the strong hand. No Western State could afford to support more than one such association without dissipating its strength. The independent trader, or interloper, was, through his weakness, at the mercy of the foreigner, and, through his irresponsibility, a source of danger to his countrymen. It was because the trade monopoly of the East India Company had outlived the conditions out of which it arose that its extinction in the nineteenth century was greeted with general and just approval.

Legislative Powers of Company

The powers of making laws and ordinances granted by the charter of Elizabeth did not differ in their general provisions from, and were evidently modelled on, the powers of making by-laws commonly exercised by ordinary municipal and commercial corporations. No copies of any laws made under the early charters are known to exist. They would doubtless have consisted mainly of regulations for the guidance of the Company's factors and apprentices. Unless supplemented by judicial and punitive powers, the early legislative powers of the Company could hardly have been made effectual for any further purpose. But they are of historical interest, as the germ out of which the Anglo-Indian codes were ultimately developed. In this connection they may be usefully compared with the provisions which, twenty-eight years after the charter of Elizabeth, were granted to the founders of Massachusetts.

Resemblance to Massachusetts Company

In 1628 Charles I granted a charter to the Governor and Company of the Massachusetts Bay in New England. It created a form of government consisting of a governor, deputy governor, and eighteen assistants, and directed them to hold four times a year a general meeting of the Company to be called the 'great and general Court', in which general court 'the Governor or deputies Governor, and such of the assistants and freemen of the Company as shall be present shall have full power and authority to choose other persons to be free of the Company and to elect and constitute such officers as they shall think fit for managing the affairs of the said Governor and Company and to make Laws and Ordinances for the Good and Welfare of the said Company and for the Government and Ordering of the said Lands and Plantation and the People inhabiting and to inhabit the same, so as such Laws and Ordinances be not contrary or repugnant to the Laws and Statutes of this our realm of England'. The charter of 1628 was replaced in 1691 by another charter, which followed the same general lines, but gave the government of the colony a less commercial and more political character. The main provisions of the charter of 1691 were transferred bodily to the Massachusetts constitution of 1780, which is now in force, and which, as Lord Bryce remarks,[1] profoundly influenced the convention that prepared the federal constitution of the United States in 1787.

Thus from the same germs were developed the independent republic of the West and the dependent empire of the East.

Other English Trading Companies

The Massachusetts Company may be taken as the type of the bodies of adventurers who during the early part of the seventeenth century were trading and settling in the newly discovered continent of the West. It may be worth while to glance at the associations of English merchants who, at the date of the foundation of the East India Company, were trading towards the East. Of these the most important were the Russia or Muscovy Company and the Levant or Turkey Company.[5]

Russia Company

The foundations of the Russia Company[6] were laid by the discoveries of Richard Chancellor. In 1553-4 this Company was incorporated by charter of Philip and Mary under the name of 'the Merchants and Adventurers for the discovery of lands not before known or frequented by any English'. It was to be governed by a court consisting of one governor (the first to be Sebastian Cabot) and twenty-eight of the most sad, discreet, and learned of the fellowships, of whom four were to be called consuls, and the others assistants. The members of the Company were to have liberty to resort, not only to all parts of the dominions of 'our cousin and brother, Lord John Bazilowitz, Emperor of all Russia, but to all other parts not known to our subjects'. And none but such as were free of or licensed by the Company were to frequent the parts aforesaid, under forfeiture of ships and merchandise—a comprehensive monopoly.

In 1566 the adventurers were again incorporated, not by charter, but by Act of Parliament, under the name of 'the fellowship of English Merchants for discovery of new trade',[7] with a monopoly of trade in Russia, and in the countries of Armenia, Media, Hyreania, Persia, and the Caspain Sea.

In the seventeenth century the members of the Company were compelled by the Czar of the time to share with the Dutch their trading privileges from the Russian Government, and by an Act of 1698, which reduced their admission fine to £5,[8] their doors were thrown open. After this they sank into insignificance.

A remnant of their ancient privileges survives in the extra-territorial character still attaching for marriage purposes to the churches and chapels formerly belonging to their factories in Russia. The Russia Company has now lost its mercantile character, and its funds are almost entirely applied to charitable purposes in connection with Russia, such as the maintenance of English chaplains in Petrograd, Moscow, and elsewhere. But it still retains its ancient constitution, and, as in the days of Sebastian Cabot, is controlled by a governor, 4 councils, and 24 assistants.[9]

Levant Company

The Levant Company was founded by Queen Elizabeth for the purpose of developing the trade with Turkey under the concessions then recently granted by the Ottoman Porte. Under arrangements made with various Christian powers and known as the Capitulations, foreigners trading or residing in Turkey were withdrawn from Turkish jurisdiction for most civil and criminal purposes. The first of the Capitulations granted to England bears date in the year 1579, and the first charter of the Levant Company was granted two years afterwards, in 1581. This charter was extended in 1593, renewed by James I, confirmed by Charles II, and, like the East India Company's charters, recognized and modified by various Acts of Parliament.

The Levant Company attempted to open an overland trade to the East Indies, and sent merchants from Aleppo to Bagdad and thence down the Persian Gulf. These merchants obtained articles at Lahore and Agra, in Bengal, and at Malacca, and on their return to England brought information of the profits to be acquired by a trade to the East Indies. In 1593 the Levant Company obtained a new charter, empowering them to trade to India overland through the territories of the Grand Signor. Under these circumstances it is not surprising to find members of the Levant Company taking an active part in the promotion of the East India Company. Indeed the latter Company was in a sense the out growth of the former. Alderman Thomas Smith, the first Governor of the East India Company, was at the same time Governor of the Levant Company, and the adventures of the two Companies were at the outset intimately connected with each other. At the end of the first volume of court minutes of the East India Company are copies of several letters sent to Constantinople by the Levant Company.

Had history taken a different course, the Levant Company might have founded on the shores of the Mediterranean an empire built up of fragments of the dominions of the Ottoman Porte, as the East India Company founded on the shores of the Bay of Bengal an empire built up of fragments of the dominions of the Great Mogul. But England was not a Mediterranean power, trade with the East had been deflected from the Mediterranean to the Atlantic, and the causes which had destroyed the Italian merchant states were fatal to the Levant Company. As the East India Company grew, the Levant Company dwindled, and in 1825 it was formally dissolved.[10]

To return to the East India Company.

The Separate Voyages

During the first twelve years of its existence, the Company traded on the principle of each subscriber contributing separately to the expense of each voyage, and reaping the whole profits of his subscription. The voyages during these years are therefore known in the annals of the Company as the 'separate voyages'. But after 1612 the subscribers threw their contributions into a 'joint stock', and thus converted themselves from a regulated company into a joint-stock company, which, however, differed widely in its constitution from the joint-stock companies of the present day.

James I's Charter of 1609

In the meantime James I had in 1609 renewed the charter of Elizabeth, and made it perpetual, subject to determination after three years' notice on proof of injury to the nation. The provisions of this charter did not, except with regard to its duration, differ in any material respect from those of the charter of Elizabeth.

Beginning of Martial Law Exercisable by Company

It has been seen that under the charter of Elizabeth the Company had power to make laws and ordinances for the government of factors, masters, mariners, and other officers employed on their voyages, and to punish offenders by fine or imprisonment. This power was, however, insufficient for the punishment of grosser offences and for the maintenance of discipline on long voyages. Accordingly, the Company were in the habit of procuring for each voyage a commission to the 'general' in command, empowering him to inflict punishments for non-capital offences, such as murder or mutiny, and to put in execution 'our law called martial'.[11]

Grant of 1615

This course was followed until 1615, when, by a Royal grant of December 16, the power of issuing commissions embodying this authority was given to the Company, subject to a proviso requiring the verdict of a jury in the case of capital offences.

Grant of 1623

By 1623 the increase in the number of the Company's settlements, and the disorderliness of their servants, had drawn attention to the need for further coercive powers. Accordingly King James I, by a grant of February 4, 162 $^{2}/_{3}$,[12] gave the Company the power of issuing similar commissions to their presidents and other chief officers, authorizing them to punish in like manner offences committed by the Company's servants on land, subject to the like proviso as to the submission of capital cases to the verdict of a jury.

Contests with Dutch and English Rivals

The history of the Company during the reigns of the first two Stuarts and the period the Commonwealth was mainly occupied with their contests with Dutch competitors and English rivals.

Massacre of Amboyna

The massacre of Ambopyna (February 16, 162 2/3) was the turning-point in the rivalry with the Dutch. On the one hand it enlisted the patriotic sympathies of Englishmen at home on behalf of their countrymen in the East. On the other hand it compelled the Company to retire from the Eastern Archipelago, and concentrate their efforts on the peninsula of India.

Courten's Association

Under Charles I the extensive trading privileges of the Company were seriously limited. Sir William Courten, through the influence of Endymion Porter, a gentleman of the Bedchamber, obtained from the kind a licence to trade to the East Indies independently of the East India Company. His association, which, from a settlement established by it at Assada, in Madagascar, was often spoken of as the Assada Company, was a thorn in the side of the East India Company for many years.

Cromwell's relations to the Company

Under the Commonwealth the intervention of the Protector was obtained for the settlement of the Company's differences both with their Dutch and with their English competitors. By the Treaty of Westminster in 1654, Cromwell obtained from the Dutch payment of a sum of £85,000 as compensation for the massacre of Amboyna and for the exclusion of the Company from trade with the Spice Islands. Difficulties arose, however, as to the apportionment of this sum among the several joint stocks of which the Company's capital was then composed, and, pending their settlement, Cromwell borrowed £50,000 of the sum for the expenses of the State. He thus anticipated the policy subsequently adopted by Montague and his successors of compelling the Company to grant public loans as a price for their privileges.

Cromwell's Charter of 1657

Ultimately the Company obtained from Cromwell in 1657 a charter under which the rump of Courten's Association was united with the East India Company, and the different stocks of the Company were united into a new joint stock. No copy of this charter is known to exist. Perhaps it was considered impolitic after the Restoration to preserve any evidence of favours obtained from the Protector.

The Company after the Restoration

During the period after the Restoration the fortunes of the Company are centred in the remarkable personality of Sir Josiah Child, and are depicted in the vivid pages of Macaulay. He has described how Child converted the Company from a Whig to a Tory Association, how he induced James II to become a subscriber to its capital, how his policy was temporarily baffled by the Revolution, how vigorously he fought and how lavishly he bribed to counteract the growing influence of the rival English Company.

Marks of royal favour are conspicuous in the charters of the Restoration period.

Charles II's Charter of 1661

The charter granted by Charles II on April 3, 1661, conferred new and important privileges on the Company. Their constitution remained practically unaltered, except that the joint-stock principle was recognized by giving each member one vote for every £500 subscribed by him to the Company's stock. But their powers were materially increased.

They were given 'power and command' over their fortresses, and were authorized to appoint governors and other officers for their government. The governor and council of each factory were empowered 'to judge all persons belonging to the said Governor and Company or that shall be under them, in all causes, whether civil or criminal, according to the laws of this kingdom, and to execute judgement accordingly'. And the chief factor and council of any place for which there was no governor were empowered to send offenders for punishment, either to a place where there was a governor and council, or to England.

The Company were also empowered to send ships of war, men, or ammunition for the security and defence of their factories and places of trade, and 'to choose commanders and officers over them and to give them power and authority, by commission under their common seal or otherwise, to continue or make peace or war with any people that are not Christians, in any place of their trade, as shall be for the most advantage and benefit of the said Governor and Company, and of their trade'. They were further empowered to erect fortifications, and supply them with provisions and ammunition, duty free, 'as also to transport and carry over such number of men, being willing thereunto, as they shall think fit,' to given them in a legal and reasonable manner, to punish them for misdemeanour, and to fine them for breach of orders. They might seize unlicensed persons and send them to England, punish persons in their employment for offences, and in case of their appealing against the sentence, seize them and send them as prisoners to England, there to receive such condign punishment as the merits of the offenders' cause should require, and the laws of the nation should allow.

Arrangements for administration of justice at Madras in Seventeenth century

With regard to the administration of justice, nothing appears to have been done towards carrying into effect the provisions of the charter of 1661 till the year 1678. At Madras, which was at that time the chief of the Company's settlements in India,[13] two or more officers of the Company used before 1678 to sit as justices in the 'choultry' to dispose of petty cases, but there was no machinery for dealing with serious crimes.[14]

In 1678 the agent and council at Madras resolved that, under the charter of 1661, they had power to judge all persons living under them in all cases, whether criminal or civil, according to the English laws, and to execute judgement accordingly, and it was determined that the governor and council should sit in the chapel in the fort on every Wednesday and Saturday to hear and judge all causes. But this high court was not to supersede the justices of the choultry, who were still to hear and decide petty cases.

Grant of Bombay to the Company

In the meantime the port and island of Bombay, which had, in 1661, been ceded to the British Crown as a part of the dower of Catherine of Braganza, were, by a charter of 1669, granted to the East India Company to be held of the Crown, 'as of the Manor of Greenwich in free and common soccage,' for the annual rent of £10.

And by the same charter the Company were authorized to take into their service such of the king's officers and soldiers as should then be on the island and should be willing to serve them. The officers and men who volunteered their services under this power became the cadets of the Company's '1st European Regiment', or 'Bombay Fusiliers', afterwards the 103rd Foot.

The Company were authorized, through their court of committees, to make laws, orders, ordinances, and constitutions for the good government and otherwise of the port and island and of the inhabitants thereof, and, by their governors and other officers, to exercise judicial authority, and have power and authority of government or command, in the island, and to repel any force which should attempt to inhabit its precincts without licence, or to annoy the inhabitants. Moreover, the principal governor of the island was empowered 'to use and exercise all those powers and authorities, in cases of rebellion, mutiny, or sedition, of refusing to serve in wars, flying to the enemy, forsaking colours or ensigns, or other offences against law, custom, and discipline military, in as large and ample manner, to all intents and purposes whatsoever, as any captain-general of our army by virtue of his office has used and accustomed, and may or might lawfully do'.

The transition of the Company from a trading association to a territorial sovereign invested with powers of civil and military government is very apparent in these provisions.

Further attributes of sovereignty were soon afterwards conferred.

Charter of 1677 Granting Powers of Coinage

By a charter of 1677 the Company were empowered to coin money at Bombay to be called by the name of 'rupees, pices, and budjrooks', or such other names as the Company might think fit. These coins were to be current in the East Indies, but not in England. A mint for the coinage of pagodas had been established at Madras some years before.

Administration of Justice at Bombay in Seventeenth Century

The commissioners sent from Surat[15] to take possession of Bombay on behalf of the Company made a report in which they requested that a judge-advocate might be appointed, as the people were accustomed to civil law. Apparently, a temporary measure, two courts of judicature wee formed, the inferior court consisting of a Company's civil officer assisted by two native officers, and having limited jurisdiction, and the supreme court consisting of the deputy governor and council, whose decisions were to be final and without appeal, except in cases of the greatest necessity.

Charter of 1683 Giving Power to raise forces and exercise martial Law, and establishing Court of Admiralty

By a charter of 1683 the Company were given full power to declare and make peace and war with any of the 'heathen nations' being natives of the parts of Asia and America mentioned in the charter, and to 'raise, arm, train, and muster such military forces as to them shall seem requisite and necessary; and to execute and use, within the said plantations, forts, and places, the law called the martial law, for the defence of the said forts, places, and plantations against any foreign invasion or domestic insurrection or rebellion'. But this power was subject to a proviso reserving to the Crown 'the sovereign right, powers, and dominion overall the forts and places of habitation', and 'power of making peace and war, when we shall be pleased to interpose our royal authority thereon'.

By the same charter the king established a court of judicature, to be held at such place or places as the Company might direct, and to consist of 'one person learned in the civil law, and two assistants', to be appointed by the Company. The court was to have power to hear and determine all cases of forfeiture of ships or goods trading contrary to the charter, and also all mercantile and maritime cases concerning persons coming to or being in the places aforesaid, and all cases of trespasses, injuries, and wrongs done or committed upon the high seas or in any of the regions, territories, countries or places aforesaid, concerning any persons residing, being, or coming within the limits of the Company's charter. These cases were to be adjudged and determined by the court, according to the rules of equity and good conscience, and according to the laws and customs of merchants, by such procedure as they might direct, and, subject to any such directions as the judges of the court should, in their best judgement and discretion, think meet and just.

The only person learned in the civil law who was sent out to India in pursuance of the charter of 1683 was Dr. John St. John. By a commission from the king, supplemented by a commission from the Company, he was appointed judge of the court at Surat.

But he soon became involved in disputes with the governor, Sir John Child,[16] who limited his jurisdiction to maritime cases, and appointed a separate judge for civil actions.

At Madras, the president of the council was appointed to supply the place of judge-advocate till one should arrive. But his arrangement caused much dissatisfaction, and it was resolved that, instead of the president's accepting this appointment, the old court of judicature should be continued, and that, until the arrival of a judge-advocate, causes should be heard under it as formerly in accordance with the charter of 1661.

Charter of 1686

In 1686 James II granted the Company a charter by which he renewed and confirmed their former privileges, and authorized them to appoint 'admirals, vice-admirals, rear-admirals, captains, and other sea officers' in any of the Company's ships within the limits of their charter, with power for their naval officers to raise naval forces, and to exercise and use 'within their ships on the other side of the Cape of Good Hope, in the time of open hostility with some other nation, the law called the law martial for defence of their ships against the enemy'. By the same charter the Company were empowered to coin in their forts any species of money usually coined by native princes, and it was declared that these coins were to be current within the bounds of the charter.

The provisions of the charter of 1683 with respect to the Company's admiralty court were repeated with some modifications, and under these provisions Sir John Biggs, who had been recorder of Portsmouth, was appointed judge-advocate at Madras.

Establishment of Municipality at Madras

Among the prerogatives of the Crown one of the most important is the power of constituting municipal corporations by royal charter. Therefore it was a signal mark of royal favour when James II, in 1687, delegated to the East India Company the power of establishing by charter a municipality at Madras. The question whether this charter should be passed under the great seal or under the Company's seal was discussed at a cabinet council. The latter course was eventually adopted at the instance of the governor and deputy governor of the Company, and the reasons urged for its adoption are curious and characteristic. The governor expressed his opinion that no persons in India should be employed under immediate commission from His Majesty, 'because the wind of extraordinary honour in their heads would probably render them so haughty and overbearing that the Company would be forced to remove them.' He was evidently thinking of the recent differences between Sir John Child and Dr. St. John, and was alive to the dangers arising from an independent judiciary which in the next century were to bring about the conflicts between Warren Hastings and the Calcutta supreme court.

Charter of 1687

Accordingly the charter of 1687, which established a municipality and mayor's court at Madras, proceeds from the Company, and not from the Crown. It recites 'the approbation of the king, declared in His Majesty's Cabinet Council[17] the eleventh day of this instant December', and then goes on to constitute a municipality according to the approved English type. The municipal corporation is to consist of a mayor, twelve aldermen, and sixty or more burgesses. The mayor and aldermen are to have power to levy taxes for the building of a convenient town house or guild hall, of a public jail, and of a school-house 'for the teaching of the Gentles or native children to speak, read, and write the English tongue, and to understand arethmetick and merchants' accounts, and for such further ornaments and edifices as shall be thought convenient for the honour, interest, ornament, security, and defence' of the corporation, and of the inhabitants of Madras, and for the payment of the salaries of the necessary municipal officers, including a school master. The mayor and aldermen are to be a court of record, with power to try civil and criminal causes, and the mayor and three of the aldermen are to be justices of the peace. There is to be an appeal in civil and criminal cases from the mayor's court to 'our supreme court of judicature, commonly called our court of admiralty'. There is to be a recorder, who must be a discreet person, skilful in the laws and constitutions of the place, and who is to assist the mayor in trying, judging, and sentencing causes of any considerable value or intricacy. And there is to be a town clerk and clerk of the peace, an able and discreet person, who must always be an Englishman born, but well skilled in the language of East India, and who is to be esteemed a notary public.

Nor are the ornamental parts of municipal life forgotten. 'For the greater solemnity and to attract respect and reverence from the common people', the mayor is to 'always have carried before him when he goes to the guild hall or other place of assembly, two silver maces gilt, not exceeding three feet and a half in length', and the mayor and aldermen may 'always upon such solemn occasions wear scarlet serge gowns, all made after one form or fashion, such as shall be thought most convenient for that hot country'. The burgesses are, on these occasions, to wear white 'pelong', or other silk gowns. Moreover, the mayor and aldermen are to have and for ever enjoy the honour and privilege of having rundelloes and kattysols[18] borne over them when they walk or ride abroad on these necessary occasions within the limits of the said corporation, and, when they go to the guild hall or upon any other solemn occasion, they may ride on horseback in the same order as is used by the Lord Mayor and aldermen of London, having their horses decently furnished with saddles, bridles, and other trimmings after one form and manner as shall be devised and directed by our President and Council of Fort St. George'.

Company's Resolution of 1680

'The charter of 1687 was the last of the Stuart charters affecting the East India Company. The constitutional history of the Company after the Revolution of 1688 may be appropriately ushered in by a reference to the resolution which was passed by them in that year:

The increase of our revenue is the subject of our care as much as our trade; 'tis that must maintain our force when twenty accidents may interrupt our trade; 'tis that must make us a nation in India; without that we are but a great number of interlopers, united by His Majesty's royal charter, fit only to trade where nobody of power thinks it their interest to prevent us; and upon this account it is that the wise Dutch, in all their general advices that we have seen, write ten paragraphs concerning their government, their civil and military policy, warfare, and the increase of their revenue, for one paragraph they write concerning trade.'

This famous resolution, which was doubtless inspired, if not penned, by Sir Josiah Child, announced in unmistakable terms the determination of the Company to guard their commercial supremacy on the basis of their territorial sovereignty and foreshadowed the annexations of the next century.

Controversies after Revolution of 1688

The Revolution of 1688 dealt a severe blow to the policy of Sir Josiah Child, and gave proportionate encouragement to his rivals. They organized themselves in an association which was popularly known as the New Company, and commenced an active war against the Old Company both in the City and in Parliament. The contending parties presented petitions to the Parliament of 1691, and the House of Commons passed two resolutions—first, that the trade of the East Indies was beneficial to the nation, and secondly, that the trade with the East Indies would be best carried on by a joint-stock company possessed of extensive privileges. The practical question, therefore, was, not whether the trade to the East Indies should be abolished, or should be thrown open, but whether the monopoly of the trade should be left in the hands of Sir Josiah Child and his handful of supporters. On this question the majority of the Commons wished to effect a compromise—to retain the Old Company, but to remodel it and to incorporate it with the New Company. Resolutions were accordingly carried for increasing the capital of the Old Company, and for limiting the amount of the stock which might be held by a single proprietor. A Bill based on these resolutions was introduced and read a second time, but was dropped in consequence of the refusal of Child to accept the terms offered to him. Thereupon the House of Commons requested the king to give the Old Company the three years' warning in pursuance of which their privileges might be determined.

Two years of controversy followed. The situation of the Old Company was critical. By inadvertently omitting to pay a tax which had been recently imposed on joint-stock companies, they had forfeited their charter and might at any time find themselves deprived of their privileges without any notice at all. At length, by means of profuse bribes, Child obtained an order requiring the Attorney-General to draw up a charter regranting to the Old Company its former privileges, but only on the condition that the Company should submit to further regulations substantially in accordance with those sanctioned by the House of Commons in 1691. However, even these terms were considered insufficient by the opponents of the Company, who now raised the constitutional question whether the Crown could grant a monopoly of trade without the authority of Parliament.[19] This question, having been argued before the Privy Council, was finally decided in favour of the Company, and an order was passed that the charter should be sealed.

Charters of 1693 and 1694

Accordingly the charter of October 7, 1693, confirmed the former charter of the Company, but was expressed to be revocable in the event of the Company failing to submit to such further regulations as might be imposed on them within a year. These regulations were embodied in two supplemental charters dated November 11, 1693, and September 28, 1694. By the first of these charters the capital of the Company was increased by the addition of £744,000. No person was to subscribe more than £10,000. Each subscriber was to have one vote for each £1,000 stock held by him up to £10,000, but no more. The governor and deputy governor were to be qualified by holding £4,000 stock, and each committee by holding £1,000 stock. The dividends were to be made in money alone. Books were to be kept for recording transfers of stock, and were to be open to public inspection. The joint stock was to continue for twenty-one years and no longer.

The charter of 1694 provided that the governor and deputy governor were not to continue in office for more than two years, that eight new committees were to be chosen each year, and that a general court must be called within eight days on request by six members holding £1,000 stock each. The three charters were to be revocable after three years' warning, if not found profitable to the realm.

By a charter of 1698 the provisions as to voting powers and qualification were modified. The qualification for a single vote was reduced to £500, and no single member could give more than five votes. The qualification for being a committee was raised to £2,000.

The affair of the Redbridge and its results

In the meantime, however, the validity of the monopoly renewed by the charter of 1693 had been successfully assailed. Immediately after obtaining a renewal of their charter the directors used their powers to effect the detention of a ship called the *Redbridge*, which was lying in the Thames and was believed to be bound for countries beyond the Cape of Good Hope. The legality of the detention was questioned, and the matter was brought up in Parliament. And on January 11, 169¾, the House of Commons passed a resolution 'that all subjects of England have equal rights to trade to the East Indies unless prohibited by Act of Parliament'.

'It has ever since been held,' says Macaulay, 'to be the sound doctrine that no power but that of the whole legislature can give to any person or to any society an exclusive privilege of trading to any part of the world.' It is true that the trade to the East Indies, though theoretically thrown open by this resolution, remained practically closed. The Company's agents in the East Indies were instructed to pay no regard to the resolutions of the House of Commons, and to show no mercy to interlopers. But the constitutional point was finally settled. The question whether the trading privileges of the East India Company should be continued was removed from the council chamber to Parliament, and the period of control by Act of Parliament over the affairs of the Company began.

Incorporation of English Company

The first Act of Parliament for regulating the trade to the East Indies was passed in 1698. The New Company had continued their attacks on the monopoly of the Old Company, a monopoly which had now been declared illegal, and they found a powerful champion in Montagu, the Chancellor of the Exchequer. The Old Company offered, in return for a monopoly secured by law, a loan of £700,000 to the State. But Montagu wanted more-money than the Old Company could advance. He also wanted to set up a new company constituted in accordance with the views of his adherents. Unfortunately these adherents were divided in their views. Most of them were in favour of a joint-stock company. But some preferred a regulated company after the model of the Levant Company. The plan which Montagu ultimately devised was extremely intricate, but its general features cannot be more clearly described than in the language of Macaulay : 'He wanted two millions to extricate the State from its financial embarrassments. That sum he proposed to raise by a loan at 8 per cent. The lenders might be either individuals or corporations, but they were all individuals and corporations, to be united in a new corporation, which was to be called the General Society. Every member of the General Society, whether individual or corporation, might trade separately with India to an extent not exceeding the amount which that member had advanced to the government. But all the members or any of them might, if they so thought fit, give up the privilege of trading separately, and unite themselves under a royal Charter for the purpose of trading in common. Thus the General Society was, by its original constitution, a regulated company; but it was provided that either the whole Society or any part of it might become a joint-stock company.'

This arrangement was embodied in an Act and two charters. The Act (9 & 10 Will. III, c. 44) authorized the Crown to borrow two millions on the security of taxes on salt, and stamped vellum, parchment, and paper, and to incorporate the subscribers to the loan by the cumbrous name of the 'General Society entitled to the advantages given by an Act of Parliament for advancing a sum not exceeding two millions for the service of the Crown of England'. The Act followed closely the lines of that by which, four years before, Montagu had established the Bank of England in consideration of a loan of £1,200,000. In each case the loan bears interest at the rate of 8 per cent., and is secured on the proceeds of a special tax or set of taxes. In each case the subscribers to the loan are incorporated and obtain special privileges. The system was an advance on that under which bodies of merchants had obtained their privileges by means of presents to the king or bribes to his ministers, and was destined to receive much development in the next generation. The plan of raising special loans on the security of special taxes has since been superseded by the National Debt and the Consolidated Fund. But the debt to the Bank of England still remains separate, and retains some of the features originally imprinted on it by the legislation of Montagu.

Of the charters granted under the Act of 1698, the first[19] incorporated the General Society as a regulated company, whilst the second[20] incorporated most of the subscribers to the General Society as a joint-stock company, under the name of 'The English Company trading to the East Indies'. The constitution of the

English Company was formed on the same general lines as that of the Old or London Company, but the members of their governing body were called directors instead of 'committees'.

The New Company was given the exclusive privilege of trading to the East Indies, subject to a reservation of the concurrent rights of the Old Company until September 29, 1701. The New Company, like the Old Company, was authorized to make by-laws and ordinances, to appoint governors, with power to raise and train military forces, and to establish courts of judicature. It was also directed to maintain ministers of religion at its factories in India, and to take a chaplain in every ship of 500 tons. The ministers were to learn the Portuguese language and to 'apply themselves to learn the native language of the country where they shall reside, the better to enable them to instruct the Gentoos that shall be the servants or slaves of the same Company or of their agents, in the Protestant religion'. Schoolmasters were also to be provided.

Union of Old and New Companies

It soon appeared that the Old Company had, to use a modern phrase, 'captured' the New Company. It had subscribed £315,000 towards the capital of two millions authorized by the Act of 1698. It had thus acquired a material interest in its rival's concern, and, at the same time, was in possession of the field. It had the capital and plant indispensable for the East India trade, and it retained concurrent privileges of trading. It soon showed its strength by obtaining a private Act of Parliament (11 & 12 Will. III, c. 4) which continued it as a trading corporation until repayment of the whole loan of two millions.

The situation was impossible; the privileges nominally obtained by the New Company were of no real value to it; and a coalition between the two Companies was the only practicable solution of the difficulties which had been created by the Act and charters of 1698.

The coalition was effected in 1702, through the intervention of Lord Godolphin, and by means of an Indenture Tripartite to which Queen Anne and the two Companies were parties, and which embodied a scheme for equalizing the capital of the two Companies and for combining their stocks. The Old Company was to maintain its separate existence for seven years, but the trade of the two Companies was to be carried on jointly, in the name of the English Company, but for the common benefit of both, under the direction of twenty-four managers, twelve to be selected by each Company. At the end of the seven years the Old Company was to surrender its charters. The New or English Company was to continue its trade in accordance with the provisions of the charter of 1698, but was to change its name for that of 'The United Company of Merchants of England trading to the East Indies'.

A deed of the same date, by which the 'dead-stock' of the two Companies was conveyed to trustees, contains an interesting catalogue of their Indian possessions at that time.

Difficulties arose in carrying out the arrangement of 1702, and it became necessary to apply for the assistance of Parliament, which was given on the usual terms. By an Act of 1707[21] the English Company was required to advance to the Crown a further loan of £1,200,000 without interest, a transaction which was equivalent to reducing the rate of interest on the total loan of £3,200,000 from 8 to 5 per cent. In consideration of this advance the exclusive privileges of the Company were continued to 1726, and Lord Godolphin was empowered to settle the differences still remaining between the London Company and the English Company. Lord Godolphin's Award was given in 1708, and in 1709 Queen Anne accepted a surrender of the London Company's charters and thus terminated its separate existence. The original charter of the New or English Company thus came to be, in point of law, the root of all the powers and privileges of the United Company, subject to the changes made by statute. Henceforth down to 1833 (see 3 & 4 Will. IV, c. 85, s. 111) the Company bears its new name of 'The United Company of Merchants of England trading to the East Indies'.

Period between 1708 and 1765

For constitutional purposes the half-century which followed the union of the two Companies may be passed over very lightly.

An act of 1711[22] provided that the privileges of the United Company were not to be determined by the repayment of the loan of two millions.

Extension of Company's Charter

The exclusive privileges of the United Company were extended for further terms by Acts of 1730[23] and 1744[24]. The price paid for the first extension was an advance to the State of £200,000 without interest, and the reduction of the rate of interest on the previous loan from 5 per cent to 4 per cent. By another Act of 1730[25] the security for the loan by the Company was transferred from the special taxes on which it had been previously charged to the 'aggregate fund', the predecessor of the modern Consolidated Fund. The price of the second extension, which was to 1780, was a further loan of more than a million at 3 per cent. By an Act of 1750[26] the interest on the previous loan of £3,200,000 was reduced, first to 3½ per cent, and then to 3 per cent.

Provisions Against Interlopers

Successive Acts were passed for increasing the stringency of the provisions against interlopers[27] and for penalizing any attempt to support the rival Ostend Company.[28]

Judicial Charters of 1726 and 1753

In 1726 a charter was granted establishing or reconstituting municipalities at Madras, Bombay, and Calcutta, and setting up or remodelling mayor's and other courts at each of these places. At each place the mayor and aldermen were to constitute a mayor's court with civil jurisdiction, subject to an appeal to the governor or president in council, and a further appeal in more important cases to the king in council. The mayor's court now also gave probates and exercised testamentary jurisdiction. The governor or president and the five seniors of the council were to be justices of the peace, and were to hold quarter sessions four times in the year, with jurisdiction over all offences except high treason. At the same time the Company was authorized, as in previous charters, to appoint generals, and other military officers, with power to exercise the inhabitants in arms, to repel force by force, and to exercise martial law in time of war.

The capture of Madras by the French in 1746 having destroyed the continuity of the municipal corporation at that place, the charter of 1726 was surrendered and a fresh charter was granted in 1753.

The charter of 1753 expressly excepted from the jurisdiction of the mayor's court all suits and actions between the Indian natives only, and directed that these suits and actions should be determined among themselves, unless both parties submitted them to the determination of the mayor's courts. But, according to Mr. W.H. Morley, it does not appear that the native inhabitants of Bombay were ever actually exempted from the jurisdiction of the mayor's court, or that any peculiar laws were administered to them in that court.[29]

The charters of 1726 and 1753 have an important bearing on the question as to the precise date at which the English criminal law was introduced at the presidency towns. This question is discussed by Sir, James Stephen with reference to the legality of Nuncomar's conviction for forgery; the point being whether the English statute of 1728 (2 Geo. II, c. 25) was or was not in force in Calcutta at the time of Nuncomar's trial. Sir James Stephen inclines to the opinion that English criminal law was originally introduced to some extent by the charter of 1661, but that the later charters of 1726, 1753, and 1774 must be regarded as acts of legislative authority whereby it was reintroduced on three successive occasions, as it stood at the three dates mentioned. If so, the statute of 1728 would have been in force in Calcutta in 1770 when Nuncomar's offence was alleged to have been committed, and at the time of his trial in 1775. But high judicial authorities in India have maintained a different view. According to their view British statute law was first given to Calcutta by the charter establishing the mayor's court in 1726, and British statutes passed after the date of that charter did not apply to India, unless expressly or by necessary implication extended to it.[30] Since the passing of the Indian Penal Code the question has ceased to be of practical importance.

Mutiny Act and Articles of War for Indian Forces

In 1744 war broke out between England and France, and in 1746 their hostilities extended to India. These events led to the establishment of the Company's Indian Army. The first establishment of that army may, according to Sir George Chesney,[31] be considered to date from the year 1748, 'when a small body of sepoys was raised at Madras, after the example set by the French, for the defence of that settlement during the course of the war which had broken out, four years previously, between France and England. At the same time a small European force was raised, formed of such sailors as could be spared from the ships on the coast, and of men smuggled on board the Company's vessels in England by the Company. An officer, Major Lawrence, was appointed by a commission from the Company to command these forces in India.' During the Company's earliest wars its army consisted mainly, for fighting purposes, of Europeans.

It has been seen that by successive charters the Company had been authorized to raise troops and appoint officers. But the more extensive scale on which the military operations of the Company were now conducted made necessary further legislation for the maintenance of military discipline. An Act of 1754[32] laid down for the Indian forces of the Company provisions corresponding to those embodied in the annual English Mutiny acts. It imposed penalties for mutiny, desertion, and similar offences, when committed by officers or soldiers in the Company's service. The Court of Directors might, in pursuance of an authority from the king, empower their president and council and their commanders-in-chief to hold courts-martial for the trial and punishment of military offences. The king was also empowered to make articles of war for the better government of the Company's forces. The same Act contained a provision, repeated in subsequent Acts, which made oppression and other offences committed by the Company's presidents or councils cognizable and punishable in England. The Act of 1754 was amended by another Act passed in 1760.[33]

Charters of 1757 and 1758 as to booty and cession of territory

The warlike operations which were carried on by the East India Company in Bengal at the beginning of the second half of the eighteenth century, and which culminated in Clive's victory at Plassey, led to the grant of two further charters to the Company.

A charter of 1757 recited that the Nabob of Bengal had taken from the Company, without just or lawful pretence and contrary to good faith and amity, the town and settlement of Calcutta, and goods and valuable commodities belonging to the Company and to many persons trading or residing within the limits of the settlement, and that the officers and agents of the Company at Fort St. George had concerted a plan of operations with Vice-

Admiral Watson and others, the commanders of our fleet employed in those parts, for regaining the town and settlement and the goods and commodities, and obtaining adequate satisfaction for their losses; and that it had been agreed between the officers of the Company, on the one part, and the vice-admiral and commanders of the fleet, on the other part, assembled in a council of war, that one moiety of all plunder and booty 'which shall be taken from the Moors' should be set apart for the use of the captors, and that the other moiety should be deposited till the pleasure of the Crown should be known. The charter went on to grant this reserved moiety to the Company, except any part thereof which might have been taken from any of the king's subjects. Any part so taken was to be returned to the owners on payment of salvage.

A charter of 1758, after reciting that powers of making peace and war and maintaining military forces had been granted to the Company by previous charters, and that many troubles had of late years arisen in the East Indies, and the Company had been obliged at very great expense to carry out a war in those parts against the French and likewise against the Nabob of Bengal and other princes or Governments in India, and that some of their possessions had been taken from them and since retaken, and forces had been maintained, raised, and paid by the Company in conjunction with some of the royal ships of war and forces, and that other territories or districts, goods, merchandises, and effects had been acquired and taken from some of the princes or Governments in India at variance with the Company by the ships and forces of the Company alone, went on to grant to the Company all such booty or plunder, ships, vessels, goods, merchandises, treasure, and other things as had since the charter of 1757 been taken or seized, *or should thereafter be taken*, from any of the enemies of the Company or any of the king's enemies in the East Indies by any ships or forces of the Company employed by them or on their behalf within their limits of trade. But this was only to apply to booty taken during hostilities begun and carried on in order to right and recompense the Company upon the goods, estate, or people of those parts from whom they should sustain or have just and well-grounded cause to fear any injury, loss, or damage, or upon any people who should interrupt, wrong, or injure them in their trade within the limits of the charters, or should in a hostile manner invade or attempt to weaken or destroy the settlements of the Company or to injure the king's subjects or others trading or residing within the Company's settlements or in any manner under the king's protection within the limits of the Company. The booty must also have been taken in wars or hostilities or expeditions begun, carried on, and completed by the forces raised and paid by the Company alone or by the ships employed at their sole expense. And there was a saving for the royal prerogative to distribute the booty in such manner as the Crown should think fit in all cases where any of the king's forces should be appointed and commanded to act in conjunction with the ships or forces of the Company. There was also *an* exception for goods taken from the king's subjects, which were to be restored on payment of reasonable salvage. These provisions, though they gave rise to difficult questions at various subsequent times, have now become obsolete. But the charter contained a further power which is still of practical importance. It expressly granted to the Company power, by any treaty of peace made between the Company, or any of their officers, servants, or agents, and any of the Indian princes or Governments, to cede, restore, or dispose of any fortresses, districts, or territories acquired by conquest from any of the Indian princes or Governments during the late troubles between the Company and the Nabob of Bengal, or which should be acquired by conquest in time coming, subject to a proviso that the Company should not have power to cede, restore, or dispose of any territory acquired from the subjects of any European Power without the special licence and approbation of the Crown. This power has been relied on as the foundation, or one of the foundations, of the power of the Government of India to cede territory.[34]

The Company as territorial Sovereign

The year 1765 marks a turning-point in Anglo-Indian history, and may be treated as commencing the period of territorial sovereignty by the East India Company. The successes of Clive and Lawrence in the struggle between the English and French and their respective allies had extinguished French influence in the south of India. The victories of Plassey[35] and Baxar[36] made the Com, any masters of the north-eastern provinces of the peninsula. In 1760 Clive returned from Bengal to England. In 1765, after five years of confusion, he went back to Calcutta as Governor and Commander-in-Chief of Bengal, armed with extraordinary powers. His administration of eighteen months was one of the most memorable in Indian history. The beginning of our Indian rule dates from the second governorship of Clive, as our military supremacy had dated from his victory at Plassey. Clive's main object was to obtain the substance, though not the name, of territorial power, under the fiction of a grant from the Mogul Emperor.

Grant of the Diwani

This object was obtained by the grant from Shah Alam of the Diwani or fiscal administration of Bengal, Bihar, and Orissa.[1]

The criminal jurisdiction in the provinces was still left with the puppet Nawab, who was maintained at Moorshedabad, whilst the Company was to receive the revenues and to maintain the army. But the actual collection of the revenues still remained until 1772 in the hands of native officials.

Thus a system of dual government was established, under which the Company, whilst assuming complete control over the revenues of the country, and full power of maintaining or disbanding its military forces, left in other hands the responsibility for maintaining law and order through the agency of courts of law.

The great events of 1765 produced immediate results in England. The eyes of the proprietors of the Company were dazzled by golden visions. On the dispatch bearing the grant of the Diwani being read to the Court of Proprietors they began to clamour for an increase of dividend, and, in spite of the Company's debts and the opposition of the directors, they insisted on raising the dividend in 1766 from 6 to 10 per cent, and in 1767 to 12½ per cent.

At the same time the public mind was startled by the enormous fortunes which 'Nabobs' were bringing home, and the public conscience was disturbed by rumours of the unscrupulous modes in which these fortunes had been amassed. Constitutional questions were also raised as to the right of a trading company to acquire on its own account powers of territorial sovereignty.[38] The intervention of Parliament was imperatively demanded.

NOTES

1. *British Dominion in India.*
2. The total amount subscribed in September, 1599, was £30,133, and there were 101 subscribers.
3. The state of things in European waters was not much better. See the description of piracy in the Mediterranean in the seventeenth century in Masson, *Historie du Commerce Francais dans le Levant*, chap. ii.
4. *American Commonwealth*, pt. 2, chap. xxxvii. See also Lyall, *British Dominion in India*, p. 54.
5. A good account of the great trading companies is given by Bonnassieux, *Les Grandes Compagnies de Commerce* (Paris, 1892). See also Causton and Keene, *The Early Chartered Companies* (1896); the article on 'Colonies, Government of, by Companies' in the *Dictionary of Political Economy*; the article on 'Chartered Companies' in the Encyclopedia of the Laws of England; and Edgerton, *Origin and Growth of English Colonies* (1903).
6. As to the Russia Company, see the Introduction to *Early, Voyages to Russia* in the publications of the Hakluyt Society.
7. This is said to have been the first English statute which established an exclusive mercantile corporation.
8. 10 & 11 Will. III, c. 6.
9. For this information I am indebted to Mr. Evelyn Hubbard, the present Governor of the Company.
10. In 1918 a new Levant Company was established, not by charter, but under the Companies Acts, with Sir Maurice de Bunsen as its first president.
11. For an example of a sentence of capital punishment under one of these commissions, see Kaye, *Administration of East India Company*, p. 66. In transactions with natives the Company's servants were nominally subject to the native courts. Rights of extra-mural jurisdiction had not yet been claimed.
12. 'The double date here and elsewhere indicates a reference to the three months, January, February, March, which according to the Old Style closed the old year, while under the New Style, introduced in 1751 by the Act 24 Geo. II, c. 23, they begin the new year.
13. The settlement of Madras or Fort St. George had been erected into a Presidency in 1651.

14. See Wheeler, *Madras in Olden Times*.

15. Bombay was then subordinate to Surat, where a factory had been established as early as 1612, and where there was a president with a council of eight members.

16. A dependent, but not a brother, of Sir Josiah Child. See Strachey, Keigwin's Rebellion, p. 21. See also H.G. Rawlinson, *British Beginnings in Western India*. Clarendon Press, 1920.

17. This formal recognition of the existence of a cabinet council is of constitutional interest. But of course the cabinet council of 1687 was a very different thing from the cabinet council of the present day.

18. Umbrellas and parasols.

19. The question had been previously raised in the great case of The *East Indian Company* v. *Sandys* (1683—85), in which the Company brought an action against Mr. Sandys for trading to the East Indies without a licence, and the Lord Chief Justice (Jeffreys) gave judgement for the plaintiffs. See the report in 10 State Trials, 371.

20. Charter of September 3, 1698.

21. Charter of September 5, 1698.

22. 6 Anne, c. 71.

23. 10 Anne, c. 35.

24. 3 Geo. II, c. 14.

25. 17 Geo. II, c. 17.

26. 3 Geo. II, c. 20.

27. 23 Geo. II, c. 22.

28. 1718, 5 Geo. I, c. 21; 1720. 7 Geo. I, Stat. 1, c. 21; 1722, 9 Geo. I, c. 26; 1732, 5 Geo. II, c. 29. See the article on 'Interlopers' in the *Dictionary of Political Economy*. For the career of a typical interloper see the account of Thomas Pitt, afterwards Governor of Madras, and grandfather of the elder William Pitt, given in vol. iii. of Yule's edition of the Diary of William Hedges and in vol. i. of Mr. Basil Williams's *Life of William* Pitt. The relations between interlopers and the East India Company in the preceding century are well illustrated by Skinner's case, which arose on a petition presented to Charles II soon after the Restoration. According to the statement signed by the counsel of Skinner there was a general liberty of trade to the East Indies in 1657 (under the Protectorate), and he in that year sent a trading ship there; but the Company's agents at Bantam, under pretence of a debt due to the Company,

seized his ship and goods, assaulted him in his warehouse at Jamba in the island of Sumatra, and dispossessed him of the warehouse and of a little island called Barella. After various ineffectual attempts by the Crown to induce the Company to pay compensation, the case was, in 1665, referred by the king in council to the twelve judges, with the question whether Skinner could have full relief in any court of law. The answer was that the king's ordinary courts of justice could give relief in respect of the wrong to person and goods, but not in respect of the house and island. The House of Lords then resolved to relieve Skinner, but these proceedings gave rise to a serious conflict between the House of Lords and the House of Commons. See Hargrave's Preface to Hale's *Jurisdiction of the House of Lords*, p. cv.

29. Charter granted by the Emperor Charles VI in 1722, but withdrawn in 1725.

30. Morley's *Digest of Cases in the Supreme Court in India*, Introduction, p. clxix.

31. Morley's Digest, Introduction, pp. xi, xxiii.

32. *Indian Polity* (3rd ed.), ch. XII, which contains an interesting sketch of the rise and development of the Indian Army. The nucleus of a European force had been formed at Bombay in 1669, *supra*, p. 18.

33. 27 Geo. II, c. 9.

34. 1 Geo. III, c. 14.

35. *Lachmi Narayanv. Raja Pratab Singh*, I. L. R. 2 All. 1.

36. Plassey (Clive), June 23, 1757; Baxar (Munro), October 23, 1764.

37. The grant is dated August 17, 1765. The 'Orissa' of the grant corresponds to what is now the district of Midnapur, and is not to be confused with the modern Orissa, which was not acquired until 1803. A good account of the condition of Bengal during the period 1765—72 will be found in Ramsay Muir's *Making of British India*, ch. iii.

38. For the arguments on this question, see Lecky, *History of England in the Eighteenth Century*, ch. xii.

6

The Period of Company's Territorial Sovereignty

Legislation of 1767

On November 25, 1766, the House of Commons resolved to appoint a committee of the whole house to inquire into the state and condition of the East India Company, and the proceedings of this committee led to the passage in 1767 of five Acts with reference to Indian affairs. The first disqualified a member of any company for voting at a general court unless he had held his qualification for six months, and prohibited the making of dividends except at a half-yearly or quarterly court. Although applying in terms to all companies, the Act was immediately directed at the East India Company, and its object was to check the trafficking in votes and other scandals which had recently disgraced their proceedings. The second Act prohibited the East India Company from making any dividend except in pursuance of a resolution passed at a general court after due notice, and directly over-ruled the recent resolution of the Company by forbidding them to declare any dividend in excess of 10 per cent per annum until the next session of Parliament. The third and fourth Acts[4] embodied the terms of a bargain to which the Company had been compelled to consent. The Company was required to pay into the Exchequer and annual sum of £400,000 for two years from February 1, 1767, and in consideration of this payment was allowed to retain its territorial acquisitions and revenues for the same period.[1] At the same time certain duties on tea were reduced on an undertaking by the Company to indemnify the Exchequer against any loss arising from the reduction. Thus the State claimed its share of the Indian spoil, and asserted its rights to control the sovereignty of Indian territories.

In 1768 the restraint on the dividend was continued for another year, and in 1769 a new agreement was made by Parliament with the East India Company for five years, during which time the Company was guaranteed the territorial revenues, but was bound to pay an annuity of £400,000, and to export a specified quantity of British goods. It was at liberty to increase its dividends during that time to 12½ per cent provided the increase did not exceed 1 per cent. If, however, the dividend should fall below 10 per cent the sum to be paid to the Government was to be proportionately reduced. If the finances of the Company enabled it to pay off some specified debts, it was to lend some money to the public at 2 per cent.

These arrangements were obviously based on the assumption that the Company was making enormous profits, out of which it could afford to pay, not only liberal dividends to its proprietors, but a heavy tribute to the State. The assumption was entirely false. Whilst the servants of the Company were amassing colossal fortunes, the Company itself was advancing by rapid strides to bankruptcy. 'It debts were already estimated at more than six millions sterling. It supported an army of about 30,000 men. It paid about one million sterling a year in the form of tributes, pensions, and compensations to the emperor, the Nabob of Bengal, and other great native personages. Its incessant wars, though they had hitherto been always successful, were always expensive, and a large portion of the wealth which should have passed into the general exchequer was still diverted to the private accounts of its servants.' Two great calamities hastened the crisis. In the south of India, Hyder Ali harried the Carnatic, defeated the English forces, and dictated peace on his own terms in 1769. In the north, the great famine of 1770 swept away more than a third of the inhabitants of Bengal.

Pecuniary embarrassments in 1772

Yet the directors went on declaring dividends at the rates of 12 and 12½ per cent. At last the crash came. In the spring session of 1772 the Company had endeavoured to initiate legislation for the regulation of its affairs. But its, the Company's, Bill was thrown out on the second reading, and in its place a select committee of inquiry was appointed by the House of Commons. In June, 1772, Parliament was prorogued, and in July the directors were obliged to confess that the sum required for the necessary payments of the next three months was deficient to the extent of £1,293,000. In August the chairman and deputy chairman waited on Lord North to inform him that nothing short of a loan of a million from the public could save the Company from ruin.

In November, 1772, Parliament met again, and its first step was to appoint a new committee with instructions to hold a secret inquiry into the Company's affairs. This committee presented its first report with unexpected rapidity, and on its recommendation Parliament in December, 1772, passed an Act prohibiting the directors from sending out to India a commission of supervision on he ground that the Company would be unable to bear the expense.

Legislation of 1773

In 1773 the Company came to Parliament for pecuniary assistance, and Lord North's Government took advantage of the situation to introduce extensive alterations into the system of governing the Company's Indian possessions.

In spite of vehement opposition, two Acts wee passed through Parliament by enormous majorities. By one of these Acts[3] the ministers met the financial embarrassments of the Company by a loan of £1,400,000 at 4 per cent, and agreed to suspend payment by the Company of the annuity of £400,000 till this loan had been discharged. The Company was restricted from declaring any dividend above 6 per cent till the new loan had been discharged, and above 7 per cent until the bond debt was reduced to £1,500,000. It was obliged to submit its accounts every half-year to the Treasury, it was restricted from accepting bills drawn by their servants in India for above £300,000 a year, and it was required to export to the British settlements within its limits British goods of a specified value.

The Regulating Act, 1773

The other Act was that commonly known as the Regulating Act.[3] To understand the object and effect of its provisions brief reference must be made to the constitution of the Company at the time when it was passed.

At home the Company was still governed in accordance with the charter of 1698, subject to a few modifications of detail made by the legislation of 1767. There was a Court of Directors and a General Court of Proprietors. Every holder of £500 stock had a vote in the Court of Proprietors, but the possession of £2,000 stock was the qualification for a director. The directors were twenty-four in number, and the whole of them were re-elected every year.

In India each of the three presidencies was under a president or governor and council, appointed by commission of the Company, and consisting of its superior servants. The numbers of council varied,[4] and some of its members were often absent from the presidency town, being chiefs of subordinate factories in the interior of the country. All power was lodged in the president and council jointly, and nothing could be transacted except by a majority of votes. So unworkable had the council become as an instrument of government, that in Bengal Clive had been compelled to delegate its functions to a select committee.

The presidencies were independent of each other. The Government of each was absolute within its own limits, and responsible only to the Company in England.

The civil and military servants of the Company were classified, beginning from the lowest rank, as writers, factors, senior-factors, and merchants. Promotion was usually by seniority. Their salaries were extremely small,[5] but they made enormous profits by trading on their own account, and by money drawn from extortions and bribes. The select committee of 1773 published an account of such sums as had been proved and acknowledged to have been distributed by the princes and other natives of Bengal from the year 1757 to 1766, both included. They amounted to £5,940,987, exclusive of the grant made to Clive after the battle of Plassey. Clive, during his second governorship, made great efforts to put down the abuses of private trade, bribery, and extortion, and endeavoured to provide more legitimate remunerations for the higher classes of the Company's civii and military servants by assigning to them specific shares in the profits derived from the salt monopoly. According to his estimates the profits from this source of a commissioner or colonel would be at least £7,000 a year; those of a factor of major, £2,000.

At the presidency towns, civil justice was administered in the mayor's courts and courts of request, criminal justice by the justices in petty and quarter sessions. In 1772 Warren Hastings became Governor of Bengal, and took steps for organizing the administration of justice in the interior of that province. In the previous year the Court of Directors had resolved to assert in a more active form the powers given them by the grant of the Diwani in 1765, and in a letter of instructions to the president and council at Fort William had announced their resolution to 'stand forth as diwan', and by the agency of the Company's servants to take upon themselves the entire care and management of the revenues.[6] In pursuance of these instructions the Court of Directors appointed a committee, consisting of the Governor of Bengal and four members of council, and these drew up a report, comprising a plan for the more effective collection of the revenue and the administration of justice. This plan was adopted by the Government on August 21, 1772, and many of its rules were long preserved in the Bengal Code of Regulations.[7]

In pursuance of this plan, a board of revenue was created, consisting of the president and members of the council, and the treasury was removed from Moorshedabad to Calcutta. The supervisors of revenue became collectors, and with them were associated native officers, styled '*diwans*'. Courts were established in each collectorship, one styled the Diwani, a civil court, and the other the Faujdari, a criminal court. Over the former the collector presided in his quality of king's diwan. In the criminal court the *kazi* and *mufti* of the district sat to expound the Mahomedan law. Superior courts were established at the chief seat of government, called the *Sadr Diwani Adalat* and the *Sadr Nazamat Adalat*. These courts theoretically derived their jurisdiction and authority, not form the British Crown, but from the native Government in whose name the Company acted as administrators of revenue. They were Company's courts, not King's courts.

Provisions of Regulating Act

By the Regulating Act of 1773 the qualification to vote in the Court of Proprietors was raised from £500 to £1,000, and restricted to those who had held their stock for twelve months. The directors, instead of being annually elected, were to sit for four years, a quarter of the number being annually renewed.

For the government of the Presidency of Fort William in Bengal, a governor-general and four counsellors were appointed, and the Act declared that the whole civil and military government of this presidency, and also the ordinary management and government of all the territorial acquisitions and revenues in the kingdoms of Bengal, Bihar, and Orissa, should, during such time as the territorial acquisitions and revenues remained in the possession of the Company, be vested in the governor-general and council of the Presidency of Fort William, in like manner as they were be at any time theretofore might have been exercised by the president and council or select committee in the said kingdoms. The avoidance of any attempt to define, otherwise than by reference to existing facts, the nature or extent of the authority claimed or exercised by the Crown over the Company in the new territorial acquisitions is very noticeable, and is characteristic of English legislation.

The first governor-general and counsellors were named in the Act. They were to hold office for five years,[8] and were not to be removable in the meantime, except by the king on the representation of the Court of Directors. A casual vacancy in the office of governor-general during these five years was to be supplied by the senior member of council. A casual vacancy in the office of member of council was during the same time to be filled by the Court of Directors with the consent of the Crown. At the end of the five years the patronage was to be vested in the Company. The governor-general and council were to be bound by the votes of a majority of those present at their meetings, and in the case of an equal division the governor-general was to have a casting vote.

Warren Hastings, who had been appointed Governor of Bengal in 1772, was to be the first governor-general. The first members of his council were to be General Clavering, Colonel Monson, Mr. Barwell, and Mr. Francis.

The supremacy of the Bengal Presidency over the other presidencies was definitely declared. The governor-general and council were to have power of superintending and controlling the government and management of the presidencies of Madras, Bombay, and Bencoolen,[9] so far and in so much as that it should not be lawful for any Government of the minor presidencies to make any orders for commencing hostilities, or declaring or making war, against any Indian princes or powers, or for negotiating or concluding any treaty with any such prince or power without the previous consent of the governor-general and council, except in such cases of imminent necessity as would render it dangerous to postpone such hostilities or treaties until the arrival of their orders, and except also in cases where special orders had been received from the Company.[20] A president and a council offending against these provisions might be suspended by order of the governor-general and council. The governors of the minor presidencies were to obey the order of the governor-general and council, and constantly and dutifully to transmit to them advice and intelligence of all transactions and matters relating to the government, revenues, or interest of the Company.

Provisions followed for regulating the relations of the governor-general and his council to the Court of Directors, and of the directors to the Crown. The governor-general and council were to obey the orders of the Court of Directors and keep them constantly informed of all matters relating to the interest of the Company. The directors were, within fourteen days after receiving letters or advices from the governor-general and council, to transmit to the Treasury copies of all parts relating to the management of the Company's revenue, and to transmit to a secretary of state copies of all parts relating to the civil or military affairs and government of the Company.

Important changes were made in the arrangements for the administration of justice in Bengal. The Crown was empowered to establish by charter a supreme court of judicature at Fort William, consisting of a chief justice and three other judges, who were to be barristers of five years' standing, and were to be appointed by the Crown. The supreme court was empowered to exercise civil, criminal, admiralty, and ecclesiastical jurisdiction, and to appoint such clerks and other ministerial officers with such reasonable salaries as should be approved by the governor-general and council, and to establish such rules of procedure and do such other things as might be found necessary for the administration of justice and the execution of the powers given by the charter. The court was declared to be at all times a court of record and a court of oyer and terminer and jail delivery in and for the town of Calcutta and factory of Fort William and the factories subordinate thereto. Its jurisdiction was declared to extend to all British subjects who should reside in the kingdoms or provinces of Bengal, Bihar, and Orissa, or any of them, under the protection of the United Company. And it was to have 'full power and authority to hear and determine all complaint is against any of His Majesty's subjects for crimes, misdemeanours, or oppressions, and also to entertain, hear, and determine any suits or actions whatsoever against any of His Majesty's subjects in Bengal, Bihar, and Orissa, and any suit, action, or complain against any person employed by or in the service of the Company or of any of His Majesty's subjects'.

But on this jurisdiction two important limitations were imposed.

First, the court was not to be competent to hear or determine any indictment or information against the governor-general or any of his council for any offence, not being treason or felony,[11] alleged to have been committed in Bengal, Bihar, or Orissa. And the governor-general and members of his council were not to be liable to be arrested or imprisoned in any action, suit, or proceeding in the supreme court.[12]

Then, with respect to proceedings in which natives of the country were concerned, it was provided that the court should hear and determine 'any suits or actions whatsoever of any of His Majesty's subjects against any inhabitant of India residing in any of the said kingdoms or provinces of Bengal, Bihar, or Orissa', on any contract in writing where the cause of action exceeded 500 rupees, and where the said inhabitant had agreed in the contract that, in case of dispute, the matter should be heard and determined in the supreme court. Such suits or actions might be brought in the first instance before the supreme court, or by appeal from any of the courts established in the provinces.

This authority, though conferred in positive, not negative, terms, appears to exclude by implication civil jurisdiction in suits by British subjects against 'inhabitants' of the country, except by consent of the defendant, and is silent as to jurisdiction in civil suits by 'inhabitants' against British subjects, or against other 'inhabitants'.

An appeal against the supreme court was to lie to the king in council, subject to conditions to be fixed by the charter.

All offences of which the supreme court had cognizance were to be tried by a jury of British subjects resident in Calcutta.

The governor-general and council and the chief justice and other judges of the supreme court were to act as justices of the peace, and for that purpose to hold quarter sessions.

Liberal salaries were provided out of the Company's revenues for the governor-general and his council and the judges of the supreme court. The governor general was to have annually £25,000, each member of his council £10,000, the chief justice £8,000, and each Puisne judge £6,000.

The governor-general and council were to have powers 'to make and issue such rules, ordinances, and regulations for the good order and civil government' of the Company's settlement at Fort William, and the subordinate factories and places, as should be deemed just and reasonable, and should not be repugnant to the laws of the realm, and to set, impose, inflict, and levy reasonable fines and forfeitures for their breach.

But these rules and regulation were not to be valid until duly registered and published in the supreme court, with the assent and approbation of the court, and they might, in effect, be set aside by the king in council. A copy of them was to be kept affixed conspicuously in the India House, and copies were also to be sent to a secretary of state.

The remaining provisions of the Act were aimed at the most flagrant of the abuses to which public attention had been recently directed. The governor-general and members of his council, and the chief justice and judges of the supreme court were prohibited from receiving presents or being concerned in any transactions by way of traffic, except the trade and commerce of the Company.

No person holding or exercising any civil or military office under the Crown or the Company in the East Indies was to receive directly or indirectly any present or reward from any of the Indian princes or powers, or their ministers or agents, or any of the nations of Asia. Any offender against this provision was to forfeit double the amount received, and might be removed to England. There was an exception for the professional remuneration of counsellors at law, physicians, surgeons, and chaplains.

No collector, supervisor, or any other of His Majesty's subjects employed or concerned in the collection of revenues or administration of justice in the provinces of Bengal, Bihar, and Orissa was, directly or indirectly, to be concerned in the buying or selling of goods byway of trade, or to intermeddle with or be concerned in the inland trade in salt, betel-nut, tobacco or rice, except on the Company's account. No subject of His Majesty in the East Indies was to lend money at a higher rate of the interest than 12 per cent per annum. Servants of the Company prosecuted for breach of public trust, or for embezzlement of public money or stores, or for defrauding the Company, might, on conviction before the supreme court at Calcutta or any other court of judicature in India, be fined and imprisoned, and sent to England. If a servant of the Company was dismissed for misbehaviour, he was not to be restored without the assent of three fourths both of the directors and of the proprietors.

If any governor-general, governor, member of council, judge of the supreme court, or any other person for the time being employed in the service of the Company committed any offence against the Act, or was guilty of any crime, misdemeanour, or offence against any of His Majesty's subjects, or any of the inhabitants of India, he might be tried and punished by the Court of King's Bench in England.

Charter of 1774 Constituting Supreme Court at Calcutta

The charter of justice authorized by the Regulating Act was dated March 26, 1774, and remained the foundation of the jurisdiction exercised by the supreme court at Calcutta until the establishment of the present high court under the Act of 1861. The first chief justice was Sir Elijah Impey. His three colleagues were Chambers, Lemaistre, and Hyde.

Difficulties arising out of Regulating Act

Warren Hastings retained the office of governor-general until 1785, when he was succeeded temporarily by Sir John Macpherson, and, eventually, by Lord Cornwallis. His appointment, which was originally for a term of five years, was continued by successive Acts of Parliament. His administration was distracted by conflicts between himself and his colleagues on the supreme council, and between the supreme council and the supreme court, conflicts traceable to the defective provisions of the regulating Act.

Difficulties in the Council

Of Hastings's four colleagues, one, Barewell, was an experienced servant of the Còmpany, and was in India at the time of his appointment. The other three, Clavering, Monson, and Francis, were sent out from England, and arrived in Calcutta with the judges of the new supreme court.

Barwell usually supported Hastings. Francis, Clavering, and Monson usually opposed him. Whilst they acted together, Hastings was in a minority, and found his policy thwarted and his decisions overruled. In 1776 he was reduced to such depression that he gave his agents in England a conditional authority to tender his resignation. The Court of Directors accepted his resignation on this authority, and took steps to supply his place. But in the meantime Clavering died (November, 1776) and Hastings was able, by means of his casting vote, to maintain his supremacy in the council. He withdrew his authority to his English agents, and obtained from the judges of the supreme court an opinion, that his resignation was invalid. These proceedings possibly occasioned the provision which was contained the Charter Act of 1793 and repeated in the Act of 1833, that the resignation of a governor-general is not valid unless signified by a formal deed.

Difficulties between Supreme Council and Supreme Court

The provisions of the Act of 1773 were obscure and defective as to the nature and extent of the authority exercisable by the governor-general and his council, as to the jurisdiction of the supreme court, and as to the relation between the Bengal Government and the court. The ambiguities of the Act arose partly from the necessities of the case, partly from a deliberate avoidance of new and difficult questions on constitutional law. The situation created in Bengal by the grant of the Diwani in 1765, and recognized by the legislation of 1773, resembled what in the language of modern international law is called a protectorate. The country had not been definitely annexed;[13] the authority of the Delhi emperor and of his native vicegerent was still formally recognized; and the attributes of sovereignty had been divided between them and the Company in such proportions that whilst the substances had passed to the latter, a shadow only remained with the former. But it was a shadow with which potent conjuring tricks could be performed. Whenever the Company found it convenient, they could play off the authority derived from the Mogul against the authority derived from the British law, and justify under the one proceedings which it would have been difficult to justify under the other. In the one capacity the Company was the all-powerful agent of an irresponsible despot; in the other it was tied and bound by the provisions of charters and Acts of Parliament. It was natural that the Company's servants should prefer to act in the former capacity. It was also natural that their Oriental principles of government should be regarded with dislike and suspicion by English statesmen, and should be found unintelligible and unworkable by English lawyers steeped in the traditions of Westminster Hall.

In the latter half of the nineteenth century Englishmen became familiar with situations of this kind, and devised appropriate formulae for dealing with them. The modern practice has been to issue an Order in Council under the Foreign Jurisdiction Act, establishing consular and other courts of civil and criminal jurisdiction, and providing them with codes of procedure and of substantive law, which are sometimes derived from Anglo-Indian sources. The jurisdiction is to be exercised and the law is to be applied in cases affecting British subjects, and, so far as is consistent with international law and comity, in cases affecting European or American foreigners. But the natives of the country are, so far as is compatible with regard to principles of humanity, left in enjoyment of their own laws and customs. If a company has been established for carrying on trade or business, its charter is so framed as to reserve the supremacy and prerogatives of the Crown. In this way a rough-and-ready system of government was provided, which would often fail to stand the application of server legal tests, but which supplied an effectual mode of maintaining some degree of order in uncivilized or semi-civilized countries.[14]

But in 1773 both the theory and the experience were lacking, which are requisite for adapting English institutions to new and foreign circumstances. For want of such experience England was destined to lose her colonies in the Western hemisphere. For want of it mistakes were committed which imperiled the empire she was building up in the East. The Regulating Act provided insufficient guidance as to points on which both the Company and the supreme court were likely to go astray; and the charter by which it was supplemented did not go far to supply its deficiencies. The language of both instruments was vague and inaccurate. They left unsettled questions of the gravest importance. The Company was vested with supreme administrative and military authority. The Court was vested with supreme judicial authority. Which of the two authorities was to be paramount? The court was avowedly established for the purpose of controlling the actions of the Company's servants, and preventing the exercise of oppression against the natives of the country. How far could it extend its controlling power without sapping the foundations of civil authority? The members of the supreme council were personally exempt from the coercive jurisdiction of the court. But how far could the court question and determine the legality of their orders?

Both the omissions from the act and its express provisions were such as to afford room for unfortunate arguments and differences of opinion.

What law was the supreme court to administer? The Act was silent. Apparently it was the unregenerate English law, insular, technical, formless, tempered in its application to English circumstances by the quibbles of judges and the obstinacy of juries, capable of being an instrument of the most monstrous injustice when administered in an atmosphere different from that in which it had grown up.

To whom was this law to be administered? To British subjects and to persons in the employment of the Company. But whom did the first class include? Probably only the class now known as European British subjects, and probably not the native 'inhabitants of India' residing in the three provinces, except such of them as were resident in the town of Calcutta. But the point was by no means clear.[15]

What constituted employment by the Company? Was a native landowner farming revenues so employed? And in doubtful cases on whom lay the burden of proving exemption from or subjection to the jurisdiction?

These were a few of the questions raised by the act and charter, and they inevitably led to serious conflicts between the council and the court.

In the controversies which followed there were, as Sir James Stephen observes,[16] three main heads of difference between the supreme council and the supreme court.

These were, first, the claims of the court to exercise jurisdiction over the whole native population, to the extent of making them plead to the jurisdiction if a writ was served on them. The quarrel on this point culminated in what was known as the Cossijurah case, in which the sheriff and his officers, when attempting to execute a writ against a *zemindar*, were driven off by a company of sepoys acting under the orders of the council. The action of the council was not disapproved by the authorities in England, and thus this contest ended practically in the victory of the council and the defeat of the court.

The second question was as to the jurisdiction of the court over the English and native officers of the Company employed in the collection of revenues for corrupt or oppressive acts done by them in their official capacity. This jurisdiction the Company was compelled by the express provisions of the Regulating Act to admit, though its exercise caused its officers much dissatisfaction.

The third question was as to the right of the supreme court to try actions against the judicial officers of the Company for acts done in the execution of what they believed, or said they believed, to be their legal duty. This question arose in the famous Patna case, in which the supreme court gave judgement with heavy damages to a native plaintiff in an action against officers of the Patna provincial council, acting in its judicial capacity. Impey's judgement in this case was made one of the grounds of impeachment against him, but is forcibly defended by Sir James Stephen against the criticisms of Mill and others, as being not only technically sound, but substantially just. Hastings endeavoured to remove the friction between the supreme court and the country courts by appointing Impey judge of the court of *Sadr Diwani Adalat*, and thus vesting in him the appellate and revisional control over the country courts which had been nominally vested in, but never exercised by, the supreme court. Had he succeeded, he would have anticipated the arrangements under which, some eighty years later, the court of *Sadr Diwani Adalat* and the supreme court were fused into the high court. But Impey compromised himself by drawing a large salary from his new office in addition to that which he drew as chief justice, and his acceptance of a post tenable at the pleasure of the Company was held to be incompatible with the independent position which he was intended to occupy as chief justice of the supreme court.

Amending Act of 1781

In the year 1781 a Parliamentary inquiry was held into the administration of justice in Bengal, and an amending Act of that year settled some of the questions arising out of the Act of 1773.

The governor-general and council of Bengal were not to be subject, jointly or severally, to the jurisdiction of the supreme court for anything counseled, ordered, or done by them in their public capacity. But this exemption did not apply to orders affecting British subjects.

The supreme court was not to have or exercise any jurisdiction in matters concerning the revenue, or concerning any act done in the collection thereof, according to the usage and practice of the country, or the regulations of the governor-general and council.

No person was to be subject to the jurisdiction of the supreme court by reason only of his being a 'landowner, landholder, or farmer of land or of land rent, or for receiving a payment or pension in lieu of any title to, or ancient possession of, land or land rent, or for receiving any compensation of share of profits for collecting of rents payable to the public out of such lands or districts as are actually farmed by himself, or those who are his under-tenants in virtue of his farm, or for exercising within the said lands and farms any ordinary or local authority commonly annexed to the possession or farm thereof or by reason of his becoming security for the payment of rent'.

No person was, by reason of his being employed by the Company, or by the governor-general and council, or by a native or descendant of a native of Great Britain, to become subject to the jurisdiction of the supreme court, in any matter of inheritance or succession to lands or goods, or in any matter of dealing or contract between parties, except in actions for wrongs or trespasses, or in civil suits by agreement of the parties.

Registers were to be kept showing the names, & c., of natives employed by the Company.

The supreme court was, however, to have jurisdiction in all manner of actions and suits against all and singular the inhabitants of Calcutta 'provided that their inheritance and succession to lands, rents, and goods, and all matters of contract and dealing between party and party, shall be determined in the case of Mahomedans, by the laws and usages of Mahomedans, and in the case of Gentus by the laws and usages of Gentus; and where only one of the parties shall be a Mahomedan or Gentu by the laws and usages of the defendant.'[17]

In order that regard should be had to the civil and religious usages of the said natives, the rights and authorities of fathers of families, and masters of families, according as the same might have been exercised by the Gentu or Mahomedan law, were to be preserved to them within their families, nor was any act done in consequence of the rule and law of caste, respecting the members of the said families only, to be held and adjudged a crime, although it might not be held justifiable by the law of England.

Rules and forms for the execution of process in the supreme court were to be accommodated to the religion and manners of the natives, and sent to the Secretary of State, for approval by the king.

The appellate jurisdiction of the governor-general and council in country cases was recognized and confirmed in cautiously general terms. 'Whereas the governor-general and council, or some committee thereof or appointed thereby, do determine on appeals and references from the country or provincial courts in civil cases,' 'the said court shall and lawfully may hold all such pleas and appeals, in the manner and with such powers as it hitherto hath held the same, and shall be deemed in law a court of record; and the judgments therein given shall be final and conclusive, except upon appeal to his Majesty, in civil suits only the value of which shall be five thousand pounds and upwards.' The same court was further declared to be a court to hear and determine on all offences, abuses, and extortions committed in the collection of revenue, and on severities used beyond what shall appear to the said court customary or necessary to the case, and to punish the same according to sound discretion provided the said punishment does not extend to death, or maiming, or perpetual imprisonment.[18]

No action for wrong or injury was to lie in the supreme court against any person whatsoever exercising any judicial office in the country courts for any judgement, decree, or order of the court, nor against any person for any act done by or in virtue of the order of the court.

The defendants in the Patna case were to be released from prison on the governor-general and council giving security (which they were required to do) for the damages recovered in the action against them; and were to be at liberty to appeal to the king in council against the judgement, although the time for appealing under the charter had expired.

The decision of Parliament, as expressed in the Act of 1781, was substantially in favour of the council and against the court on all points. Sir James Stephen argues that the enactment of this Act 'shows clearly that the supreme court correctly interpreted the law as it stood.'[19] But this contention seems to go too far. A legislative reversal of a judicial decision shows that, in the opinion of the legislature, the decision is not substantially just, but must not necessarily be construed as an admission that the decision is technically correct. It is often more convenient to cut a knot by legislation than to attempt its solution by the dilatory and expensive way of appeal.

The Act of 1781 contained a further provision which was of great importance in the history of Indian legislation. It empowered the governor-general and council 'from time to time to frame regulations for the provincial courts and councils'. Copies of these regulations were to be sent to the Court of Directors and to the Secretary of State. They might be disallowed or amended by the king in council. But were to remain in force unless disallowed within two years.

On assuming the active duties of revenue authority in Bengal in 1772, the president and council had made general regulations for the administration of justice in the country by the establishment of civil and criminal courts. And by the Regulating Act of 1773 the governor-general and council were expressly empowered to make rules, ordinances, and regulations. But regulations made under this power had to be registered in the supreme court,[20] with the consent and approbation of that court. In 1780 the governor-general and council made regulations, in addition to those of 1772, for the more effectual and regular administration of justice in the provincial civil courts, and in 1781 they issued a revised code superseding all former regulations. If these regulations were made under the power given by the Act of 1773 they ought to have been registered. But it does not appear that they were so registered, and after the passing of the Act of 1781 the governor-general and council preferred to act under the powers which enabled them to legislate without any reference to the supreme court. However, notwithstanding the limited purpose for which the powers of 1781 were given, it was under those powers that most of the regulation laws for Bengal purported to be framed. Regulations so made did not require registration or approval by the supreme court. But it was for some time doubtful whether they were binding on that court.[21]

Further Legislation of 1781

The Act of 1781 for defining the powers of the supreme court was not the only legislation of that year affecting the East India Company. The Company had by 1778 duly repaid its loan of £1,400,000 from the Exchequer, and subsequently reduced the bond debt to the limits prescribed by an Act of that year.[22] By an Act passed in 1781[3] the Company was required to pay a single sum of £400,000 to the public in discharge of all claims to a share in its territorial revenues up to March 1 in that year, and its former privileges were extended until three years' notice after March 1, 1791. By the same Act it was authorized to pay a dividend of 8 per cent out of its clear profits, but three-fourths of the remainder were to go as a tribute to the public.

By way of repayment of the military expenses incurred by the State on its behalf, the Company was required to pay two lacs of rupees annually for each regiment of 1,000 men sent to India at the Company's desire. The Act further authorized the Company to enlist soliders[4] and punish deserters, and prohibited British subjects from residing more than ten miles from any of the Company's principal settlements without a special licence.

Parliamentary inquiries of 1781

Two Parliamentary committees on Indian affairs were appointed in the year 1781. The object of the first, of which Burke was the most prominent members, was to consider the administration of justice in India. Its first fruits were the passing of the Act, to which reference has been made above, for further defining the powers of the supreme court. But it continued to sit for many years and presented several reports, some written by Burke himself. The other committee, which sat in secret, and of which Dundas was chairman, was instructed to inquire into the cause of the recent war in the Carnatic and the state of the British government on the coast. This committee did not publish its report until 1782, by which time Lord North's Government had been driven out of office by the disastrous results of the American war, and had been succeeded by the second Rockingham ministry. The reports of both committees were highly adverse to the system of administration in India, and to the persons responsible for that administration, and led to the passing of resolutions by the House of Commons requiring the recall of Hastings and Impey, and declaring that the powers given by the Act of 1773 to the governor-general and council ought to be more distinctly ascertained. But the Court of Proprietors of the Company persisted in retaining Hastings in office in defiance both of their directors and of the House of Commons, and no steps were taken for further legislation until after the famous coalition ministry of Fox and North had come into office. Soon after this event, Dundas, who was now in opposition, introduced a Bill which empowered the king to recall the principal servants of the Company, and invested the Governor-General of Bengal with power which was little short of absolute. But a measure introduced by a member of the opposition had no chance of passing, and the Government were compelled to take up the question themselves.

Fox's East India Bill

It was under these circumstances that Fox introduced his famous East India Bill of 1783. His measure would have completely altered the constitution of the East India Company. It was clear that the existing distribution of powers between the State, the Court of Directors, and the Court of Proprietors at home, and the Company's servants abroad, was wholly unsatisfactory, and led to anarchy and confusion. Dundas had proposed to alter it by making the governor-general practically independent, and vesting him with absolute power. Fox adopted the opposite course of increasing the control of the State over the Company at home and its officers abroad. His Bill proposed to substitute for the existing Courts of Directors and Proprietors a new body, consisting of seven commissioners, who were to be named in the Act, were during four years to be irremovable, except upon an address from either House of Parliament, and were to have an absolute power of placing or displacing all persons in the service of the Company, and of ordering and administering the territories, revenues, and commerce of India. Any vacancy in the body was to be filled by the king. A second or subordinate body, consisting of nine assistant directors chosen by the legislature from among the largest proprietors, was to be formed for the purpose of managing the details of commerce. For the first five years they were given the same security of tenure as the seven commissioners, but vacancies in their body were to be filled by the Court of Proprietors.

The events which followed the introduction of Fox's East India Bill belong rather to English than to Indian constitutional history. Everybody is supposed to know how the Bill was denounced by Pitt and Thurlow as a monstrous device for vesting the whole government and patronage of India in Fox and his Whig satellites; how, after having been carried through the House of Commons by triumphant majorities, it was defeated in the House of Lords through the direct intervention of the king; how George III contumeliously drove Fox and North out of office after the defeat of their measure; how Pitt, at the age of twenty-five, ventured to assume office with a small minority at his back; and how his courage, skill, and determination, and the blunders of his opponents, converted that minority into a majority at the general election of 1784.

Pitt's Act of 1784

Like other ministers, Pitt found himself compelled to introduce and defend when in office measures which he had denounced when in opposition. The chief ground of attack on Fox's Bill was its wholesale transfer of patronage from the Company to nominees of the Crown. Pitt steered clear of this rock of offence. He also avoided the appearance of radically altering the constitution of the Company. But his measure was based on the same substantial principle as that of his predecessor and rival, the principle of placing the Company in direct and permanent subordination to a body representing the British Government.

The Act of 1784[24] began by establishing a board of six commissioners, who were formally styled the 'Commissioners for the Affairs of India' but were popularly known as the Board of Control. They were to consist of the Chancellor of the Exchequer and one of the secretaries of state for the time being and of four other Privy Councillors, appointed by the king, and holding office during pleasure. There was to be a quorum of three, and the president was to have a casting vote. They were unpaid, and had no patronage, but were empowered 'to superintend, direct, and control all acts, operations, and concerns which in anywise relate to the civil or military government or revenues of the British territorial possessions in the East Indies'. They were to have access to all papers and instruments of the Company, and to be furnished with such extracts or copies as they might require. The directors were required to deliver to the Board of Control copies of all minutes, orders, and other proceedings of the Company, and of all dispatches sent or received by the directors or any of their committees, and to pay due obedience to, and be bound by, all orders and directions of the Board, touching the civil or military government and revenues of India. The Board might approve, disapprove, or modify the dispatches proposed to be sent by the directors, might require the directors to send out the dispatches as modified, and in case of neglect or delay, might require their own orders to be sent out without waiting for the concurrence of the directors.

A committee of secrecy, consisting of not more than three

members, was to be formed out of the directors, and, when the Board of Control issued orders requiring secrecy, the committee of secrecy was to transmit these orders to India, without informing the other directors.

The Court of Proprietors lost its chief governing faculty, for it was deprived of the power of revoking or modifying any proceeding of the Court of Directors which had received the approval of the Board of Control.[25]

These provisions related to the Government of India at home. Modifications were also made in the governing bodies of the different presidencies in India.

The number of members of the governor-general's council was reduced to three, of whom the commander-in-chief of the Company's forces in India was to be one and to have precedence next to the governor-general.

The Government of each of the Presidencies of Madras and Bombay was to consist of a governor and three counsellors, of whom the commander-in-chief in the presidency was to be one, unless the commander-in-chief of the Company's forces in India happened to be in the presidency, in which case he was to take the place of the local commander-in-chief. The governor-general or governor was to have a casting vote.

The governor-general, governors, commander-in-chief, and members of council were to be appointed by the Court of Directors. They, and any other person holding office under the Company in India, might be removed from office either by the Crown or by the directors. Only covenanted servants of the Company were to be qualified to be members of council. Power was given to make provisional and temporary appointments. Resignation of the office of governor-general, governor, commander-in-chief, or member of council was not to be valid unless signified in writing.[26]

The control of the governor-general and council over the government of the minor presidencies was enlarged, and was declared to extend to 'all such points as relate to any transactions with the country powers, or to war or peace, or to the application of the revenues or forces of such presidencies in time of war'.

A similar control over the military and political operations of the governor-general and council was reserved to the Court of

Directors. 'Whereas to pursue schemes of conquest and extension of dominion in India are measures repugnant to the wish, the honour, and policy of this nation', the governor-general and his council were not, without the express authority of the Court of Directors, or of the secret committee, to declare war, or commence hostilities, or enter into any treaty for making war, against any of the country princes or States in India, or any treaty for guaranteeing the possession of any country prince or State, except where hostilities had actually been commenced, or preparations actually made for the commencement of hostilities, against the British nation in India, or against some of the princes of States who wee dependent thereon, or whose territories were guaranteed by any existing treaty.[27]

The provisions of the Act of 1773 for the punishment of offences committed by British subjects in India were repeated and strengthened. Thus the receipt of presents by persons in the employment of the Company or the Crown was to be deemed extortion, and punishable as such, and there was an extraordinary provision requiring the servants of the Company, under heavy penalties, to declare truly on oath the amount of property they had brought from India.

All British subjects wee declared to be amenable to all courts of competent jurisdiction in India or in England for acts done in Native States, as if the act had been done in British territory.[28] The Company was not to release or compound any sentence or judgement of a competent court against any of its servants, or to restore any such servant to office after he had been dismissed in pursuance of a judicial sentence. The governor-general was empowered to issue his warrant for taking into custody any person suspected of carrying on illicit correspondence with any native prince or other person having authority in India.[29]

A special court, consisting of three judges, four peers, and six members of the House of Commons, was constituted for the trial in England of offences committed in India.[30]

The Company was required to take into consideration its civil and military establishments in India, and to give orders 'for every practicable retrenchment and reduction', and numerous internal regulations, several of which had been proposed by Fox, were made for Indian administration. Thus, promotion was to be as a rule by seniority, writers and cadets were to be between the ages of fifteen and twenty-two when sent out, and servants of the Company who had been five years in England were not to be capable of appointment to an Indian post, unless they could show that their residence in England was due to ill health.

The double government established by Pitt's Act of 1784, with its cumbrous and dilatory procedure and its elaborate system of checks and counter-checks, though modified in details, remained substantially in force until 1858. In practice the power vested in the Board of Control was exercised by the senior commissioner, other than the Chancellor of the Exchequer or Secretary of State. He became known as the President of the Board of Control, and occupied a position in the Government of the day corresponding to some extent to that of the modern Secretary of State for India. But the Board of Directors, though placed in complete subordination to the Board of Control, retained their rights of patronage and their powers of revision, and were thus left no unsubstantial share in the home direction of Indian affairs.[31]

Legislation of 1780

The first important amendments of Pitt's Act were made in 1786. In that year Lord Conrnwallis[32] was appointed governor-general, and he made it a condition of his accepting office that his powers should be enlarged. Accordingly an Act was passed which empowered the governor-general in special cases to override the majority of his council and act on his own responsibility, and enabled the offices of governor-general and commander-in-chief to be united in the same person.

By another Act of the same session the provision requiring the approbation of the king for the choice of governor-general was repealed. But as the Crown still retained the power of recall this repeal was not of much practical importance.

A third Act repealed the provisions requiring servants of the Company to disclose the amount of property brought home by them, and amended the constitution and procedure of the special court under the Act of 1784. It also declared (s. 29) that the criminal jurisdiction of the supreme court at Calcutta was to extend to all criminal offences committed in any part of Asia, Africa, or America, beyond the Cape of Good Hope to the Straits of

Magellan, within the limits of the Company's trade, and (s. 30) that the governor or president and council of Fort St. George, in their courts of oyer and terminer and jail delivery, and the mayor's court at Madras should have civil and criminal jurisdiction over all British subjects residing in the territories of the Company on the coast of Coromandel, or in any other part of the Carnatic, or in the Northern Circars, or within the territories of the Soubah of the Deccan, the Nabob of Arcot, or the Rajah of Tanjore.

Legislation of 1788

In 1788 a serious difference arose between the Board of Control and the Board of Directors as to the limits of their respective powers. The Board of Control, notwithstanding the objections of the directors, ordered out four royal regiments to India, and charged their expenses to Indian revenues. They maintained that they had this power under the Act of 1784. The directors on the other hands argued that under provisions of the Act of 1781, which were still unrepealed, the Company could not be compelled to bear the expenses of any troops except those sent out on their own requisition. Pitt proposed to settle the difference in favour of the Board of Control by means of an explanatory or declaratory Act. The discussions which took place on this measure raised constitutional questions which have been revived in later times.[34]

It was objected that troops raised by the Company in India would suffice and could be much more cheaply maintained. It was also argued on constitutional grounds that no troops ought to belong to the king for which Parliament did not annually vote the money.

In answer to the first objection Pitt confessed that, in his opinion, the army in India ought to be all on one establishment, and should all belong to the king, and declared that it was mainly in preparation for this reform that the troops were to be conveyed.[35]

With respect to the second objection he argued that the Bill of Rights and the Mutiny Act, which were the only positive enactments on the subject, were so vague and indefinite as to be almost nugatory, and professed his willingness to receive any suggestions made for checking an abuse of the powers proposed to be conferred by the Bill.

The questions were eventually settled by a compromise. The Board of Control obtained the powers for which they asked, but a limit was imposed on the number of troops which might be charged to Indian revenues. At the same time the Board of Control were prevented from increasing any salary or awarding any gratuity without the concurrence of the directors and of Parliament, and the directors were required to lay annually before Parliament an account of the Company's receipts and disbursements.[36]

Charter Act of 1793

In 1793, towards the close of Lord Cornwallis's governor-generalship, it became necessary to take steps for renewal of the Company's charter. Pitt was then at the height of his power; his most trusted friend, Dundas,[37] was President of the Board of Control; the war with France, which had just been declared, monopolized English attention; and Indian finances were, or might plausibly be represented as being, in a tolerably satisfactory condition. Accordingly the Act of 1793, which was introduced by Dundas, passed without serious opposition, and introduced no important alternations. It was a measure of consolidation, repealing several previous enactments, and runs to an enormous length, but the amendments made by it relate to matters of minor importance.

The two junior members of the Board of Control were no longer required to be Privy Councillors. Provision was made for payment of the members and staff of the Board out of Indian revenues.

The commander-in-chief was not to be a member of the council at Fort William unless specially appointed by the Court of Directors. Departure from India with intent to return to Europe was declared to vacate the office of governor-general, commander-in-chief, and certain other high offices. The procedure in the councils of the three presidencies was regulated, the powers of control exercisable by the governor-general were emphasized and explained, and the power of the governor-general to overrule the majority of his council was repeated and extended to the Governors of Madras and Bombay. The governor-general, whilst visiting another presidency, was to supersede the governor, and might appoint a vice-president to act for him in his absence. A series of elaborate provisions continued the exclusive privileges of trade for a further term of twenty years, subject to modifications of detail. Another equally elaborate set of sections regulated the application of the Company's finances. Power was given to raise the dividend to 10 per cent, and provision was made for payment to the Exchequer of an annual sum of £500,000 out of the surplus revenue which might remain after meeting the necessary expenses, paying the interest on, and providing for reduction of capital of, the Company's debt, and payment of dividend. It is needless to say that this surplus was never realized. The mutual claims of the Company and the Crown in respect of military expenses were adjusted by wiping out all debts on either side up to the end of 1792, and providing that thenceforward the Company should defray the actual expenses incurred for the support and maintenance of the king's troops serving in India. Some supplementary provisions regulated matters of civil administration in India. The admiralty jurisdiction of the supreme court of Calcutta was expressly declared to extend to the high seas. Power was given to appoint covenanted servants of the Company or other British inhabitants to be justices of the peace in Bengal. Power was also given to appoint scavengers for the presidency towns, and to levy what would now be called a sanitary rate. And the sale of spirituous liquors was made subject to the grant of a licence.

Legislation between 1793 and 1813

A few parliamentary enactments of constitutional importance were passed during the interval between the Charter Acts of 1793 and 1813.

The lending of money by European adventurers to native princes on exorbitant terms had long produced grave scandals, such as those which were associated with the name of Paul Bentham, and were exposed by Burke in his speech on the Nabob of Arcot's debts. An Act of 1797[1] laid down an important provision which was reproduced in the Act of 1915 (s. 125), and which prohibited, under heavy penalties, unauthorized loans by British subjects to native princes.

The same Act reduced the number of judges of the supreme court at Calcutta to three, a chief justice and two *puisnes*, and authorized the grant of charters for the constitution of a recorder's court instead of the mayor's court at Madras and Bombay. It reserved native laws and customs in terms similar to those contained in the Act of 1781. It also embodied an important provision giving an additional and express sanction to the exercise of a local power of legislation in the Presidency of Bengal. One of Lord Cornwallis's regulations of 1793 (Reg. 41) had provided for forming into a regular code all regulations that might be enacted for the internal government of the British territories of Bengal. The Act of 1797 (s. 8) recognized and confirmed this 'wise and salutary provision', and directed that all regulations which should be issued and framed by the Governor-General in Council at Fort William in Bengal, affecting the rights, persons, or property of the natives, or of any other individuals who might be amenable to the provincial courts of justice, should be registered in the judicial department, and formed into a regular code and printed, with translations in the country languages, and that all the grounds of each regulation should be prefixed to it. The provincial courts of judicature were directed to be bound by these regulations, and copies of the regulations of each year were to be sent to the Court of Directors and to the Board of Control.[38]

An Act of 1799[39] gave the Company further powers for raising European troops and maintaining discipline among them. Under this Act the Crown took the enlistment of men for serving in India into its own hands and, on petition from the Company, transferred recruits to them at an agreed sum per head for the cost of recruiting. Authority was given to the Company to train and exercise recruits, not exceeding 2,000, and to appoint officers for that purposes (bearing also His Majesty's commission) at pay not exceeding the sums stated in the Act. The number which the Crown could hold for transfer to the Company was limited to 3,000 men, or such a number as the Mutiny Act for the time being should specify. All the men raised were liable to the Mutiny Act until embarked for India.

An Act of 1800[40] provided for the constitution of a supreme court at Madras, and extended the jurisdiction of the supreme court at Calcutta over the district of Benares (which had been ceded in 1775) and all other districts which had been or might thereafter be annexed to the Presidency of Bengal.

An Act of 1807 gave the governors and councils at Madras and Bombay the same powers of making regulations, subject to approval and registration by the supreme court and recorder's court, as had been previously vested in the Government of Bengal, and the same power of appointing justices of the peace.

Charter Act of 1813

The legislation of 1813 was of a very different character from that of 1793. It was preceded by the most searching investigation which had yet taken place into Indian affairs. The vigorous policy of annexation carried on by Lord Wellesley during his seven years' tenure of office (1798—1805) had again involved the Company in financial difficulties, and in 1808 a committee of the House of Commons was appointed to inquire, amongst other things, into the conditions on which relief should be granted. It continued its sittings over the four following years, and the famous Fifth Report, which was published in July, 1812, is still a standard authority on Indian land tenures, and the best authority on the judicial and police arrangements of the time. When the time arrived for taking steps to renew the Company's charter, a Dundas[41] was still at the Board of Control, but it was no longer found possible to avoid the questions which had been successfully shirked in 1793. Napoleon had closed the European ports, and British traders imperatively demanded admission to the ports of Asia. At the end of 1811 Lord Melville told the Court of Directors that His Majesty's ministers could not recommend to Parliament the continuance of the existing system unless they were prepared to agree that the ships, as well as goods, of private merchants should be admitted into the trade with India under such restrictions as might be deemed reasonable.

The Company struggled hard for their privileges. They began by arguing that their political authority and commercial privileges were inseparable, that their trade profits were dependent upon their monopoly, and that if their trade profits were taken away their revenues would not enable them to carry on the government of the country. But their accounts had been kept in such a fashion as to leave it very doubtful whether their trade profits, as distinguished from their territorial revenues, amounted to anything at all. And this ground of argument was finally cut from under their feet by the concession of a continued monopoly of the tea trade, from which it was admitted that the commercial profits of the Company were principally, if not wholly, derived.

Driven from this position the Company dwelt on the political dangers which would arise from an unlimited resort of Europeans to India. The venerable Warren Hastings was called from his retreat to support on this point the views of the Company before the House of Commons, and it was on this occasion that the members testified their respect for him by rising as a body on his entrance into the House and standing until he had assumed his seat near the bar. His evidence confirmed the assertions of the Company as to the danger of unrestricted European immigration into India, and was supplemented by evidence to a similar effect from Lord Teignmouth (Sir J. Shore), Colonel (Sir John) Malcolm, and Colonel (Sir Thomas) Munro. Experience had proved, they affirmed, that it was difficult to impress even upon the servants of the Company, whilst in their novitiate, a due regard for the feelings and habits of the people, and Englishmen of classes less under the observation of the supreme authorities were notorious for the contempt with which, in their natural arrogance and ignorance, they contemplated the usages and institutions of the natives, and for their frequent disregard of the dictates of humanity and justice in their dealings with the people of India. The natives, although timid and feeble in some places, were not without strength and resolution in others, and instances had occurred where their resentment had proved formidable to their oppressors. It was difficult, if not impossible, to afford them protection, for the Englishman was amenable only to the courts of British law established at the presidencies, and although the local magistrate had the power of sending him further for trial, yet to impose upon the native complainant and witness the obligation of repairing many hundred miles to obtain redress was to subject them to delay, fatigue, and expense, which would be more intolerable than the injury they had suffered.

That their apprehensions were unfounded no one who is acquainted with the history or present conditions of British India would venture to deny. But they were expressed by the advocates of the Company in language of unjustifiable intemperance and exaggeration. Thus Mr. Charles Grant, in the course of the debate in the House of Commons, dwelt on the danger of letting loose among the people of India a host of desperate needy adventurers, whose atrocious conduct in America and in Africa afforded sufficient indication of the evil they would inflict upon India.

The controversy was eventually compromised by allowing Europeans to resort to India, but only under a strict system of licences.

Closely connected with the question of the admission of independent Europeans into India was that of missionary enterprise. The Government were willing to take steps for the recognition and encouragement of Christianity by the appointment of a bishop and archdeacons. But a large number of excellent men, belonging mainly to the Evangelical party, and led in the House of Commons by Wilberforce, wee anxious to go much further in the direction of committing the Indian Government to the active propagation of Christianity among the natives of India. On the other hand, the past and present servants of the Company, including even those who, like Lord Teignmouth, were personally in sympathy with the Evangelical school, were fully sensitive to the danger of interfering with the religious convictions or alarming the religious prejudices of the natives.

The proposals ultimately submitted by the Government to Parliament in 1813 were embodied in thirteen resolutions.[42]

The first affirmed the expediency of extending the Company's privileges, subject to modifications, for a further term of twenty years.

The second preserved to the Company the monopoly of the China trade and of the trade in tea.

The third threw open to all British subjects the export and import trade with India, subject to the exception of tea, and to certain safeguards as to warehousing and the like.

The fourth and fifth regulated the application of the Company's territorial revenues and commercial profits.

The sixth provided for the reduction of the Company's debt, for the payment of a dividend at the rate of 10½ per cent per annum, and for the division of any surplus between the Company and the public in the proportion of one-sixth to the former and five-sixths to the latter.

The seventh required the Company to keep its accounts in such manner as to distinguish clearly those relating to the territorial and political departments from those relating to the commercial branch of its affairs.

The eighth affirmed the expediency, in the interests of economy, of limiting the grants of salaries and pensions.

The ninth reserved to the Court of Directors the right of appointment to the offices of governor-general, governor, and commander-in-chief, subject to the approbation of the Crown.

Under the tenth, the number of the king's troops in India was to be limited, and any number exceeding the limit was; unless employed at the express requisition of the Company, to be at the public charge. This modified in a sense favourable to the Company, Pitt's declaratory Act of 1788.

Then followed a resolution that it was expedient that the Church establishment in the British territories in the East Indies should be placed under the superintendence of a bishop and three archdeacons, and that adequate provision should be made from the territorial revenues of India for their maintenance.

The twelfth resolution declared that the regulations to be framed by the Court of Directors for the colleges at Haileybury and Addiscombe ought to be subject to the regulation of the Board of Control, and that the Board ought to have power to send instructions to India about the colleges at Calcutta[43] and Madras.

It was round the thirteenth resolution that the main controversy raged, and its vague and guarded language shows the difficulty that was experienced in settling its terms. The resolution declared 'that it is the duty of this country to promote the interest and happiness of the native inhabitants of the British dominions in India, and that such measures ought to be adopted as may tend to the introduction amongst them of useful knowledge and of religious and moral improvement. That in the furtherance of the above objects, sufficient facilities shall be afforded by law to persons desirous of going to and remaining in India for the purpose of accomplishing these benevolent designs, provided always, that the authority of the local Governments, respecting the intercourse of Europeans with the interior of the country, be preserved, and that the principles of the British Government, on which the natives of India have hitherto relied for the free exercise of their religion, be inviolably maintained.' One discerns the planter following in the wake of the missionary, each watched with a jealous eye by the Company's servants.

The principles embodied in the Resolutions of 1813 were developed in the Act of the same year. The language of the preamble to the Act is significant. It recites the expediency of continuing to the Company for a further term the possession of the territorial acquisitions in India, and the revenues thereof, 'without prejudice to the undoubted sovereignty of the Crown of the United Kingdom of Great Britain and Ireland in and over the same.'[44] The constitutional controversy of he preceding century was not to be reopened.

The Act then granted the Indian possessions and revenues to the Company for a further term of twenty years, reserved to it for the same time the China trade and the tea trade, but threw open the general Indian trade, subject to various restrictive conditions.

The thirty-third section after reciting the thirteenth resolution, and the expediency of making provision for granting permission to persons desirous of going to and remaining in India, for the purposes mentioned in the resolution (missionaries) 'and for other lawful purposes' (traders), enabled the Court of Directors or, on their refusal, the Board of Control, to grant licences and certificates entitling the applicants to proceed to any of the principal settlements of the Company, and to remain in India as long as they conducted themselves properly, but subject to such restrictions as might for the time being be judged necessary. Unlicensed persons were to be liable to the penalties imposed by earlier Acts on interlopers, and to punishment on summary conviction in India. British subjects allowed to reside more than ten miles from a presidency town were to procure and register certificates from a district court.

A group of sections related to the provision for religion, learning, and education, and the training of the Company's civil and military servants. There was to be a Bishop of Calcutta, with three archdeacons under him. The colleges at Calcutta and elsewhere were placed under the regulations of the Board of Control. One lac of rupees in each year was to be 'set apart and applied to the revival and improvement of literature and the encouragement of the learned natives of India, and for the introduction and promotion of a knowledge of the sciences among the inhabitants of the British territories in India'. The college at Haileybury and the military seminary at Addiscombe[45] were to be maintained, and no person was to be appointed writer unless he had resided four terms at Haileybury, and produced a certificate that he had conformed to the regulations of the college.

Then came provisions for the application of the revenues,[46] for keeping the commercial and territorial accounts distinct, and for increasing and further defining the powers of superintendence and direction exercised by the Board of Control.

The patronage of the Company was preserved, subject to the approval of the Crown in the case of the higher offices, and of the Board of Control in certain other cases.

The number of king's troops to be paid for out of the Company's revenues was not to exceed 20,000, except in case of special requisition. In order to remove doubts it was expressly declared that the Government in India might make laws, regulations, and articles of war for their native troops, and provide for the holding of courts martial.

The local Governments were also empowered to impose taxes on persons subject to the jurisdiction of the supreme court, and to punish for non-payment.

Justices of the peace were to have jurisdiction in cases of assault or trespass committed by British subjects on natives of India, and also in cases of small debts due to natives from British subjects. Special provision was made for the exercise of jurisdiction in criminal cases over British subjects residing more than ten miles from a presidency town; and British subjects residing or trading, or occupying immovable property, more than ten miles from a presidency town were to be subject to the jurisdiction of the local civil courts.

And, finally, special penalties were enacted for theft, forgery, perjury, and coinage offences, the existing provisions of the common or statute law being apparently considered insufficient for dealing adequately with these offences.

Legislation between 1813 and 1833

The imperial legislation for India during the interval between 1813 and 1833 does not present many features of importance.

An Act of 1814 removed doubts about the powers of the Indian Government to levy duties of customs and other taxes.

An Act of 1815 gave power to extend the limits of the presidency towns, and amended some of the minor provisions of the Act of 1813.

An Act of 1818 removed doubts about the validity of certain Indian marriages, a subject which has always presented much difficulty, but which has now been dealt with by Indian legislation.

An Act of 1820 enabled the East India Company to raise and maintain a corps of volunteer infantry.

An Act of 1823 charged the revenues of India with the payment of additional sums for the pay and pensions of troops serving in India, and regulated the pensions of Indian bishops and archdeacons, and the salaries and pensions of the judges of the supreme courts.

The same Act authorized the grant of a charter for a supreme court of Bombay in substitution for the recorder's court.

The prohibition on settling in India without a licence was still retained. But restrictions on Indian trade were gradually removed, and a consolidating Act of 1823 expressly declared that trade might be carried on in British vessels with all places within the limits of the Company's charter except China.

Another Act of 1823 consolidated and amended the laws for punishing mutiny and desertion of officers and soldiers in the Company's service.

An Act of 1824 transferred the island of Singapore to the East India Company.

Acts of 1825 and 1826 further regulated the salaries of Indian judges and bishops, and regulated the appointment of juries in the presidency towns.

An Act of 1828 declared the real estates of British subjects dying within the jurisdiction of the supreme courts at the presidency towns to be liable for payment of their debts. Other

Acts of the same year applied the East India Mutiny Act to the force known as the Bombay Marine, and extended to the East Indies sundry amendments of the English criminal law.

And an Act of 1832[9] authorized the appointment of persons other than covenanted civilians to be justices of the peace in India, and repealed the provisions requiring jurors to be Christians.

Charter Act of 1853

When the time came round again for renewing the Company's charter, Lord William Bentinck's peaceful regime had lasted for five years in India; the Reform Act had just been carried in England, and Whig principles were in the ascendant. Bentham's views on legislation and codification were exercising much influence on the minds of law reformers. Macaulay was in Parliament, and was secretary to the Board of Control, and James Mill, Bentham's disciple, was the examiner of India correspondence at the India House. The Charter Act of 1833,[48] like that of 1813, was preceded by careful inquires into the administration of India. It introduced important changes into the constitution of the East India Company and the system of Indian administration.

The territorial possessions of the Company were allowed to remain under its government for another term of twenty years; but were to be held by the Company 'in trust for his Majesty, his heirs and successors, for the service of the Government of India.

The Company's monopoly of the China trade, and of the tea trade, was finally taken away.

The Company was required to close its commercial business and to wind up its affairs with all convenient speed. Its territorial and other debts were charged on the revenues of India, and it was to receive out of those revenues and annual dividend at the rate of £10s. per cent on the whole amount of its capital stock (i.e. £630, 000 a year), but this dividend was to be subject to redemption by Parliament on payment of £200 sterling for every £100 stock, and for the purpose of this redemption a sum of two million pounds was to be paid by the Company to the National Debt Commissioners and accumulated with compound interest until it reached the sum of twelve millions.[49]

The Company, while deprived of its commercial functions,

retained its administrative and political powers, under the system of double government instituted by previous Acts, and, in particular, continued to exercise its rights of patronage over Indian appointments. The constitution of the Board of Control was modified, but as the powers of the Board were executed by its president the modifications had no practical effect. The Act reenacted provisions of former Acts as to the 'secret committee' of the Court of Directors, and the dispatches to be sent through that committee, and it simplified the formal title of the Company by authorizing it to be called the East India Company.

No very material alteration was made in the system on which the executive government was to be carried on in India. The superintendence, direction, and control of the whole civil and military government were expressly vested in a governor-general and counsellors, who were to be styled the Governor-General of India in Council'.[50] This council was increase by the addition of a fourth ordinary member, who was not to be one of the Company's servants, and was not to be entitled to act as member of council except for legislative purposes.[51] It need hardly be stated that the fourth member was Macaulay.

The overgrown Presidency of Bengal[52] was to be divided into two distinct presidencies, to be called the presidency of Fort William and the Presidency of Agra. But this provision never came into operation. It was suspended by an enactment of 1835 (5 & 6 Will. IV, c. 52), and the suspension was continued indefinitely by the Charter Act of 1853 (16 & 17 Vict. c. 95, s. 15).

The intention was that each of the four presidencies, Fort William, Fort St. George, Bombay, and Agra, should have, for executive purposes, a governor and council of its own. But the governor-general and his council were to be, for the present, the governor and council of Fort William, and power was given to reduce the members of the council, or even suspend them altogether and vest the executive control in a governor alone.[53]

Important alterations were made by the Act of 1833 in the legislative powers of the Indian Government. 'At that date there were five different bodies of statute law in force in the (Indian) empire. First, there was the whole body of statue law existing so far as it was applicable, which was introduced by the Charter of George I and which applied, at least, in the presidency towns.

Secondly, all English Acts subsequent to that date, which were expressly extended to any part of India. Thirdly, the regulations of the governor-general's council, which commence with the Revised Code of 1793, containing forty-eight regulations, all passed on the same day (which embraced the results of twelve years' antecedent legislation), and were continued down to the year 1834. They only had force in the territories of Bengal. Fourthly, the regulations of the Madras council, which spread over the period of thirty-two years, from 1802 to 1834, and are [were] in force in the Presidency of Fort St. George. Fifthly, the regulations of the Bombay Code, which began with the revised code of Mr. Mountstuart Elphinstone in 1827, comprising the results of twenty-eight years' previous legislation, and were also continued into 1834, having force and validity in the Presidency of Fort St. David.'[54]

'In 1833', says Mr. Cowell in continuation, 'the attention of Parliament was directed to three leading vices in the process of Indian government. The first was in the nature of the laws and regulations; the second was in the ill-defined authority and power from which these various laws and regulations emanated; and the third was the anomalous and sometimes conflicting judicatures by which the laws were administered.'

The Act of 1833 vested the legislative power of the Indian Government exclusively in the Governor-General in Council, who had been, as has been seen, reinforced by the addition of a fourth legislative member. The four Presidential Governments were merely authorized to submit to the Governor-General in Council 'drafts or projects of any laws or regulations which they might think expedient', and the Governor-General in Council was required to take these drafts and projects into consideration and to communicate his resolutions thereon to the Government proposing them.

The Governor-General in Council was expressly empowered to make laws and regulations –

a) for repealing, amending, or altering any laws or regulations whatever, for the time being in force in the Indian territories;

b) for all persons, whether British or native, foreigners or others, and for all courts of justice, whether established by character or otherwise, and the jurisdiction there of;

c) for all places and things whatsoever within and throughout the whole and every part of the said territories;

d) for all servants of the Company within the dominions of princes and States in alliance with the Company; and

e) as articles of war for the government of the native officers and soldiers in the military service of the Company, and for the administration of justice by courts-martial to be holden on such officers and soldiers.

But this power was not to extend to the making of any laws and regulations—

(i) which should repeal, vary, or suspend any of the provisions of the Act of 1833, or of the Acts for punishing mutiny and desertion of officers and soldiers in the service of the Crown or of the Company; or

(ii) which should affect any prerogative of the Crown, or the authority of Parliament, or the constitution or rights of the Company, or any part of the unwritten laws or constitutions of the United Kingdom, whereon may depend the allegiance of any person to the Crown, or the sovereignty or dominion of the Crown over the Indian territories; or

(iii) without the previous sanction of the Court of Directors, which should empower any court other than a chartered court to sentence to death any of His Majesty's natural-born subjects born in Europe, or their children, or abolish any of the chartered courts.

There was also an express saving of the right of Parliament to legislate for India and to repeal Indian Acts and, the better to enable Parliament to exercise this power, all Indian laws were to be laid before Parliament.

Laws made under the powers given by the Act were to be subject to disallowance by the Court of Directors, acting under the Board of Control, but, when made, were to have effect as Acts of Parliament, and were not to require registration or publication in any court of justice.

The laws made under the Act of 1833 were known as Acts, and took the place of the 'regulations' made under previous Acts of Parliament.

A comprehensive consolidation and codification of Indian laws was contemplated. Section 53 of the Act recited that it was 'expedient that subject to such special arrangements as local circumstances may require, a general system of judicial establishments as police, to which all persons whatsoever, as well Europeans as natives, may be subject, should be established in the said territories at an early period; and that such laws as may be applicable in common to all classes of the inhabitants of the said territories, due regard being had to the rights, feelings, and peculiar usages of the people, should be enacted; and that all laws and customs having the force of law within the same territories should be ascertained and consolidated, and as occasion may require, amended'.

The Act then went on the direct the Governor-General in Council to issue a commission, to be known as the 'Indian Law Commission', which was to inquire into the jurisdiction, powers, and rules of the existing courts of justice and police establishments in the Indian territories, and all existing forms of judicial procedure, and into the nature and operation of all laws, whether civil criminal written or customary, prevailing and in force in any part of the Indian territories, to which any inhabitants of those territories were then subject. The commissioners were to report to the Governor-General in Council, setting forth the results of their inquiries, and suggestion alterations, and these reports were to be laid before Parliament.

This was the first Indian Law Commission, of which Macaulay was the most prominent member.[55] Its labours resulted directly in the preparation of the Indian Penal Code, which, however, did not become law until 1860, and, indirectly and after a long interval of time, in the preparation of the Codes of Civil and Criminal Procedure and other codes of substantive and adjective law which now form part of the Indian Statute Book.

Important provisions were made by the Act of 1833 for enlarging the rights of European settlers, and for protecting the natives of the country, and ameliorating their condition.

It was declared to be lawful for any natural-born subject of His Majesty to proceed by sea to any port or place having a custom-house establishment within the Indian territories, and to reside thereat, or to proceed to and reside on or pass through any part of the territories which were under the Company's government on January 1, 1800, or any part of the countries ceded by the Nabob of the Carnatic, of the province of Cuttack, or of the settlements of Singapore and Malacca. These rights might be exercised without the requirement of any licence. But every subject of His Majesty not being a native was, on his arrival in India from abroad, to signify on entry, to an officer of customs, his name, place of destination, and objects of pursuit in India. A licence was still required for residence in any part of India other than those above mentioned, but power was reserved to the Governor-General in Council, with the previous approbation of the Court of Directors, to declare any such part open, and remove the obligation of a licence.

Another section expressly enabled any natural-born subject of the Crown to acquire and hold lands in India.

The regulations as to licences have long since been abolished or fallen into desuetude. But by s. 84 of the Act of 1833 the Governor-General in Council was required, as soon as conveniently might be, to make laws or regulations providing for the prevention or punishment of the illicit entrance into or residence in British India of persons not authorized to enter or reside therein. Effect was given to this requirement by Act III of 1864, under which, as now amended by Act III of 1915, the Government of India and local Governments can order foreigners to remove themselves form British India, and apprehend and detain them if they refuse to obey the order. Under the same Act the Governor-General in Council can apply to British India, or any part thereof, special provisions as to the reporting and licensing of foreigners.[56]

An echo of the fears expressed in 1813 as to the dangers likely to arise from the free settlement of interlopers is to be found in the section which, after reciting that 'the removal of restrictions on the intercourse of Europeans with the said territories will render it necessary to provide for any mischief or dangers that may arise therefrom, requires the Governor-General in Council, by laws and regulations, to provide, with all convenient speed, for the protection of the natives of the said territories from insult and outrage in their persons, religions, and opinions.[57]

Section 87 of the Act declared that 'no native of the said territories, nor any natural-born subject of His Majesty resident therein, shall, by reason only of his religion, place of birth, descent, colour, or any of them, be disabled form holding any place, office, or employment under the Company'. The policy of freely admitting natives of India to a share in the administration of the country has never been more broadly or emphatically enunciated.

And finally, the Governor-General in Council was required forthwith to take into consideration the means of mitigating the state of slavery, and of ameliorating the condition of slaves, and of extinguishing slavery throughout the Indian territories so soon as such extinction should be practicable and safe, and to prepare and submit to the Court of Directors drafts of laws on the subject.[58] In preparing these drafts due regard was to be had to the laws of marriage and the rights and authorities of fathers and heads of families.

The sections of the Act which follow these broad declarations of policy are concerned mainly with regulations relating to the ecclesiastical establishments in India and increasing the number of bishoprics to three, and with regulations for the college of Haileybury.

The Act of 1833, as sent out to India, was accompanied by an explanatory dispatch from the Court of Directors, "which, according to a tradition in the India Office, was drafted by James Mill.[59]

Legislation between 1833 and 1853

'During the twenty years' interval between the Charter Act of 1833 and that of 1853 there was very little Parliamentary legislation on India.

An Act of 1835 (5 & 6 Will. IV, c. 52) suspended the provisions of the Act of 1833 as to the division of the Presidency of Bengal into two presidencies,[60] and authorized the appointment of a lieutenant-governor for the North-Western Provinces.[61] The project of establishing on executive council for the Bengal and North-

An Act of 1840 (3 & 4 Vict. c. 37) consolidated and amended the Indian Mutiny Acts, and empowered the Governor-General in council to make regulation for the Indian Navy.

An Act of 1848 (11 & 12 Vict. c. 21) enacted for India a law of insolvency, which has been repealed and re-enacted for the presidency towns by Act III of 1909.

Charter Act of 1853

In 1853, during the governor-generalship of Lord Dalhousie, it became necessary to take steps for renewing the term of twenty years which had been created by the Act of 1833, and accordingly the last of the Charter Acts (16 & 17 Vict. c. 95) was passed in that year.

It differed from the previous Charter Acts by not fixing any definite term for the continuance of the powers, but simply providing that the Indian territories should remain under the government of the Company, in trust for the Crown, until, Parliament should otherwise direct.

The Act reduced the number of the directors of the Company from twenty-four to eighteen, and provided that six of these should be appointed by the Crown.

It continued indefinitely, until the Court of directors and Board of Control should otherwise direct, the suspension of the division of the Bengal Presidency contemplated by the Act of 1835, but authorized the appointment of a separate governor for that presidency, distinct from the governor-general.[62] However, the Act went on the provide that, unless and until this separate governor was appointed, the Court of Directors and Board of Control might authorize the appointment of a lieutenant–governor of Bengal. The power of appointing a separate governor was not brought into operation until the year 1912, but the power of appointing a lieutenant-governor was exercised in 1854, and continued until 1912.

By the following section, power was given to the directors either constitute one new presidency, with the same system of a governor and council as in the Presidencies of Madras and Bombay, or, as an alternative, to authorize the appointment of a lieutenant–governor. The power of constitute a new presidency was not exercised, but a new lieutenant-governership was created for the Punjab in 1859.

Further alterations were made by the Act of 1853 in the machinery for Indian legislation. The 'fourth' or legislative members of the governor-general's council was placed on the same footing with the older or 'ordinary' members of the council by being given a right to sit and vote at executive meetings. At the same time the council was enlarged for legislative purposes by the addition of legislative members, of whom two were the Chief Justice of Bengal and one other supreme court judge, and the others were Company' servants of ten years' standing appointed by the several local Governments. The result was that the council as constituted for legislative purposes under the Act of 1853 consisted of twelve[63] members, namely-

The governor-general.

The commander-in-chief.

The four ordinary members of the governor-general's council.

The chief justice of Bengal.

A puisne judge.

Four representative members (paid)[64] from Bengal, Madras, Bombay, and the North-Western Provinces.

The settings of the legislative council were made public and their proceedings were officially published.

The Indian Law commission appointed under the Act of 1833 has ceased to exist before 1853. It seems to have lost much of its vitality after Macaulay's departure from India. It lingered on for many years, published periodically ponderous volumes of reports, on which, in many instances, Indian Acts have been based, but did not succeed in effecting any codification of the laws or customs of the country, and was finally allowed to expire.[65] Efforts were, however, made by the Act of 1853 to utilized its labours, and for this purpose power was given to appoint a body of English commissioners, with instructions to examine and consider the recommendations of the Indian Commission.[66]

And, finally, the right of patronage to Indian appointments was by the Act of 1853 taken away from the Court of Directors and directed to be exercised in accordance with regulations framed and directed to be exercised in accordance with regulations framed by Board of Control. These regulations threw the covenanted civil service open to general competitions.[67]

In 1855 an Act was passed (18 & 19 Vict. c. 53) which prohibited the admission of further students to Haileybury College after January 25, 1856, and directed the college to be closed on January 31, 1858.

Establishment of Chief Commissionerships

In 1854 was passed an Act which has had important administrative results in India. Under the old system the only mode of providing for the government of newly acquired territory was by annexing it to one of the three Presidencies. Under this system of annexations the Presidency of Bengal had grown to unwieldy dimensions. Some provision had been made for the relief of its government by the constitution of a separate lieutenant-governorship for the North-Western Provinces in 1836. The Act of 1853 had provided for the constitution of a second lieutenant–governorship, and, if necessary, of a fourth presidency. These powers were, however, not found sufficient, and it was necessary to provide for the administration of territories which it might not be advisable to include in any presidency or lieutenant-governorship.[68]

This provision was made by the Act of 1854, which empowered the Governor-General of India in Council, with the sanction of the court of Directors and the Board of Control, to take by proclamation under his immediate authority and management any part of the territories for the time being in the possession or under the government of the East India Company, and thereupon to give all necessary orders and directions respecting the administration of that part, or otherwise provide for its administration. The mode in which this power was practically exercised was by the appointment of chief commissioners, to whom the Governor-General in Council delegates such powers as need not be reserved to the Central Government. In this way chief commissionerships were established for Assam,[69] the Central Provinces, Burma, and other parts of India. But the title of chief commissioner was not directly recognized by Act of Parliament,[70] and the territories under the administration of chief commissioners are technically 'under the immediate authority and management' of the Governor-General in Council within the meaning of the Act of 1854.

The same Act empowered the Government of India, with the sanction of the Home authorities, to define the limits of the several provinces in India; expressly vested in the Governor-General in Council all residuary authority not transferred to the local Government of the provinces into which the old Presidency of Bengal had been divided; and directed that the governor-general was no longer to bear the title of governor of that presidency.

The Government of India Act, 1858

The Mutiny of 1857 gave the deathblow to the system of 'double government', with its division of powers and responsibilities. In February, 1858, Lord Palmerston introduced a Bill for transferring the government of India to the Crown. Under his scheme the home administration was to be conducted by a president with the assistance of a council of eight persons. The members of the council were to be nominated by the Crown, were to be qualified either by having been directors of the Company or by service or residence in India, and were to hold office for eight years, to retiring by rotation in each year. In other respects the scheme did not differ materially from that eventually adopted. The cause of East India Company was pleaded by John Stuart Mill in a weighty State paper, but the second reading of the Bill was carried, by a large majority.

Shortly afterwards, afterwards, however, Lord Palmerton was turned out of office on the Conspiracy to Murder Bill, and, was succeeded by Lord Derby, with Mr. Disraeli as Chancellor of the Exchequer and Lord Ellenborough as President of the Board of Control. The Chancellor of the Exchequer promptly introduced a new Bill for the Government of India, of which the most remarkable feature was a council consisting partly of nominees of the Crown and partly of persons elected on a complicated and elaborate system, by citizens of Manchester and other large towns, holders of East India stock, and others. This scheme died of ridicule, and when the House assembled after the Easter recess no one could be found to defend it.[71] Mr. Disraeli grasped eagerly at a suggestion by Lord John Russell that the Bill should be laid aside, to be succeeded by another based on resolutions of the

House. In the meantime Lord Ellenborough had been compelled to resign in consequence of disapproval of his dispatch censuring Lord Canning's Oudh proclamation, and had been succeeded by Lord Stanley, on whom devolved the charge of introducing and piloting through the House the measure which eventually became law as the Act for the better government of India.

This Act declared that India was to be governed directly by and in the name of the Crown, acting through a Secretary of State, to whom were to be transferred the powers formerly exercised either by the Court of Directors or by the Board of Control. Power was given to appoint a fifth principal Secretary of State for this purpose.

The Secretary of State was to be aided by a council of fifteen members, of whom eight were to be appointed by the Crown and seven elected by the directors of the East India Company. The major part both of the appointed and of the elected members were to be persons who had served or resided in India for ten years, and, with certain exceptions, who had not left India more than ten years before their appointment. Future appointments or elections were to be so made that nine at least of the members of the council itself as to others. The members of the council should hold these qualifications. The power of filling vacancies was vested in the crown as to Crown appointments, and in the council itself as to others. The members of the council were to hold office during good behavior, but to be removable on an address by both Houses of Parliament, and were not to be capable of sitting or voting in Parliament.

The council was charged with the duty of conducting, under the direction of the Secretary of State, the business transacted in the United Kingdom in relation to the government of India and the correspondence with India. The Secretary of State was to be the president of the council, with power to overrule in case of difference of opinion, and to send, without reference to the council, any dispatches which might under the former practice have been sent through the secret committee.

The officers on the home establishment both of the Company and of the Board of Control were to form the establishment of the new Secretary of State in Council, and a scheme for a permanent establishment was to be submitted.

The patronage of the more important appointments in India was vested either in the Crown or in the Secretary of State in Council. Lieutenant-governors were to be appointed by the governor-general subject to the approval of the Crown.

As under the Act of 1853, admission tot he covenanted civil service was to be open to all natural-born subjects of Her Majesty, and was to be granted in accordance with the results of an examination held under rules to be made by the Secretary of State in Council with the assistance of the Civil Service Commissioners.

The patronage to military cadetships was to be divided between the Secretary of State and his Council.

The property of the Company was transferred to the Crown. The expenditure of the revenues of India was to be under the control of the Secretary of State in Council, but was to be charged with a dividend on the Company's stock and with their debts, and the Indian revenues remitted to Great Britain were to be paid to the Secretary of State in Council and applied for Indian purposes. Provision was made for the appointment of a special auditor of the accounts of the Secretary of State in Council.

The Board of Control was formally abolished. With respect to contracts and legal proceedings, the Secretary in State of Council was given a quasi-corporate character for the purpose of enabling him to assert the rights and discharge the liabilities devolving upon him as successor to the East India Company.

The Indian Army

It has been seen that under the authority given by various Acts the Company raised and maintained separate military forces of their own. The troops belonging to these forces, whilst in India, were governed by a separate Mutiny Act, perpetual in duration, though re-enacted from time to time with amendments.[72] The Company also had a small naval force, once known as the Bombay Marine, afterwards as the Indian Navy, and now represented by the Royal Indian Marine.

The Act of 1858 transferred to the service of the Crown the naval and military forces of the Company, retaining, however, their separate local character, with the same liability to local service of the pay and privileges as if they were in the service of the Company. Many of the European troops refused to acknowledge the authority of Parliament to make this transfer. They demanded re-engagement and bounty as a condition of the transfer of their services,[73] and, failing to get these terms, were offered their discharge.

In 1860 the existence of European troops as a separate force was brought to an end by an Act (23 & 24 Vict. c. 100) which, after reciting that it is not expedient that a separate European force should be continued for the local service of Her Majesty in India, formally repealed the enactments by which the Secretary of State in Council was authorized to give directions for raising such forces.

In 1861 the officers and soldiers formerly belonging to the Company's European forces were invited to join, and many of them were transferred to, the regular army under the authority of an Act of that year (24 & 25 Vict. c. 74). Thus the European army of the late East India Company, except a small residue, became merged in the military forces of the Crown.[74]

The naval force of the East India Company was not amalgamated with the Royal Navy, but came to an end in 1863, when it was decided that the defence of India against serious attack by sea should be undertaken by the Royal Navy, which was also to provide for the performance of the duties in the Persian Gulf which had been previously undertaken by the Indian Navy.[75]

The change effected by the Government of India Act, 1858, was formally announced in India by the Queen's Proclamation of November 1, 1858.

In 1859 the Government of India Act, 1859 (22 & 23 Vict. c. 41), was passed for determining the officers by whom, and the mode in which, contracts on behalf of the Secretary of State in Council were to be executed in India.

NOTES

1. This was apparently the first direct recognition by Parliament of the territorial acquisitions of the Company. See *Damodhar Gordhan* v. *Deoram Kanji* (the *Bhaunagar* case), L.R. 1 App. Cas. 332, 342.
2. The history of the East India Company tends to show that whenever a chartered company undertakes territorial sovereignty

on an extensive scale the Government is soon compelled to accept financial responsibility for its proceedings, and to exercise direct control over its actions. The career of the East India Company as a territorial power maybe treated as having begun in 1765, when it acquired the financial administration of the provinces of Bengal, Bihar, and Orissa. Within seven years it was applying to Parliament for financial assistance. In 1773 its Indian operations were placed directly under the control of a governor-general appointed by the Crown, and in 1784 the Court of Directors in England were made directly subordinate to the Board of Control—that is, to a minister of the Crown.

3. This Act is described in its 'short title' as an Act of 1772 because Acts then dated from the beginning of the session in which they were passed.
4. They were usually from twelve to sixteen.
5. In the early part of the eighteenth century a writer, after five years' residence in India, received £10 a year, and the salaries of the higher ranks were on the same scale. Thus a member of council had £80 a year. When Thomas Pitt was appointed Governor of Madras in 1698 he received £300 a year for salary and allowances, and £100 for outfit.
6. Letter of August 28, 1771.
7. The office of 'diwan' implied, not merely the collection of the revenue, but the administration of civil justice. The *'nizamut'* comprised the right of arming and commanding the troops, and the management of the whole of the police of the country, as well as the administration of criminal justice. Morley, *Digest of Cases in the Supreme Courts in India,* p. xxxi. See a fuller account of Warren Hastings's plan, ibid., p. xxxiv.
8. It has been suggested that this enactment is the origin of the custom under which the tenure of the more important offices in India, such as those of governor-general, governor, lieutenant-governor, and member of council, is now limited to five years. The limitations not imposed by statute or by the instrument of appointment.
9. Bencoolen, otherwise Fort Marlborough, is in Sumatra. It was founded by the English in 1686, and was given to the Dutch by the London Treaty, March 11, 1824, in exchange for establishments on the continent of India and for the town and fort of Malacca and its dependencies, which were handed over to the East India Company by 5 Geo. IV, c. 108.

10. This was the first assertion of Parliamentary control over the treaty relations of the Company.

11. Could it then try the governor-general for treason or felony?

12. The saving appears to be limited to civil proceedings. It would exempt against arrest on mesne process.

13. On May 10, 1773, the House of Commons, on the motion of General Burgoyne, passed two resolutions, *(1)* that all acquisitions made by military force or by treaty with foreign powers do of right belong to the State; *(2)* that to appropriate such acquisitions to private use is illegal. But the nature and extent of the sovereignty exercised by the Company was for a long time doubtful. See *Mayor of Lyons* v. *East India Company*, 3 State Trials, new series, 647, 707; 1 Moore P.C. 176.

14. See the Orders in Council under the successive Foreign Jurisdiction Acts, printed in the Statutory Rules and Orders Revised, and the charters granted to the Imperial British East Africa Company (Hertslet, *Map of Africa by Treaty*, i. 118), to the Royal British South Africa Company (ibid. I. 274), and to the Royal Niger Company (ibid. i. 446).

15. *Nuncomar and Impey*, ii. 237.

16. 21 Geo. III, c. 70.

17. This proviso was taken from Warren Hastings's plan for the administration of justice prepared and adopted in 1772, when the Company first 'stood forth as diwan'. It is interesting as a recognition of the personal law which played so important a part during the break-up of the Roman Empire, but has, in the West, been gradually superseded by territorial law.

18. See *Harington's Analysis*, i. 22. But it seems very doubtful whether the council or any of the council had in fact ever exercised jurisdiction as a court of *Sadr Diwani Adalat*. See *Nuncomar and Impey*, ii. 189.

19. *Nucomar and Impey*, ii. 192.

20. As French laws had to be registered by the *Parliament*, and as Acts of Parliament affecting the Channel Islands still have to be registered by the Royal Courts.

21. See Cowell's *Tagore Law Lectures*, 1872, and *In the matter of Ameer Khan*, 6 Bengal Law Reports, 392. 408. The power of legislation was recognized and extended in 1797 by 37 Geo. III, c. 142, s. 8.

22. The Company was unable to meet the payments required by this Act, and successive Acts had to be passed for extending the terms

fixed for payment (22 Geo. III, c. 51; 23 Geo. III, cc. 36, 83; 24 Geo. III, sees. 1, c. 3).

23. This was the first Act giving Parliamentary sanction to the raising of European troops by the Company. Clode, *Military Forces of the Crown*, i. 269.

24. Many of the provisions of this Act were re-enacted in the subsequent Acts of 1793, 1813, and 1833.

25. The Court of Proprietors had recently overruled the resolution of the Court of Directors for the recall of Warren Hastings.

26. s. 28. This was probably enacted in consequence of the circumstances attending Hastings's resignation of office.

27. s. 34. This enactment with its recital was substantially reproduced by a section of the Act of 1793 (33 Geo. III, c. 52, s. 42).

28. s. 44. Re-enacted by 33 Geo. III, c. 52, s. 67.

29. s. 53. This section was re-enacted in substance by 33 Geo. III, c. 52, ss. 45, 46.

30. ss. 66-80. The elaborate enactment constituting the court and regulating its procedure were amended by an Act of 1786 (26 Geo. III, c. 57), but appear never to have been put in force. 'In 149 b.c., on the proposal of Lucius Calpurnius Piso, a standing Senatorial Commission *(quacstio ordinaria)* was instituted to try in judicial form the complaints of the provincials regarding the extortions of their Roman magistrates.' Mommsen, 3, 73.

31. As to the practical working of the system at the close of the eighteenth century see Kaye's *Administration of the East India Company*, p. 129.

32. 'The first of the new dynasty of Parliamentary Governors-General.' Lyall, *British Dominion in India*, p. 218.

33. 26 Geo. III, c. 16. Lord Cornwallis, though holding the double office of governor-general and commander-in-chief, still found his powers insufficient, and was obliged to obtain in 1791 a special Act (31 Geo. III, c. 40) confirming his orders and enlarging his powers. The exceptional powers given to the governor-general by the Act of 1786 were reproduced in the Act of 1793 (33 Geo. III, c. 52, ss. 47—51).

34. See the discussion in 1878 as to the employment of Indian troops in Malta, Hansard, cxl. 14, and Anson, *Law and Custom of the Constitution*, vol. ii, pt. II. P. 174 (3rd ed.).

35. Lord Cornwallis was at this time considering a scheme for the combination of the king's and Company's forces. See Cornwallis Correspondence, i. 251, 341; ii. 316, 572.

36. Clode, *Military Forces of the Crown*, i. 270.

37. Henry Dundas, who afterwards became the first Viscount Melville. He did not become president till June 22, 1793, but had long been the most powerful member of the Board.

38. See Harington's *Analysis of Bengal Laws and Regulations*, 1-9.

39. See Clode, *Military Forces of the Crown*, i. 289.

40. The charter under this Act was granted in December, 1801. Bombay did not acquire a supreme court until 1823 (3 Geo. IV, c. 74).

41. Robert Dundas, who, on his father's death in 1811, became the second Viscount Melville.

42. Printed in an appendix to vol. vii. of Mill and Wilson's *British India*.

43. The college at Calcutta had been founded by Lord Wellesley for the training of the Company's civil servants.

44. The sovereignty of the Crown had been clearly reserved in the charter of 1698. But at that time the territorial possessions were insignificant.

45. The names of these places are not mentioned.

46. An interesting discussion of these provisions is to be found in the correspondence of 1833 between Mr. Charles Grant and the Court of Directors. According to Mr. Grant the principle established by the Acts of 1793 and 1813 was that the profit accruing from the Company's commerce should, in the first instance, be employed in securing the regular payment of dividends to the proprietors of stock, and should then be applied for the benefit of the territory. The last-mentioned applications to be suspended only so long as the burden of debt on the territory continued below a certain specified amount.

47. Singapore was placed under the Colonial Office by the Straits Settlements Act, 1866 (29 & 30 Vict., c. 115, s. 1).

48. 3 & 4 Will. IV, c. 85. The Act received the Royal Assent on August 28, 1833, but did not come into operation, except as to appointments and the like, until April 22, 1834 (s. 117).

49. As to the financial arrangements made under these provisions, see the evidence of Mr. Melvile before the Lords Committee of 1852.

50. It will be remembered that the Governor-General had been previously the Governor-General of Bengal in Council.

51. The duty of the fourth ordinary member' (under the Act of 1833)

was confined entirely to the subject of legislation; he had no power to sit or vote except at meetings for the purpose of making laws and regulations; and it was only by courtesy, and not by right, that he was allowed to see the papers or correspondence, or to be made acquainted with the deliberations of the Government upon any subject not immediately connected with legislation. 'Minute by Sir Barnes Peacock of November 3, 1859.

52. It had been increased by the addition of Benares in 1775, of the modern Orissa in 1803, of large territories in the North-West in 1801—3, and of Assam, Arakan, and Tenasserim in 1824.

53. The power of reduction was exercised in 1833 by reducing the number of ordinary members of the Madras and Bombay councils from three to two (Political Dispatch of December 27, 1833). The original intention was to abolish the councils of the minor presidencies, but, at the instance of the Court of Directors, the irretention was left optional.

54. Cowell, *Tagore Lectures* of 1872. For 'Fort St. David' read 'Bombay'. See also Harington's *Analysis of the Bengal Regulations.*

55. His colleagues were another English barrister, Mr. Cameron, afterwards law member of council, and two civil servants of the Company, Mr. Macleod of the Madras Service, and Mr. (afterwards Sir William) Anderson of the Bombay Service. Sir William Macnaghten of the Bengal Service was also appointed, but did not accept the appointment.

56. See *Alter Caufman* v. *Government of Bombay,* [1894] I. L.R. 18 Bombay, 636. As to the general powers of excluding aliens form British territory, see *Musgrove* v. *Chun Teeong Toy,* [1891] L. R. A. C. 272 (exclusion of Chinese from Australia), and an article in the *Law Quarterly Review* for 1897 on 'Alien Legislation and the Prerogative of the Crown'.

57. See ss. 295—8 of the Indian Penal Code.

58. See Act V of 1843 and ss. 370, 371 of the Indian Penal Code. See also Mr. Cameron's evidence before the Select Committee of the House of Lords in 1852, and Minutes by Sir H. S. Maine, No. 92.

59. Kaye, *Administration of the East India Company,* P. 137

60. By s. 15 of the Character Act of 1853 (16 & 17 Vict. c. 95) this suspension was continued until the Court of Directors and Board of Control should otherwise direct.

61. The first appointment was made in 1836.

62. Under the Act of 1833 the Governor-General of India was also Governor of Bengal, but during his frequent absences from

Calcutta used to delegate his functions in the latter capacity to the senior member of his council. See the evidence of Sir Herbert Maddock and Mr. F. Millett before the Select Committee of the House of Lords in 1852.

63. Power was given by the Act of 1853 to the governor-general to appoint, with the sanction of the Home Government, two other members from the civil service, but this power was never exercised.

64. They received salaries of £5,000 a year each.

65. As to the proceedings of the Commission, see the evidence given in 1852 before the Select Committee of the House of Lords on the East India Company's charter by Mr. F. Millett and Mr. Hay Cameron. Mr. Millett was the first secretary, and was afterwards member of the Commission, Mr. Cameron was one of the first members of the Commission, and was afterwards legislative member of the governor-general's council.

66. The commissioners appointed under this power were Sir John (afterwards Lord) Romilly, Sir John Jervis (Chief Justice of Common Pleas), Sir Edward Ryan, C.H. Cameron, J. N. Macleod, J.A. F. Hawkins, Thomas Flower Ellis, and Robert Lowe (Lord Sherbrooke). They were instructed by the Board of Control to consider specially the preparation of a simple and uniform code of procedure for Indian courts, and the amalgamation of the supreme and *Sadr* courts. (Letter of November 30, 1853, from the Board of Control to the Indian Law Commission.)

67. They were prepared in 1854 by a committee under the presidency of Lord Macaulay.

68. See preamble to Act of 1854.

69. The chief commissionership of Assam was abolished in 1908, but restored in 1912. Burma was placed under a lieutenant-governor in 1897.

70. It was afterwards recognized by the Act of 1870 (33 Vict. c. 3), ss. 1, 3, and is recognized in the Act of 1915.

71. It was to this Bill that Lord Palmerston applied the Spanish boy's remark about Don Quixote, and said that whenever a man was to be seen laughing in the streets he was sure to have been discussing the Government of India Bill.

72. The first of these Acts was an Act of 1753 (27 Geo. II, c. 9), and the last was an Act of 1857 (20 & 21 Vict. c. 66), which was repealed in 1863 (26 & 27 Vict. c. 48).

73. In 1859 they made a 'demonstration' which, from the small stature of the recruits enlisted during the Indian Mutiny, was sometimes called the 'Dumpy Mutiny'. Pritchard, *Administration of India*, i. 36.

74. Under existing arrangements all the troops sent to India are placed on the Indian establishment, and from that time cease to be voted on the Army Estimates. The number of the forces in the regular army as fixed by the annual Army Act is declared to be 'exclusive of the number actually serving within Her Majesty's Indian possessions.'

75. See Sir Charles Wood's letter to the Admiralty of October 20, 1862.

7

Period of Government by the Crown Towards Representative Government

Legislation of 1861

Three Acts of great importance were passed in the year 1861.

Indian Civil Service Act, 1861

Under the Chapter Act of 1793 rank and promotion in the Company's civil service were strictly regulated by seniority and all offices in the 'civil line' of the Company's service in India under the degree of councilor were strictly reserved to the civil servants of the presidency in which the office was held. But by reason of the exigencies of the public service, numerous civil appointments had been made in India in disregard of these restrictions. The Indian Civil Service Act, 1861 (24 & 25 Vict. c. 54), validated all these irregular appointments in the past, but scheduled a number of appointments which, in the future, were to be reserved to members of the covenanted civil service.

At the same time it abolished the rule as to seniority and removed all statutory restrictions on appointments to offices not in the schedule. And, even with respect to the reserved offices, it left a power of appointing outsiders under exceptional circumstances. This power could only be exercised where it appeared to the authority making the appointment that, under the circumstances of the case, it ought to be made without regard to statutory conditions. The person appointed was required to have resided for at least seven years in India. If the post was in the Revenue or Judicial Departments, the person appointed had to pass the same examinations and tests as were required in the case of the covenanted civil services. The appointment was provisional only, and was to be forthwith reported to the Secretary of State in Council with the special reasons for making it, and unless approved within twelve months by the Secretary of State it became void.

Indian Councils Act, 1861

The Indian Councils Act, 1861 (24 & 25 Vict. c. 67), modified the constitution of the governor-general's executive council and remodeled the Indian legislatures. A fifth ordinary member was added to the governor-general's council. Of the five ordinary members, three were required to haye served for ten years in India under the Company or the Crown, and one was to be a barrister or advocate of five years' standing. Power was retained to appoint the commander-in-chief an extraordinary member.

Power was given to the governor-general, in case of his absence from headquarters, to appoint a president of the council, with all the powers the governor-general except those with respect to legislation. And, in such case, the governor-general might invest himself with all the powers exercisable by the Governor-General in Council, except the powers with respect to legislation.

For purposes of legislation the governor-general's council was reinforced by additional members, not less than six nor more than twelve in number, nominated by the governor-general and holding office for two years. Of these additional members, not less than one-half were to be non-official, that is to say, person, not in the civil or military service of the Crown. The lieutenant-governor of a province was also to be an additional member whenever the council held a legislative sitting within his province.

The Legislative Council established under the Act of 1853 had modelled its procedure on that of Parliament, and had shown what was considered an inconvenient degree of independence by asking questions as to, and discussing the propriety of, measures of the Executive Government.[1] The functions of the new Legislative Council were limited strictly to legislation, and the Council was expressly forbidden to transact any business except the consideration and enactment of legislative measures, or to entertain any motion except a motion for leave to introduce a Bill, or having reference to a Bill actually introduced.[2]

Measures relating to the public revenue or debt, religion, military or naval matters, or foreign relations, were not to be introduced without the governor-general's sanction. The assent of the governor-general was required to every Act passed by the council, and any such Act might be disallowed by the queen, acting through the Secretary of State.

The legislative power of the Governor-General, in Council was declared to extend to making laws and regulations for repealing, amending, or altering any laws or regulations for the time being in force in the 'Indian territories now under the dominion of Her Majesty',[3] and making to laws and regulations for all persons, whether British or native foreigners or others, and for all courts of justice, and for all places and things within the said territories, and for all servants of the Government of India within the dominions of princes and States in alliance with Her Majesty.[4] But there were express savings for certain Parliamentary enactments, for the general authority of Parliament, and for any part of the unwritten laws or constitution of the United Kingdom whereon the allegiance of the subject or the sovereignty of the Crown may depend.

An exceptional power was given to the governor-general, in cases of emergency, to make without his council, ordinances, which were not to remain in force for more than six months.

Doubts had for some time existed about the proper mode of legislative for newly acquired territories of the Company. When Benares and the territories afterwards known as the North-Western Provinces were annexed, the course adopted was to extend to them, with some variations, the laws and regulations in force in the older-provinces of Bengal, Bihar, and Orissa. But when the Saugor and Nerbudda territories were acquired from the Marathas by Lord Hastings, and when Assam, Arakan and Tenasserim were conquered in 1824, and Pegu in 1852, these regions were specially exempted from the Bengal Regulations, instructions, however, been given to the officer administrating them to conduct their procedure in accordance with the spirit of the regulations, so far as they were suitable to the circumstances of the country.[5] And when the Punjab was annexed the view taken was that the Governor-General in Council had power to make laws for the new territory, not in accordance with the forms prescribed by the Chapter Acts for legislation, but by executive order, corresponding to the Orders in Council made by the Crown for what are called Crown Colonies. Provinces in which this power was exercised were called 'non-regulation provinces' to distinguish them from the 'regulation provinces', which were governed by regulations formally made under the Charter Acts. A large body of laws had been passed under this power or assumed power, and in order to remove any doubts as to their validity a section was introduced into the Indian Council Act, 1861, declaring that no rule, law, or regulation made before the passing of the Act by the governor-general or certain other authorities should be deemed invalid by reason of not having been made in conformity with the provisions of the Charter Acts.[6]

The power of legislation which had been taken away from the governments of Madras and Bombay by the Charter Act of 1833 was restored to them by the Act of 1861. The councils of the governors of Madras and Bombay were expanded for legislative purposes by the addition of the advocate general and of other members nominated on the same principles as the additional members of the governor-general's council. No line of demarcation was drawn between the subjects reserved for the central and the local legislature respectively; but the previous sanction of the governor-general was made requisite for legislature by the local legislature in certain cases, and all Acts of the local legislature required the subsequent assent to the governor-general in addition to that of the Governor, and were made subject to this allowance by the Crown, as in the case of Acts of the governor-general's council. There were also the same restrictions on the proceedings of the local legislature.

The governor-general was directed to establish, by proclamation, a legislative council for Bengal,[7] and was empowered to establish similar councils for the North-Western Provinces and for the Punjab.[8] These councils were to consist of the lieutenant-governor and of a certain number of nominated councilors, and were to be subject to the same provisions as the local legislatures for madras and Bombay.

The Act also gave power to constitute new provinces for legislative purposes and appoint new lieutenant- governors, and to alter the boundaries of existing provinces.

Indian High Courts Act, 1861

The amalgamation of the supreme and sadr courts, that is to say, of the courts representing the Crown and the Company respectively at the presidency towns, had long been in contemplation, and was carried into effect by the Indian high Courts Act, 1861.[9]

By this Act the Queen was empowered to establish, by letters patent,[4] high courts of judicature in Calcutta, Madras, and Bombay and on their establishment the old chartered supreme courts and the old 'Sadr Adalat' Courts were to be abolished , the jurisdiction and the powers of the abolished courts being transferred to the new high courts.

Each of the high courts was to consist of a chief justice and not more than fifteen judges, of whom not less than one-third, including the chief justice, were to be barristers, and not less than one-third were to be members of the covenanted civil service. All the judges were to be appointed by and to hold office during the pleasure of the Crown. The high courts were expressly given superintendence over, and power to frame rules of practice for, all the courts subject to their appellate jurisdiction.

Power was given by the Act to establish another high court, with the same constitution and powers as the high courts established at the presidency towns.[11]

Legislation after 1861

The Indian High Courts Act of 1861 closed the series of constitutional statutes consequent on the transfer of the Government of India to the Crown. Until the end of the nineteenth century the Acts of Parliament subsequently passed for India did little more than amend, with reference to minor points, the acts of 1858 and 1861.

Indian High Courts Act, 1865

The Indian High Courts Act, 1865,[12] empowered the Government-General in Council to pass orders altering the limits of the jurisdiction of the several chartered high courts and enabling them to exercise their jurisdiction over native Christian subjects of Her Majesty resident in Native States.

Government of India Act, 1865

Another Act of the same year, the Government of India Act, 1865[13], extended the legislative powers of the governor-general's council to all British subjects in Native States, whether servants of the Crown or not, and enabled the Governor- General in Council to define and alter, by proclamation, the territorial limits of the various presidencies and lieutenant-governorships.

Government of India Act, 1869

The Government of India Act, 1869[1] vested in the Secretary of State the right of filling all vacancies in the Council of India, and changed the tenure of members of the council from a tenure during good behaviour to a term of ten years. It also transferred to the Crown from the Secretary of State in Council the right of filling vacancies in the offices of the members of the councils in India.

Indian Councils Act, 1869

The Indian Councils Act, 1869[15] still further extended the legislative powers of the governor-general's council by enabling it to make laws for all native Indian subjects of Her Majesty in any part of the world, whether in India or not.

Government of India Act, 1870 and Legislation by Regulation

A very important modification in the machinery for Indian legislation was made by the Government of India Act, 1870[16]. It has been seen that for a long time the governor-general, believed himself to have the power of legislating by executive order for the non-regulation provinces. The Indian Councils Act of 1861, whilst validating rules made under this power in the past, took away the power for the future. The Act of 1870 practically restored this power by enabling the governor-general to legislate in a summary manner for the less advanced parts of India.[17] The machinery provided was as follows. The Secretary of State in Council was, by resolution, to declare the provisions of Section 1 of the Act of 1870 applicable to some particular part of a British

Indian province. Thereupon the Governor in Council, lieutenant-governor, lieutenant–governor in Council, or chief commissioner of the province, might at any time propose to the Governor-General in Council drafts of regulations for the peace and good government of that part, and these drafts, when approved and assented to by the Governor-General in Council, and duly gazetted, were to have the same force of law as if they had been formally passed at sitting of the Legislative Council. This machinery was extensively applied to the less advanced districts of the different Indian provinces, and numerous regulations have been made under it.

Statutory Civilians

The same Act of 1870 contained two other provisions of considerable importance. One of them (s. 5) repeated and strengthened the power of the governor-general to overrule his council.[18] The other (s. 6), after reciting the expediency of giving additional facilities for the employment of natives of India 'of proved merit and ability' in the civil service of Her Majesty in India, enabled any native of India to be appointed to any 'office, place, or employment' in that service, notwithstanding that he had not been admitted to that service in the manner directed by the Act of 1858, *i.e.* by competition in England. The conditions of such appointments were to be regulated by rules made by the Governor-General in Council, with the approval of the Secretary of State in Council. The result of these rules was the 'statutory civilian', who has now been merged in or superseded by the 'Provincial Service'.

Indian Councils Act and Indian Bishops Act, 1871

Two small Acts were passed in 1871, the Indian Councils Act, 1871 (34 & 35 Vict. c. 34),[19] which made slight extensions of the powers of local legislatures, and the Indian Bishops Act, 1871 (34 & 35 Vict. c. 62), which regulated the leave of absence of Indian bishops.

An Act of 1873 (36 Vict. c. 17) formally dissolved the East India Company as from January 1, 1874.

Indian Councils Act, 1874

The Indian Councils Act., 1874 (37 & 38 Vict. c. 91), enabled a sixth member of the governor-general's council to be appointed for public works purposes.

Council of India Act, 1876

The Council of India Act, 1876 (39 & 40 Vict. c. 7), enabled the Secretary of State, for special reasons, to appoint any person having professional or other peculiar qualifications to be a member of the Council of India, with the old tenure, during good behavior, which had been abolished in 1869.[20]

Royal Titles Act, 1870

In the same year was passed the Royal Titles Act, 1876 (39 & 40 Vict. c. 10), which authorized the Queen to assume the title of Empress of India.

Indian Salaries and Allowances Act, 1880

The Indian Salaries and Allowances Act, 1880 (43 & 44 Vict. c. 3), enabled the Secretary of State to regulate by order certain salaries and allowances which had been previously fixed by statute.

Indian Marine Service Act, 1884

The Indian Marine Services Act, 1884 (47 & 48 Vict. c. 38), enabled the Governor-General in Council to legislate for maintaining discipline in a small marine establishment, now called the Royal Indian Marine, the members of which were neither under the Naval Discipline Act nor under the Merchant Shipping Acts.

Council of India Reduction Act, 1889

The Council of India Reduction Act, 1889 (52 & 53 Vict. c. 65), authorized the Secretary of State to abstain from filling vacancies in the Council of India until the number should be reduced to ten.

Indian Councils Act, 1892 Introduction of elective principle and expansion of functions of Councils.

The Indian Councils Act, 1892 (55 & 56 Vict. c. 14), passed when Lord Kimberley was Secretary of State for India and Lord Lansdowne was Governor-General, enlarged the size of the legislative councils; and also their functions. The regulations under which the non-official members were to be nominated provided for recommendations, which, in practice, were always adopted, and thus introduced the elective principle into the constitution of the councils, whilst scrupulously avoiding the name of election. The restrictions imposed by the Act of 1861 on the functions of the councils were relaxed by giving power to make rules authorizing the discussion of the annual financial statement, and the asking of questions, but no member was to have power to submit or propose any resolution, or to divide the council, in respect of any such financial discussion or the answer to any question.

These provisions were pregnant with consequence which were developed by later legislation.

The Act also cleared up a doubt about the meaning of an enactment in the Indian Councils Act of 1861, modified some of the provisions of that Act about the office of 'additional members' of legislative councils, and enabled local legislatures, with the previous sanction of the governor-general, to repeal or alter Acts of the governor-general's council affecting their province.[21]

Madras and Bombay Armies Act, 1893

The Madras and Bombay Armies Act, 1893 (56 & 57 Vict. c. 62), abolished the offices of commanders-in-chief of the Madras and Bombay armies, and thus made possible a simplification of the Indian military system which had been asked for persistently by four successive viceroys.[22]

Contracts (India Office) Act, 1903

The Contracts (India Office) Act, 1903 (3 Edw. VII, c. 11), declared the mode in which certain contracts might be made by the Secretary of State in Council.

Indian Councils Act, 1904

The Indian Councils Act, 1904 (4 Edw. VII, c. 26), while continuing the power to appoint a sixth member of the Governor-General's Council, removed the necessity for appointing him specifically for public works purposes.

Partition of Bengal

The partition of Bengal effected by Lord Curzon's government in 1905 did not require any parliamentary legislation. It was subsequently modified in a manner described later on.

Council of India Act, 1907

The Council of India Act, 1907 (7 Edw. VII, c. 35), modified the constitution of the Council of India.

Indian Councils Act, 1909

The Indian Councils Act, 1909 (9 Edw. VII, c.4), the passage of which will always be associated with the name of Lord Morley of Blackburn, made important changes in the constitution and functions of the Indian legislative councils, and gave power to make changes in the executive governments of the Indian provinces.

The introduction of the measure was preceded by discussions and correspondence, which began in Lord Morley's first year of office as Secretary of State for India, and extended over a period of nearly three years.

Lord Minto's Minute

In 1906 the Viceroy, Lord Minto, drew up a minute in which he reviewed the political situation in India, and pointed out how the growth of education, encouraged by British rule, had led to the rise of important classes claiming equality of citizenship, and aspiring to take a larger part in shaping the policy of the government. He then appointed a committee of his council to consider the group of questions arising out of these novel conditions. From the discussion thus commenced was developed a tentative project of reform, which was outlined in a Home Department letter to local governments dated August 24, 1907. This letter, after having received approval by the Secretary of State in Council, was laid before Parliament, and was published in England and India. The local governments to whom it was addressed were instructed to consult important bodies and individuals representative of various classes of the community before submitting their own conclusions to the Government of India. The replies were received in due course, and are to be found in the 'colossal blue books' appended to a letter from the Government of India, dated October 1, 1908, in which the situation was again reviewed, and revised proposals were formulated. The views of the Secretary of State on these proposals were expressed in a dispatched dated November 27, 1908, and were expounded by Lord Morley in a speech delivered in the House of Lords on December 17, 1908.

Objects of Morley-Minto Reforms

The main objects of Lord Morley's proposals were to give the Indian legislative councils a more truly representative character, among other things by increasing their numbers, by substituting election for nomination in constructing them, and by a liberal extension of their freedom of discussion.

The Bill embodying his proposals was introduced by him in the House of Lords in February, 1909, passed through both Houses of Parliament with only one important alteration, and became law before the end of May. Like other Acts relating to India it was couched in wide and general terms, leaving all details, and some matters of principle, to be determined by regulations made by the authorities in India.

The provisions of the Act of 1909, that is to say, that Act, as supplemented by the regulations under it, were as follows:

(1) Size of Legislative Councils

The size of the legislative councils was materially enlarged. Thus the maximum number of members[23] was raised, for the Governor- General's council, from 16 to 60, for Bengal, Madras and Bombay from 20 to 50, and for the United Provisions from 15 to 50.

(2) Principle of election specifically recognized and nominated members

The Act required that members of the legislative councils should include elected as well as nominated members. It left the number or proportion of elected members to be fixed by regulations, but it expressly recognized the principle of election which was latent in the regulations under the Act of 1892. The regulations under the Act of 1909 were framed, first, with the object of securing to the Government a sufficient official representation, and secondly, of obtaining, as far as possible, a fair representation of the different classes and interests in the country. Nomination was retained *(a)* for the appointment of official members, and *(b)* for the appointment of non-official members to supplement the elected members. There were thus three classes of 'additional members' in each council— nominated official members, nominated non-official members, elected members. The nomination of non-official members worked alongside of election as a means of representing special interests for whose representation it seemed impracticable to provide by election, or special qualifications such as those of experts. The elected members were returned by constituencies such as municipalities, district and local boards, universities, chambers of commerce, and trade associations, and group of persons such as land-holders or tea-planters. Mohammedans also succeeded in obtaining separate representation.

(3) Composition of Councils

The Act prescribed that at least one half of the additional members of the legislative councils of the Governor-General and of the governors of Madras and Bombay, and at least one-third of the members of the other legislative councils, should be persons not in the civil or military service of the Crown. This left is still permissible to maintain an official majority on each council. But, in pursuance of the policy announced by the Secretary of State, the regulations created non-official majorities in all the provincial legislative councils, and maintained an official majority only in the Governor-General's legislative council.[24] This, however, did not imply that in the provincial legislative councils the majority was to consist wholly of elected members.

(4) Enlargement of functions of Councils

The functions of the legislative council were enlarged. Under the Act of 1892, as has been seen, there was power to discuss the financial statement, and to ask questions, but there was no power to move resolutions, or to divide the council, on any topic, financial or other. The practice had been to allot one or two days annually in every council to the discussion of a budget already settled by the executive government. Under the Act of 1909, there was power to move resolutions, not only on the budget, but on any matter of general public interest, and to divide the council upon them. The resolutions were to take the form of recommendations to the executive government, recommendations on which the government were not bound to act. The government, as Lord Morley said in his speech of December, 1908, 'will deal with these resolutions as carefully, or as carelessly, as they think fit, just as governments do here'. The power to put questions was extended by permitting supplementary questions, subject to disallowance by the president.

(5) Vice-Presidents

The Governor-General, the governors of presidencies, and lieutenant-governors having executive councils, were required to appoint members of their councils to be vice-presidents of the councils, with power, in the temporary absence of their chief, to act for them, and preside at meetings of their councils.

(6) Expansion of size of executive councils in Madras and Bombay

The maximum number of ordinary members of the executive councils for Madras and Bombay was raised from two to four, but two at least of them were to be persons who at the time of their appointment had been in the service of the Crown in India for at least twelve years.

(7) Power to create executive councils in other provinces

The Governor-General in Council was given power to establish by proclamation executive councils for lieutenant governors, but except in the case of Bengal, any such proclamation was to be subject to disallowance by either House of Parliament. The provision giving this power in the case of all lieutenant governorships was struck out by the House of Lords, and the ultimate form of the clause was the result of a compromise between the two Houses. The proclamation which gave an executive council to the United Provinces was vetoed by the House of Lords in 1915.

Lord Morley, in his speech of December, 1908, spoke of his proposals as 'the opening of a very important chapter in the history of Great Britain and India', and again as 'opening a chapter in constitutional reform.' Similar expressions have since been applied to later projects of legislation. A thread of continuity connects the successive stages of English legislation for India, and any division of the series of enactments is open to the charge of being arbitrary. But perhaps the Act of 1909 has a better claim than either its predecessor of 1892, or its successor of 1919, to close one period and to open another, that of constitutional experiments.[25]

Effect of Morley-Minto Act on Constitutional Changes

In any case the Act of 1909 undoubtedly accelerated the pace of constitutional changes, a pace which was further accelerated by the events of the great war. Both Lord Morley and Lord Minto expressly disclaimed any desire or intention to advance towards parliamentary or responsible government. But events are stronger than reformers, and the goal which was emphatically disclaimed in 1908, was as emphatically and authoritatively announced in August 1917.

Appointment of Indians to Executive Councils and to Councils of India

In the course of the debates on the Bill of 1909, much was said about Lord Morley's announcement of his intention to appoint a native of India to a post on the Governor-General's council. This subject was not strictly relevant to the Bill, because the power of making these appointments is free from any restriction as to race, creed, or place of birth. Effect was given to Lord Morley's intention by the appointment in March, 1909, of Mr. Sinha (now Lord Sinha) to the post of law member of the Governor-General's executive council. This appointment carried a step further the policy adopted in 1907, when two natives of India were placed on the Secretary of State's council. In pursuance of the same policy natives of India were subsequently placed on the executive councils for Bengal, Madras, and Bombay, and for Bihar and Orissa.

Indian High Courts Act, 1911

The Indian High Courts Act, 1911 (1 & 2 Geo. V, c. 18):

(1) raised the maximum number of judges of an Indian High Court from sixteen to twenty,

(2) gave power to establish new high courts from time to time as, occasion may require, and to make consequential changes in the jurisdiction of the courts, and

(3) gave power to appoint temporary additional judges of any high court for a term not exceeding two years.

The construction placed on the power to establish a new high court given by s. 16 of the Indian High Courts Act, 1861, had been, that the power was not recurrent and had been exhausted by the establishment of a high court at Allahabad.

India Office Pensions

The Government of India Act Amendment Act, 1911 (1 & 2 Geo. V, c. 25), amended the pension provisions of the Government of India Act, 1858, an authorizing the grant of allowances to the personal representatives of deceased members of the India Office staff.

King-emperor's Delhi Durbar, 1911, and further constitutional changes

On December 12, 1911, at a Durbar held at Delhi, King George V commemorated in person his coronation in Westminster Abbey as King of the United Kingdom of Great Britain and Ireland, and of the British dominions beyond the seas, and as emperor of India. The event was unprecedented in the annals of British India. Never before had an English king worn his imperial crown in India: indeed, never before had a British sovereign set foot on Indian soil. There had been a general expectation that an exceptional occasion would be signalized by exceptional announcements. The expectation was not disappointed. At the great Durbar, the King-Emperor, accompanied by the Queen-Empress, was surrounded by a vast assemblage, which included the governors and great officials of his Indian empire, the great feudatory princes and chiefs of India, representatives of the Indian peoples, and representatives from the military forces of the Indian dominions. Three announcements were made. The first was made by the King-Emperor himself and expressed his personal feelings and those of the Queen Empress. The second was made by the Governor–General on behalf of the King-Emperor, and declared the grants, concessions, reliefs and benefactions which His Imperial Majesty had been pleased to bestow upon this glorious and memorable occasion. The third was made by the King-Emperor in person and announced the transfer of the seat of the Government of India from Calcutta to the ancient capital Delhi, the simultaneously and as a consequence of that transfer, the creation at as early a date as possible of a Governorship for the Presidency of Bengal of a new Lieutenant-Governorship in Council administering the areas of Bihar, Chota Nagpur, and Orissa, and of a chief commissionership of Assam, with the necessary administrative changes and redistribution of boundaries.

The King's announce. Transfer of Capital to Delhi, appointment of Governor in Council in Bengal and creation of new provinces of Bihar and Orissa.

The decisions thus announced had been for many months the subject of discussions in the English Cabinet, at the India Office, and in the Governor-General's Council, and of correspondence between the Government of India and the Secretary of State in England. But the secret had been well kept, and the result of these deliberations was not disclosed, either in England or in India, before the King-Emperor's announcement was made.

The Delhi Dispatch and the Reply

The correspondence which led up to the Durbar announcements is embodied in a dispatch from the Government of India dated August 25, 1911, and in the Secretary of State's reply of November 1, 1911. The dispatch states very fully the nature of the proposals submitted to the Secretary of State, and the reasons for them. The reply conveys a general assent.

The dispatch beings by elaborating the proposal of the Government of India to make Delhi the future capital, because, it said, 'we consider this the keystone of the whole project'. It was certain that in the course of time the just demands of Indians for a larger share in the government of the country would have to be satisfied, and the question would be how this devolution of power could be conceded without impairing the supreme authority of the Governor-General in Council. The only possible solution of the difficulty would appear to be gradually to give the Provinces a larger measure of self-government until at last India would consist of a number of administrations, autonomous in all provincial affairs, with the Government of India above them all, and possessing power to interfere in cases of misgovernment, but ordinarily restricting their functions on matters of Imperial concern. In order that this consummation might be attained, it was essential that the Supreme Government should not be associated with any particular Provincial Government. The removal of the Government of India from Calcutta was therefore a measure which would materially facilitate the growth of local self-government on sound and safelines.

The question of providing a separate capital for the Government of India had often been debated, but generally with the object of finding a site where that Government could spend all seasons of the year. Such a solution would be ideal, but was impracticable. The various sites suggested were either difficult of access or devoid of historical associations. 'Delhi is the only possible place.' It had splendid communications, the climate was good for seven months in the year, and its salubrity could be ensured at a reasonable cost. Both on administrative on political grounds the claims of Delhi to be the capital of India were unrivalled.

Starting from the proposition that Delhi must be the future capital, and examining the weight of Calcutta objections, the dispatch went on to discuss the best mode of dealing with the Presidency of Bengal.

Simple rescission of the partition effected in 1905, and a reversion to the previous state of things, were manifestly impossible, both on political and on administrative grounds. But the partition should be remodelled, and the dispatch indicated the lines on which, in the opinion of the Government of India, the remodelling ought to take place.

The policy foreshadowed by the correspondence and announced at the Durbar embodied two great administrative changes; a transfer of the capital of India from Calcutta to Delhi and a remodelling of the partition of Bengal.

Lord Curzon's Partition of Bengal, 1905

In October, 1905, the huge province under the Lieutenant-Governor of Bengal had been divided into two lieutenant-governorships. Of these the western retained the old name of Bengal and the old seat of government at Calcutta, whilst the eastern was augmented by the addition of Assam, previously under a chief Commissioner, was called Eastern Bengal and Assam, and had for its seat of government Dacca.

The rearrangement effected in pursuance of the Durbar announcements made the following changes:

1. It reunited the five Bengali-speaking divisions of the old province of Bengal, and formed them into a presidency administered by a governor in council. The area of this presidency or province is approximately 70, 000 square miles, and its population about 42,000,000.
2. It created a lieutenant-governorship in council, consisting of Bihar, Chota Nagpur, and Orissa, with legislative council, and a capital at Patna. The area of this province is approximately 113, 000 square miles, and its population about 35,000,000.
3. It detached Assam from Eastern Bengal and placed it again under a chief commissioner. Assam has an area of about 56, 000 square miles, and a population of about 5,000,000.

These administrative changes were mainly effected under powers conferred by Acts relating to the government of India, but some supplementary legislation was required, both in India and in England.

The Secretary of the State for India in Council made a formal declaration that the Governor-General of India should no longer be the governor of the presidency of Fort William in Bengal, but that a separate governor should be appointed for that presidency.

By a royal warrant dated March 21, 1912, Lord Carmichael, previously governor of Madras, was appointed governor of the presidency of Fort William in Bengal.

Proclamations giving effect to Delhi Durbars

By a proclamation notified on March 22, 1912, a new province was carved out of the previous lieutenant-governorship of Bengal, was called Bihar and Orissa, and was placed under a lieutenant-governor.

By another proclamation of the same date the territories that were in future to constitute the Presidency of Fort William in Bengal were delimited.

And by a third proclamation of the same date the territories which had before 1905 constituted the chief commissionership of Assam were taken under the immediate authority and management of the Governor-General in Council, and again formed into a chief commissionership, called the chief commissionership of Assam.

Before the Consolidation Act of 1915, the authorities for the powers thus exercised could only be found by diligent search in the tangled mass of enactments relating to the government of India, and require some explanation.

By s. 16 of the Government of India Act, 1853 (16 & 17 Vict. c. 95), the court of directors of the East India Company, acting under the direction and control of the board of control, were empowered to declare that the Governor-General in Council should not be governor of the presidency of Fort William in Bengal, but that a separate governor was to be from time to time appointed in like manner as the governors of Madras and Bombay. In the meantime, and until a governor was appointed, there was power under the same section to appoint a lieutenant–governor of such part of the presidency of Bengal as was not under the lieutenant-governorship of the North-West (now United) Provinces. The power to appoint a lieutenant-governor was exercised, and during the continuance of its exercise, the power to appoint a governor remained in abeyance. But it still existed, was inherited by the Secretary of State from the Court of Directors and the Board of Control, and was exercised in March, 1912, when a governorship was substituted for a lieutenant-governorship of Bengal.

The power to constitute the new province of Bihar and Orissa and to appoint a lieutenant-governor of it was given by s. 46 of the Indian Councils Act, 1861.

The power to delimit the territories of the presidency or province of Bengal was given by s. 47 of the Indian Councils Act, 1861, and s. 4 of the Government of India Act, 1865.

The power to take Assam under the immediate authority and management of the Governor-General in Council and to place it under a chief commissioner was given by s. 3 of the Government of India Act, 1854.

The territorial redistributions made by the proclamations of March 22 took effect on the following April 1. Under s. 47 of the Indian Councils Act, 1861, laws in force in territories severed from a province remained in force until superseded by further legislation. But it was found in 1912, as it had previously been found after the alteration of provinces made in 1905, that a few minor adaptations were immediately needed to make the old laws fit the new conditions. These adaptations were made by an Act of the Governor-General in Council, which was framed on the lines of the Bengal and Assam Laws Act of 1905 (Act VII of 1905), and was, as a measure of urgency, passed through all its stages on March 25, 1912. The Act among other things, constituted a board of revenue for the province of Bihar and Orissa.

Further legislative provision, mostly of a technical character, was made by an Act of Parliament, the Government of India Act 1912, which received the Royal Assent on June 25, 1912.[26]

Government of India Act, 1912

The Act recited the proclamations of March 22, 1912, and then went on, by s.1, to declare and explain the powers and position of the new governor of Bengal and his council.

When the Government of India Act, 1833, became law, the intention was to divide the overgrown presidency of Bengal into two presidencies (Fort William and Agra) and to have four presidencies, Fort William (Bengal), Fort St. George (Madras), Bombay and Agra; and each of these four presidencies was to have a governor and council of its own. But this intention was not carried out. The presidency of Agra was never constituted, the governor-general and his council continued to be, under what had been meant to be a temporary provision, the governor and council of Fort William, and lieutenant-governors were in course of time appointed for the North-West (now United) Provinces and for Bengal. But the provisions of the Act of 1833 were still applicable to the governor in council of Bengal, if and when constituted. What was needed, when that event took place in 1912, was apply to the governor and council of Bengal those provisions, mostly in Acts subsequent to 1833, which applied exclusively to the governors and councils of Madras and Bombay. Among the provisions so applied were those which relate to legislative councils, to the right of the governor to act as governor-general in the governor-general's absence, to the salaries of the governors and their councils, and to the number and qualifications, under s. 2 of the Act of 1909, of the members of the executive councils.

Creation of Executive Council for Bihar and Orissa, and power to create such Councils in other provinces.

The Act of 1912 (s. 2) authorized the creation of an executive council for the new province of Bihar and Orissa. The Act of 1909 had-authorized the creation of an executive council to assist the lieutenant-governor of Bengal. It had also given power to create by proclamation an executive council for any other province under a lieutenant –governor, but in any such case the power was not to be exercised until the proclamation had been laid before each house of Parliament, and either house might object. In order to facilitate the immediate establishment of an executive council for Bihar and Orissa, the Act of 1912 dispensed with further references to Parliament.

Creation of Legislative Councils in Assam and Central Provinces

Another Section (s. 3) of the Act of 1912 authorized the establishment of legislative councils for provinces under chief commissioners. Under the previous law legislative councils could only be established for provinces under lieutenant-governors. The new power was required primarily to enable continuance of government with a legislative council for Assam, but was wide enough to cover other provinces, such as the Central Provinces. A legislative council was established for Assam on November 14, 1912, and a legislative council for the Central Provinces on November 10, 1913.

Formation of Separate Province of Delhi

In the past the transfer of territories for the purpose of forming a chief commissionership had been effected under the power given by s. 3 of the Government of India Act, 1854 (17 & 18 Vict. c. 77). This power was exercised in 1901 to transfer territories from the lieutenant-governorship of the Punjab to the chief commissionership of the North–West Frontier Province. In September, 1912, it was similarly exercised to transfer the city of Delhi and part of the Delhi district from the same lieutenant-governorship, take it under the immediate authority and management of the Governor-General in Council, and form it into a chief commissionership known as the Province of Delhi. An Indian Act, the Delhi Laws Act, 1912 (XIII of 1912), had adapted the old laws to the new conditions. The intention was to make the site of the new capital and its surroundings an *enclave* occupying the same kind of position as Washington and the District of Columbia in the United States.

Government of India Act, 1915

In 1915 was passed the first measure for consolidating the numerous Acts of Parliament relating to the government of India. The Government of India Act, 1915 (5 & 6 Geo. V, c. 61), gave effect to a project which has engaged the intermittent attention of the Government of India and the India Office for more than forty years. It was based on the 'Digest of Statutory Enactments relating to the Government of India' which formed the nucleus of the book entitled *The Government of India.*[27] It repealed, with a few omissions, the unrepealed provisions of 47 Acts, beginning with an Act of 1770, and consolidated them in a single Act of 135 Sections with 5 schedules. It was introduced in the House of Lords, and was after second reading, committed to a joint committee of the two Houses of Parliament. The Committee sat under the chairmanship of Lord Loreburn went very carefully through the Bill, eliminated some proposals which appeared to go beyond the scope of consolidation, and recommended it for adoption. The Bill was passed in July, 1915, and came into operation on January 1, 1916.

Government of India (Amendment) Act, 1916

An amending measure, embodying some provisions struck out from the Bill of 1915 as beyond the scope of consolidation, was introduced and passed in 1916, and became law as the Government of India. (Amendment) Act, 1916 (6 & 7 Geo. V, c. 37). The alterations which it made in the law were of a minor character.

First consolidation of the law relating to India further constitution Reforms.

The Consolidation Act of 1915 , with its modest supplement of 1916, made the English statue law relating to India easier to understand, and therefore easier to amend. The need for substantial amendment was soon made apparent. The great war which begin in 1914 materially changed the political atmosphere in India. The magnificent war services of the princes and peoples of India were recognized by the admission of representatives of India to the Imperial War Conference, to the Imperial War Cabinet, and among the Imperial Delegates at the Peace Conference. These things inspired or quickened among the politically minded classes in India the sense of being an integral part of a world-wide empire. The Morley-Minto reforms, from which so much had been expected, and by which so much had been achieved, were now condemned as no longer adequate to Indian needs.

Responsible Government and announcement of August 20, 1917

Indian politicians talked much about 'home rule' and about 'self-government' on the lines of the British self-governing dominions. The 'Home Rule' movement, started by Mrs. Besant, found formal expression on September 6, 1916, when the Home Rule League was formally established at a meeting in Madras. A month later nineteen elected members of the Indian Legislative Council submitted to the Government of India a memorandum of proposed reforms. In December 1916, the Indian National Congress and the Muslim League, in a series of meetings held at Lucknow, agreed to joint action in favour of political reform. Both bodies adopted the proposals known as the Congress League scheme, which was an elaboration of the proposal of the nineteen members, with the addition of special provisions to secure Muslim interests; and both agreed to co-operate with the Home Rule League in its propaganda. The phrase which ultimately found most favour in official quarters as indicating the lines on which reform should proceed was 'Responsible Government'. In 1909 Mr. Berriedale Keith, of the Colonial Office, published a little book, since much expanded, on Responsible Government in the British Dominions. When Mr. Lionel Curtis, the well-known publicist, after visiting other parts of the British Empire, made a long stay in India in the autumn of 1916, he applied the phrase to Indian conditions. It obtained much vogue, and, in course of time, formal and authoritative recognition.

In the meantime much important correspondence on Indian reforms had been carried on between the India Office and the Government of India. On August 20, 1917, Mr. Montagu, the Secretary of State for India, when answering a question in the House of Commons, made a declaration of government policy, which became widely known as the 'announcement' or 'pronouncement' of that date. 'The policy of His Majesty's Government,' he said, 'with which the Government of India are in complete accord, is that of the increasing association of Indians in every branch of the administration, and the gradual development of self-governing institutions, with a view to the progressive realization of responsible government in India as an integral part of the British Empire.'

Montagu Chelmsford Report

Mr. Montagu's visit to India followed in the autumn of 1917 and resulted in the famous Montagu-Chelmsford Report, which was signed by the Secretary of State and the Viceroy and bears date April 22, 1918.

NOTES

1. It had, among other things, discussed the propriety of the grant to the Mysore princes. See Proceedings of Legislative Council for 1860, pp. 1343—1402.
2. 24 & 25 Vict. c. 67, s. 19. As to the object with which this section was framed, see paragraph 24 of Sir Charles Wood's dispatch of August 9, 1861.
3. Explained by 55 & 56 Vic. c. 14, s. 3.
4. These powers were extended by 28 & 29 Vict. c. 17, s. 1. And 32 & 33 Vict. c. 98, s. 1.
5. Indian legislation subsequently became necessary for the purpose of ascertaining and determining the rules which had been thus validated in general terms. See Sir James Stephen's speech in the Legislative Council in the debate on the Punjab Laws Acts, March 26, 1872, and the chapter contributed by him to Sir W. Hunter's *Life of Lord Mayo*, vol. ii, pp. 214—221
6. A legislative council for Bengal was established by a proclamation of January 18, 1862.
7. A legislative council was established for the North-Western Provinces and Oudh (now United Provinces of Agra and Oudh) in 1886, and for the Punjab in 1897.
8. 24 & 25 Vict. c. 104.
9. The letters patent or characters now in force with respect to these three high courts bear date December 28, 1865.
10. s.16. Under this power a high court was established at Allahabad in 1866. It is probable that the power was thereby exhausted.

11. 28 & 29 Vict. c. 15.
12. 28 & 29 Vict. c. 17.
13. 32 & 33 Vict. c. 97.
14. 32 & 33 Vict. c. 98.
15. 33 & 34 Vict. c. 3.
16. This restoration of a power of summary legislation was strongly advocated by Sir H. S. Maine. See Minutes by sir H.S. Maine, pp. 153, 156.
17. It will be remembered that Lord Lytton acted under this power when he exempted imported cotton goods from duty in 1879.
18. This Act was passed in consequence of the decision of the Bombay High Court in R. v. Reay, 7 Bom. Cr. 6.
19. This power was exercised in the case of Sir H. S. Maine, and was probably conferred with special reference to him.
20. In the absence of this power the sphere of action of the then new legislature for the North-Western Provinces and Oudh was confined within an infinitesimal area.
21. Administrative reforms in India are not carried out with undue precipitancy. The appointment of a single commander-in-chief for India, with four subordinate commanders under him, was recommended by Lord William Bentinck, Sir Charles Metcalfe, and others in 1833. (Further Papers respecting the East India Company's Charter, 1833.)
22. Excluding those who, as members of the executive council, were *ex-offcio* members of the legislative council.
23. In Bombay the official members had been in a minority for some years before the Act of 1909.
24. The difficulties which Lord Morley had to encounter and the formidable nature of the opposition which he had to face, are illustrated by his correspondence with Lord Minto, published in 1917 in the second volume of his *Recollections*.
25. For the debates in Parliament on the Coronation Durbar announcements and on the Government of India Act, 1912, see the Parliamentary Debates in the House of Lords on 12 December, 1911, and 21 and 22 February, 26 March, 12, 17, 18, and 20 June, and 29 July, 1912, and in the House of Commons of 12 December, 1911, and 14 February, 22 and 24 April, and 7 and 10 June, 1912.
26. First edition 1898, third edition January 1915.

8

Progressive Realization of Responsible Government

The report suggested the appointment of three special committees, of which two were to sit in India, and which were to supplement the work embodied in the report by recommendations on three subjects : (1) the franchise for the legislative councils; (2) the division of functions between the central and provincial governments, and, in the provincial governments, between the executive councils and the 'ministers' whom it was proposed to appoint; and (3) the changes required in the home administration of Indian affairs.

Lord South-boroughs Committees

The constitution of the first two of these committees, commonly known as the Franchise Committee and the Functions Committee, and the terms of reference to them were publicly announced in October 1918, and the committees reported in February 1919. The third committee sat in England with Lord Crewe as chairman, and reported on June 21, 1919.

The Government of India Act, 1919

After the arrival in England of the supplementary Indian reports no time was lost in converting the Montagu-Chelmsford proposals into legislative form.[1] The Bill introduced in the House of Commons by Mr. Montagu on June 2, 1919, was based upon the Montagu-Chelmsford Report, and followed closely its recommendations. After second reading of June 5, it was referred to a joint committee of the two Houses of which Lord Selborne was chairman. In the months of July and August the joint committee set in public and heard evidence on the proposals of the Bill from a large number of witnesses, many of whom had come from India for the purpose. When Parliament met again after the autumn recess the committee sat in private, made many important amendments to the Bill and submitted a special report.[2] The Bill as amended passed through both Houses and received the Royal Assent on December 23, 1919.

On the same day the King-Emperor, by a royal proclamation[1] of that date, notified in India that he had given his assent to an Act which would take its place among the great historic measures passed by Parliament for the better Government of India and for the greater contentment of her people. The proclamation reviewed the course of parliamentary legislation for India. 'The Acts of 1773 and 1784 were designed to establish a regular system of administration and justice under the Honuorable East India Company. The Act of 1833 opened the door for Indians to public office and employment. The Act of 1858 transferred the administration from the Company to the Crown and laid the foundations of public life which exist in India to-day. "The Act of 1861 sowed the seed of representative institutions, and the seed was quickened into life by the Act of 1909. The Act which has now become law entrusts the elected representatives of the people with a definite share in the Government and points the way to full responsible Government hereafter.'

Purpose and scope of Act of 1919

The Act of 1919 begins with a preamble which recites the declaration of August 20, 1917. This recital, which appeared in a shorter form in the Bill presented to the House of Commons, was much expanded by the joint committee on the Bill. It is of great importance as embodying the promises made to the peoples of India, and as indicating the policy which underlies the provisions of the Act.

It seems desirable, for historical purposes, to summarize fully the provisions of the Act of 1919, not only because of its importance, but because it has been merged in a measure of consolidation[4] combining its provisions with those of the Acts of 1915 and 1916. It will therefore be convenient to show clearly the changes made by the legislation of 1919 in the previous law as embodied in the Acts of 1915 and 1916.[5]

The need for greater provincial autonomy was the point on which there was the largest measure of agreement among India reformers, and Part I of the Act deals with Local Governments. In its first section it enunciates the principles on which powers and responsibilities are to be distributed between the central governments and the local governments, leaving all details to be worked out by statutory rules. Subjects are to be classified by rules as 'central subjects' and 'provincial subjects'. Provincial subjects are to be divided into 'reserved subjects' and 'transferred subjects'. Reserved subjects are to be under the control of the Governor in his executive Council, transferred subjects are to be under the control of the Governor acting with ministers to be chosen from the elected members of the provincial legislature.[6]

Thus the plan embodied in the Act partitions the domain of provincial government into two fields, one of which is made over to ministers chosen from the elected members of the provincial legislature, while the other remains under the administration of a Governor in Council.

'This scheme', said the joint committee on the Bill,[7] 'has evoked apprehensions which are not unnatural in view of its novelty. But the committee, after a most careful consideration of all suggested alternatives, are of opinion that it is the best way of giving effect to the declared policy of his Majesty's Government.' So the committee, whilst making many important changes in the measure submitted for their consideration, retained this fundamental feature.

It will be observed that there is a primary divisions between 'central subjects' and 'provincial subjects', and that the latter class is divided into 'reserved subjects' and 'transferred subjects'. The administration of 'reserved subjects' is in each province, to be under the control of the governor in his executive council, that of 'transferred subjects' under the control of the governor 'acting with ministers appointed under this Act'. This is the famous system of 'diarchy' or 'dyarchy' (for authorities differ on the spelling), about which so much was heard in the discussions on Mr. Montagu's Bill. The word, however spelt, simply mean 'double government', a phrase formerly applied to the system under which the government of British India was partly under the Crown and partly under the East India Company.

The Act goes on to enable local governments to borrow money on the security of their own provincial revenues.[8]

Governors' Provinces

It alters the system of executive government for eight Indian provinces. These are the three old presidencies of Bengal, Madras, and Bombay, and five other provinces, namely, the United Provinces, the Punjab, Bihar and Orissa, the Central Provinces, and Assam. These eight provinces', are called in the Act 'governors' provinces', and each of them is to be under a governor in council for reserved subjects and a governor acting with ministers for transferred subjects.[9]

The provisions of previous Acts applying to presidencies are, speaking broadly, to apply to the five other provinces, but, though the appointment of governors of these provinces rests with the Crown, it is to be made after consultation with the Governor-General.[10]

Burma, under its lieutenant-governor, and the areas under the chief commissioners, were left outside the range of 'governor's provinces', but their governments were made local governments for certain purposes of the Act.

The joint committee on the bill, after hearing evidence, did not advise that Burma should be included within the scheme of government laid down by the new Act, But the position of Burma has, since the date at which that committee reported, been made the subject qf a further parliamentary inquiry with the results that the provisions of the Act of 1919 have now been applied to that province also.

Ministers and Councils Secretaries

The Act provides for the appointment of 'ministers' and 'Council secretaries'. A minister is to be appointed by the governor and to hold office during the governor's pleasure. He is not to be a member of the governor's executive council, or an official as defined by s. 46 of the Act. He is to draw the same salary as is payable to a member of the executive council unless the local legislature fixes a lower salary. He is not to hold office for more than six months, unless he is or becomes an elected member of the local legislature.[11]

In relation to transferred subjects, ' the governor is to be guided by the advice of his ministers, unless he sees sufficient cause to dissent from their opinion, in which case he must require action to be taken in accordance with their advice.'[12]

The position of 'council secretaries' under this section will correspond roughly to that of under-secretaries in Parliament.

Under s.5[13] only one member of a governor's executive council need have served for twelve years under the Crown in India, and the commander-in-chief, when resident at Calcutta, Madras, or Bombay, is no longer to be on the governor's executive council.

Section 6[14] regulates the conduct of business by the governor in council and by the governor with ministers. Orders and other proceedings of the government of a governor's province are to be expressed to be made by the government of the province, and are to be authenticated as the governor by rule directs, but provision must be made by rule for distinguishing orders and other proceedings relating to transferred subjects from other orders and proceedings. The legal validity of orders or proceedings so authenticated is not to be questioned on the ground that they were not duly made. The governor is empowered to make rules and orders for the transaction of business in his executive council and with his ministers and for regulating the relations between his executive council and his ministers.

Changes in constitution of Legislative Councils

Another Section of the Act (s. 7)[15] deals with the composition of governors' legislative councils. These are to consist of the members of the executive council and of members nominated or elected as provided by the Act. The governor is not to be a member of the legislative council, but is to have the right of addressing it and, for that purpose, of requiring its attendance. The proportion of official members and elected members is fixed at a maximum of 20 per cent official members and a minimum of 70 per cent elected members. The total number of members of each council is provisionally fixed by the first schedule to the Act, but may be increased, subject to the maintenance of the above proportions. The governor has also power to nominate specialists for the purpose of particular Bills, one in the case of Assam, two in the case of other provinces. The numbers fixed by the schedule materially enlarge the size of the councils. Thus, under Lord Morley's Act, there were, for Bengal, Madras, Bombay, and the United Provinces respectively, 50 members, exclusive of the members of executive councils. Under the schedule to the Act of 1919, the total number for Bengal is 125, for Madras and the United Provinces 118, and for Bombay 111.[16]

All matters relating to the qualification of members and electors, and the mode of election, including the vexed question of communal electorates, were to be regulated by statutory rules.[17] The comprehensive rules made for this purpose were based upon those proposed by the Franchise Committee, but materially modified.[18]

Under s.8[2] the life of a governor's legislative council is normally three years, but may be terminated by dissolution, and extended, in special circumstances, for a ,limited period. The governor fixes the times and places for holding the sessions and has power to prorogue the council. The person presiding at a meeting of the council has power to adjourn it. Questions are determined by a majority of votes of the members present, and in case of equality of votes the person presiding has a casting vote.

Elected Presidents of Councils

For each of the governors' legislative councils there is to be (s. 9)[20] a president, appointed for the first four years by the governor, but subsequently elected by the council from among its members and approved by the governor. There is also to be a deputy president, elected and approved in like manner. The salary of an appointed president is to be fixed by the governor, the salaries of elected presidents and vice-presidents are to be fixed by Act of the local legislature. The report of the joint committee on the Bill contains important observations on the position of these presidents.

Section 10 of the Act of 1919[21] was so framed as to include under the expression 'local legislature' not only the legislative councils of governors' provinces, but any legislative council of a lieutenant-governor[22] or chief commissioner. The alterations which this section makes in the previous law consist mainly in attempts to make more careful adjustments between the powers of the central executive and the central legislature and the powers of the local legislatures. Thus a local legislature may, certain cases specially exempted by statutory rules, impose a new tax without the previous sanction of the Governor-General, but may not, without such sanction, make a law regulating any 'central-subject', or any 'provincial subject', which has been declared by statutory rule to be either in whole or in part subject to legislation by the Indian Legislature, in respect of any matter to which this declaration applies.

Power to vote or withhold supply, subject to safeguards

The provisions of s. 11[23] relating to the business and procedure in governors' legislative councils mark a great advance in the direction of parliamentary methods, particularly in conceeding the right to vote supplies. There is to be an annual statement of estimated expenditure and revenues, and the proposals of the local government for the appropriation of provincial revenues in any year are to be submitted to the vote of the council in the form of demands for grants. The council may assent, or refuse its assent, to a demand, or may reduce the amount demanded either by a reduction of the whole grant or by the omission or reduction of any of its items. A proposal for appropriation of revenues is not to be made except on the recommendation of the governor, communicated to the council. The voted 'grants' only cover the kind of expenditure which in England is made out of 'moneys provided by Parliament'. Certain charges of a special or recurring character, set out in the section, are outside the range of voted 'grants'. The distinction will be recognized as corresponding roughly to the English distinction between charges on the votes and charges on the consolidated fund. So far the procedure is based on English practice. But the executive government is given exceptional powers of authorizing expenditure in case of need. If a demand relates to a 'reserved subject', and the governor certifies that the expenditure is essential to the discharge of his responsibility for the subject, the local government has power, in relation to any demand, to act as if it had been assented to, notwithstanding the withholding of the assent, or the reduction of the amount, asked for.

The joint committee on the Bill wished it 'to be perfectly clear that this power is real and that its exercise should not be regarded as unusual or arbitrary. Unless the governor has the right to secure supply for those services for which he remains responsible to Parliament, that responsibility cannot justly be fastened upon him'.

The governor also has power, in cases of emergency, to authorize such expenditure as may be, in his opinion, necessary for the safety or tranquillity of the province, or for the carrying on of any department. In addition to his powers for authorizing expenditure, the governor has, under the same section, powers for stopping dangerous or mischievous legislation. When any Bill has been introduced or is proposed to be introduced, or any amendment to a Bill is moved or proposed to be moved, the governor may certify that the Bill or any clause of it, or the amendment, affects the safety or tranquillity of his province or any part of it or of another province, and may direct that no proceedings or no further proceedings shall be taken by the council in relation to the Bill, clause or amendment, and effect is to be given to any such direction.

The provisions of this important section are left to be worked out in detail by statutory rules and standing orders. The standing orders are to supplement the rules, and must not be inconsistent with them. They are to be made in the first instance by the governor in council, but may be altered by the local legislature, with the assent of the governor.

The section concludes by declaring that 'subject to the rules and standing orders affecting the council there shall be freedom of speech in the governors' legislative councils. No person shall be liable in any proceedings in any court by reason of his speech or vote in any such council, or by reason of anything contained in any official report of the proceedings of any such council.'

Reservation of Bills

Under previous Acts the governor, lieutenant-governor, or chief commissioner had power either to assent to, or to withhold his assent from, legislative measures passed by, the local legislature. If he assented, the measure was sent up for the assent of the Governor-General. He is now, by s. 12[24] given alternative powers. He may, instead, of either granting or refusing assent to a Bill, return the Bill to his council, for reconsideration, either in whole or in part, together with any amendments which he may recommend. Or he may, in cases prescribed by rules, and in some cases must, reserve the Bill for the consideration of the Governor–General.

The same section gives the Governor –General further powers of dealing with measures of local legislatures submitted for his assent or reserved for his consideration.

Section 11 of the new Act[25] had, as stated above, given the governor power to stop mischievous legislation. Section 13[26] deals with the still more difficult case of failure to pass necessary legislation.

Power vested in the Governor to secure essential legislation

The Montagu-Chelmsford Report, and the government Bill as introduced, proposed to solve this difficult problem by sending Bills to grand committees on which the Government could secure a majority. But the joint committee rejected this solution. The 'official bloc' was not in good odour, and it was thought preferable to fix responsibility more directly on the governor. Under s.13 of the Act, where a governor's legislative council has refused leave to introduce, or has failed to pass in a form recommended by the governor, any Bill relating to a reserved subject, the governor may certify that the passage of the Bill is essential to the discharge of his responsibility for the subject, and thereupon the Bill, not withstanding that the council have not consented thereto, is to be deemed to have passed, and will, on signature by the governor, become an Act of the local legislature, in the form of the Bill as originally introduced or proposed to be introduced, or (as the case may be) in the form recommended to the council by the governor. The Act will be expressed to be made by the governor, and an authentic copy will be sent to the Governor-General, who will reserve it for His Majesty's pleasure. But if, in the opinion of the Governor-General, a state of emergency exists which justifies such action, he may give his assent, and thereupon the Act is to come into force at once, but is to be subject to disallowance by His Majesty in Council.

An Act made under this section must, as soon as practicable after being made, be laid before each House of Parliament, and, if it has to be presented for His Majesty's assent, it is not to be so presented until copies have been laid before both Houses of Parliament for not less than eight days on which the House has sat.

Section 14[27] provides for the vacation of seats on local legislative councils. An 'official' is not qualified for election as a member of such a council, and if any non-official member of such a council, whether elected or nominated, accepts any office in the service of the Crown in India, he vacates his seats.

Power to create new Governors provinces and to exclude 'backward tracts' from the operation of the Act

The next Section (15)[28] provides for the constitution of new provinces, and makes provision for 'backward tracts'. The Governor-General in Council may, by notification, after obtaining an expression of opinion from the local government and local legislature affected, constitute a new governor's province, or place part of a province under a deputy governor. The Governor-General in Council may also by notification declare any territory in British India to be a 'backward tract', and exclude it from the operation of laws applying to the province in which it is situate, or make exceptions or modifications in the application of these laws to the tract. Local legislatures may be authorized to make similar exceptions and modifications with respect to such tracts. These 'backward tracts ' will take the place of the scheduled districts under the previous laws.

Provisions relating to central Government Constitution of new bicameral Indian Legislature

Part II of the Act relates to the Central Government of India, and the provisions of this part of the measure were extensively changed in their passage through the joint committee on the Bill. There are still, as originally proposed, to be two chambers of the central legislature, a Council of State and a Legislative Assembly.[29] But the composition and functions of each chamber are materially altered. The Council of State is not to be a device for passing measures which cannot be got through the Legislative Assembly. It is to be, in the language of the joint committee, a 'true second chamber'. Except as otherwise prescribed by or under the Act, a Bill is not to be deemed to have been passed by the Indian legislature unless it has been agreed to by both chambers, either without amendment or with agreed amendments.

Council of State

The Council of State is to consist of not more than 60 members, nominated or elected in accordance with statutory rules. Of these not more than 20 are to be official members. The Governor-General has power to appoint from among its members a president and other persons to preside in the president's absence.[30]

Legislative Assembly

The Legislative Assembly is also to consist of members nominated or elected in accordance with statutory rules. The total number was provisionally fixed at 140, 100 elected, 40 non-elected; and of the non-elected 40, 26 must be official. But there is power, by statutory rule, to increase the total number, and to vary the proportion between the classes of members , so however that at least five-sevenths must be elected members and at least one-third of the other members must be non-officials.[31]

The Governor-General is not to be a member of the Council of State or of the Legislative Assembly, but may address either of these bodies and may for that purpose require the attendance of its members.[32]

As in the case of the provincial legislatures, there is to be a president of the Legislative Assembly, appointed for the first four years by the Governor-General, and subsequently elected by the Assembly and approved by the Governor-General.[33] In these and other respects the provisions for the president and deputy president correspond generally to those for the provincial legislatures.

The normal life of the Council of State is fixed at five years, that of the Legislative Assembly at three years, but as in the case of provincial legislatures there are powers to shorten and extend these periods.[34] And there are corresponding provisions about times, places, and adjournments of meetings and discussion of questions.

An official cannot be an elected member of either chamber, and if an elected member accepts office he vacates his seat. No person can be a member of both chambers. If a person is elected to both, he must choose between them. Every member of the Governor-General's executive council must be nominated to one of the two chambers, and has the right to attend in and address the other.[35]

Principle of responsible Government not formally recognized in Central Government

'It was not', remarked the joint committee, 'within the scheme of the Bill to introduce at the present stage any measure of responsible government into the central administration, 'and accordingly the plan of government through ministers, and the division between 'reserved' and 'transferred subjects', find no place in Part II of the Act. But in most of the provisions about the composition, power, and proceedings of the legislatures there is a pretty close resemblance between Part I and Part II.[36] In fact the provisions of Part II on these subjects may be described as being based on those of Part I, with the necessary modifications. In both Parts there is power for the executive government to authorize necessary expenditure and to make necessary laws.

The new Act removes the statutory limit on the number of members of the Governor-General's executive council, and adds to the statutory qualifications for the member of the council having legal experience that of being a pleader of an Indian High Court.[37]

There is power, as in the case of local legislatures, to appoint council secretaries.[38]

Transfer of Secretary of State's salary and other India office expenditure to British estimates

Part III of the Act deals with the Secretary of State in Council. It requires the salary of the Secretary of State for India, and enables any other expenses of his department, to be paid out of moneys provided by Parliament, instead of being paid out of the revenues of India.[39] In the opinion of the joint committee, all charges of the India Office, not being agency charges, ought to be paid out of moneys provided by Parliament. This important change brings the administration of the India Office under the direct and recurrent criticism of Parliament, like that of other departments of the British Government. The rather formal and ineffectual debates of previous years on going into committee on the East India revenue accounts have now become things of the past, and the policy of the Secretary of State for India, like that of other Ministers of the Crown, can be challenged on the vote for his salary. The first occasion which provided this opportunity was on July 8, 1920, when the action of the Secretary of State with respect to the proceedings of General Dyer at Amritsar was made the subject of an acrimonious debate.

Changes in constitution and procedure of Councils of India

The report of Lord Crewe's Committee on the India Office engaged the attention of the joint committee on the Government Bill. The joint committee were not in favour of a abolishing the Council of India. They thought that, at any rate for some time to come, it would be absolutely necessary that the Secretary of State should be advised by persons of Indian experience, and they were convinced that, if no such Council existed, the Secretary of State would have to form an informal one, if not a formal one. Accordingly they contended themselves with recommending alterations in the constitution and procedures of the Council, and these alterations are embodied in the Act (ss. 31, 32, 34).[1] The minimum and maximum number of members are to be eight and twelve instead of ten and fourteen. Half of them must have recently served or resided in India (not merely British India). The term of office is reduced from seven years to five. Any member of the council who was at the time of his appointment domiciled in India is to get, in addition to his annual salary of £1,200, an annual subsistence allowance of £600. Service on the Council is to count towards pension for service in India. These changes make it easier to place Indians on the Council of India. The rigid statutory provisions about the business and procedure of the Council are superseded by more elastic regulations.

Relaxation of Secretary of State's power of control over Indian Administration

The relations of the Secretary of State with the Government of India, and through it with the provincial governments, form the subject of another section (33).[41] These relations were given careful consideration by the joint committee on the Bill, and the important conclusions at which they arrived are to be found in their report. The changes in the direction of giving more independence and responsibility both to the central government and to the provincial governments in India were, in the opinion of the committee, to be made, in the main, rather by a change of conventions than by statutory provisions. They were matters of policy rather than of legislation direct or subsidiary. But in some cases restrictions by statutory rules would be necessary. The section confers power to deal with such cases, and provides security for effective parliamentary criticism of rules made under the power.

High Commissioner for India

The last Section (35)[42] of this Part of the Act carries out the recommendation of Lord Crewe's committee, that a High Commissioner of India, paid of Indian revenues, be appointed to perform for India functions of agency, as distinguished from political functions, analogous to those performed in the offices of the High Commissioner of the Dominions.[43]

Provisions relating to civil services

Part IV of the Act deals with the position of the civil services in India under the new constitution. Subject to the provisions made by statute of statutory rule, any person in the civil service of the Crown in India is declared (by s. 36)[44] to hold office during His Majesty's pleasure, and may be employed in any manner required by a proper authority within the scope of his duty. But he may not be dismissed by any authority subordinate to that by which he was appointed, and may, if dismissed, he reinstated by the Secretary of State in Council. If a person appointed by the Secretary of State in Council thinks himself wronged by an order of an official superior in a governor's province, he has a statutory right to complain to the Governor, who is directed to examine the complaint and require such action to be taken therein as may appear to him to be just and equitable.

By the same Section (s.36) the Secretary of State in Council is empowered to make rules for regulating the classification of the civil services in India, the methods of their recruitment, their conditions of service, pay and allowances, and discipline and conduct. Powers for dealing with such matters may be delegated to Indian authorities and legislatures. Pension rights under existing rules are preserved, but the rules may be varied without prejudice to existing rights. Doubts had been entertained about the validity of some of the existing rules about civil servants, and about the authority under which they had been made. For the removal of such doubts, the concluding paragraph of the section confirms 'all rules or other provisions in operation at the time of the passing of the Act, whether made by the Secretary of state in Council, or by any other authority, relating to the civil service of the Crown in India', but enables them to be revoked, varied, or added to by rules under the new Act.'

If the third schedule to the 1919 Act and the second schedule to the Government of India Act are compared with the third schedule to the Act of 1915 it will be found that some changes have been made in the list of offices reserved to the Indian Civil Service.

Another section (37)[45] amends the power under s. 97 of the Act of 1915 to appoint to the Indian Civil Service persons domiciled in India.

Public Service Commission

The Secretary of State is to establish in India (s. 38)[46] a Public Service Commission, to discharge, in regard to recruitment and control of the public services in India, such functions as may be assigned thereto by rules made by the Secretary of State in Council.

Auditor General

Section 39[47] provides for financial control of Indian administration. There is to be an auditor general in India appointed by the Secretary of State in Council, and having his first position regulated by rules made by that authority. Subject to any rules made by the Secretary of State in Council, no office may be added to or withdrawn from the public services, and the emoluments of no post are to be varied, except after consultation with such financial authority as may be designated in the rules, being, as the case requires, either an authority of the province or of the Government of India.

All rules under this Part of the Act require the concurrence of a majority of votes at a meeting of the Council of India.[48]

Statutory Commission to report progress

Part V of the Act (s. 41)[49] provides for the appointment of a Statutory Commission, to report, after a due interval, on the condition of India, under its new constitution. The commission is not to be appointed until the expiration of ten years from the passing of the Act, and the joint committee express an opinion that no changes of substance in the constitution, whether in the franchise, or in the lists of transferred and reserved subjects, should be made in the interval. The Commission is to inquire into the working of the system of government, the growth of education, and the development of representative institutions in British India, and to report as to whether and to what extent it is desirable to establish the principle of responsible government, or to extend, modify, or restrict the degree of responsible government then existing in British India, including the question whether the establishment of second chambers of the local legislatures is or is not desirable.

Part VI of the new Act contains some general or supplementary provisions.

Members of the central and local governments may (s. 42)[50] be allowed, under restrictions, to retain their interest in their trade or business, but are not, during their term of office, to take part in its direction or management. A proposal to this effect was considered in connection with the amending Bill of 1916, but was eventually dropped. Any assent or disallowance which, under the previous law, has to be signified through the Secretary of State in Council, is now (s. 43) to be signified by His Majesty in Council.

Procedure for the making of rules under the Act

Another section (s. 44)[51] regulates the machinery for making statutory rules. Where any such rules require the approval of Parliament, two alternative methods are permitted. Either the rules must lie on the table of each House for a limited number of days in accordance with the common practice about any English statutory rules and orders, or drafts of the proposed rules must be submitted for the express approval of each House. In the case of the rules made in 1920, the latter method was adopted.

The amending Act of 1916 contained a 'printing clause' under which the amending provisions were to be incorporated with, and printed as part of, the Consolidation Act of 1915. This clause is now superseded by a similar provision (s. 45) for incorporating the new provisions of 1919 in the principal Act of 1915-16. The second schedule to the Act of 1919 shows the mode in which the new provisions are to be incorporated, and the consequential modifications which are to be made in the 'principal Act'.

Part III of the schedule shows how certain provisions of the 'principal Act', which are obsolete or unnecessary or require amendment in detail', are repealed or modified or otherwise dealt with in the law as it now stands.

The last Section (47) provides a short title, dates (very elastic) at which the new provisions are to come into operation, rules of interpretation, and 'transitory' provisions. Executive powers are conferred for dealing with difficulties which may arise in connection with first giving effect to the provisions of the new law.

All the statutory rules[52] required for the election and constitution of the new provincial councils and for the central legislature received the necessary parliamentary approval in the course of the year 1920. The first elections were held at the end of that year, and the sittings of the legislature were formally opened at the beginning of 1921.

At an early date in the parliamentary session of 1921, a joint committee of the two Houses of Parliament was set up for the consideration of all India affairs as might be referred to it. This step was taken in pursuance of a recommendation made in the report (par. 6) of the joint committee on the Bill of 1919. The Montagu-Chelmsford Report had recommended a standing committee of the House of Commons. The joint committee of 1921 considered and reported on the House of Lords Bill of that session for regulating the Government of Burma.

Inauguration of new legislature by Duke of Connaught

It was on February 9, 1921, that the new Indian Legislature, consisting of the Council of State and the Legislative Assembly, was formally opened at Delhi. The proceedings were inaugurated by the reading of a message from the King-Emperor, and by speeches from the Viceroy (Lord Chelmsford) and from the Duke of Connaught representing the King-Emperor.

The royal message contained the following significance's passage. 'For years, it may be for generations, patriotic and loyal

Indians have dreamed of *Swaraj* for their Motherland. To-day you have the beginnings of *Swaraj* within my Empire, and the widest scope and ample opportunity for progress to the liberty which my other Dominions enjoy.' The Viceroy's speech traced the course of evolution of British policy in India, indicated the successive stages in the history of constitutional developments in India under British rule, and expounded the principles on which the Act of 1919 based. The Duke of Connaught, in the course of an important and interesting speech, said that autocratic as was the Government inaugurated when India became a dependency of British Crown, it was based on principles laid down by Queen Victoria in her proclamation of 1858 to the peoples of India; and he quoted as the keynote of that proclamation the following words: 'In their prosperity will be our strength, in their contentment our security, and in their gratitude our best reward.' Speaking on behalf of His Majesty and with the assent of his Government, he repudiated in the most emphatic manner the idea that the administration of India had been, or ever could be based on principles of force or terrorism. The principle of autocracy had now been abandoned. Its retention would have been incompatible with that contentment which had been declared by Queen Victoria to be the aim of British rule, and would have been inconsistent with the legitimate demands and aspirations of the Indian people, and the stage of political development they have attained. Henceforward, in an ever-increasing degree, India would have to bear her own burden.

The message and speeches of February 9, 1921, strike the note on which the foregoing brief summary of British Parliamentary legislation for India may appropriately be brought to a conclusion. The Act of 1919 is the most adventurous experiment which has yet been tried in British India. The ideal aimed at by the British Government in India had previously been a benevolent despotism administrated by an intelligent bureaucracy. That ideal has now reconciled with the desire for self-government with which all Englishmen are bound by their instincts and traditions to sympathize, and which no Englishman can afford to condemn. The reconciliation has been attempted by English communities in all parts of the world, by different methods, and with varying different degree of success. It is for India to profit by these experiences, whether of failure or of success, and the executive and legislature at Westminster can best discharge their imperial responsibilities by giving as free a scope as possible to the trial of the great experiment which they have authorized, and by refraining from any form of unnecessary, captious or irritating criticism. Some ten years hence, when the Statutory Commission has reported, it will be easier to say where, how and why the experiment has succeeded or failed. In the meantime our watchword should be patient, sympathy, and hope.

NOTES

1. The Montagu-Chelmsford Report is published as Report on Indian Constitutional Reforms, 1918, Cd. 9109. The supplementary Indian Reports as 1919, Cd. 141, 103
2. 1919, Cd. 203. It is also to be found in the report published officially under the title *India in 1919*.
3. The proclamation has been published as a parliamentary paper, Cd. 610, and also in the volume published officially as *India in 1919*.
4. The title of this Consolidation Act is 'The Government of India Act', without date. It was published by the Stationery Office.
5. The text of the Act of 1919 will be found in the official volume *India in 1919*.
6. 1919 Act, s. 1; Government of India Act, s.45 A.
7. Joint Committee's Report, par. 4.
8. 1919 Act, s. 2; G. of I. Act, s. 30 (I A).
9. 1919 Act, s. 3; G. of I. Act, s. 46.
10. 1919 Act, s. 3; G. of I. Act, s. 46.
11. 1919 Act, s. 4; G. of I. Act, s. 52.
12. On this point reference should be made to par. 5 of the joint committee's report, and to their note on clause 6 of the Bill.
13. G. of I. Act, s. 47
14. G. of I. Act, s. 49
15. G. of I. Act, s. 72 A.
16. 'For the numbers as fixed by statutory rules *see* table in Appendix II to *India in 1920*.
17. G. of I. Act. S. 72 A (4).
18. The draft rules for elections to provincial legislative councils as approved by the joint committee on the Bill were, under the

proviso to s. 44 (3) of the Act, laid before each House of Parliament, and were, after amendment, approved by both Houses in July 1920. On the whole question of franchise important expression of opinion are to be found in the joint committee's report on clause 7 of the Bill.

19. G. of I. Act, s. 72 B.
20. G. of I. Act, s. 72 C
21. G. of I. Act, s. 80 A
22. There was then a lieutenant-governor of Burma.
23. G. of I. Act, s. 72 D.
24. G of I. Act, s. 81 A.
25. G of I. Act, s. 72 D.
26. G of I. Act, s. 72 E.
27. G of I. Act, s. 80 B.
28. G of I. Act, s. 52 A.
29. S. 17; G. of I. Act, s. 63.
30. S. 18; G. of I. Act, s. 63 A.
31. S. 19; G. of I. Act, s. 63 B. The actual number, as fixed by rule, is 144.
32. Ss. 18, 19; G. of I. Act, ss. 63 A, 63 B.
33. S. 20; G. of I. Act, s. 63 C.
34. S. 21; G. of I. Act, s. 63 D.
35. S. 22; G. of I. Act, s. 63 E
36. See ss. 24—27; G. of I. Act, ss. 67-67B.
37. S. 28; G. of I. Act, s. 36.
38. S. 29 G. of I. Act, s. 43 A.
39. S. 30; G. of I. Act, s. 2 [3].
40. See G. of I. Act, ss. 3-14. Repeal and ommission of ss. 12, 13, 14, 16.
41. G. of I. Act, s. 19 A.
42. G. of I. Act, s. 29 A.
43. The office of the High Commissioner for India was created by an Order in Council, dated 13 August, 1920.
44. G. of I. Act, S. 96 D.
45. G. of I. Act, s. 97 (2 A).
46. G. of I. Act, s. 96 C.

47. G. of I. Act, s. 96 D.
48. S. 40; G. of I. Act, s. 96 E.
49. G. of I. Act, s. 84 A.
50. G. of I. Act, s. 124, Proviso.
51. G. of I. Act, s. 129 A.
52. They have been published by the Stationery Office in a collected form under the title Rules under the Government of India Act.

9

The Government of India Act of 1919

Events Leading to the Passing of the Act

The disillusionment created by the Act of 1909 in the political atmosphere of India aggravated and reinforced the demand for self-government. The Indian people found that self-government would not descend upon them as a gift of the British. Meanwhile, they had a fairly clear idea of what was meant by self-government. As Gokhale remarked: 'The political philosophy and axioms of the West have become an essential part of Indian life, and when its education came to India it brought with it the politics of Nationality, Liberalism and Freedom.'

Events were moving fast both in India and abroad. The Resolution for Provincial Autonomy of 1911 and the transfer of the Capital from Calcutta to Delhi were, indeed, significant developments. Indian aspirations were quickened by the outbreak of the First World War in 1914. Political theorists became active in formulating new schemes for India. One of the first was that of Gokhale.[1] Next came the scheme of Lionel Curtis of *The Round Table*, which advocated 'Dyarchy'—a dual government in which political power was shared by British and Indian representatives. Mention should also be made of the scheme prepared by nineteen members of the Viceroy's Legislative Council, which was subsequently adopted by both the Indian National Congress and the Muslim League in 1916. Its main features were direct elections to Provincial Councils, the binding character of the council resolutions on the Governor, a four-fifth majority of elected members in the Central Legislature, Indianization of half the membership in the Executive Council and the election of these members by the elected members of the Legislatures.

The discussions on these schemes and others were making the political atmosphere tense when on 20 August, 1917 Montagu, the then Secretary of State, made the following announcement in the House of Commons:

> The policy of His Majesty's Government, with which the Government of India are in complete accord, is that of the increasing association of Indians in every branch of the administration and the gradual development of self-governing institutions with a view to the progressive realisation of responsible government in India as an integral part of the British Empire.

Soon after the announcement, Montagu visited India. Along with the viceroy, Lord Chelmsford, he toured all over the country studying the Indian political problem. They published a joint report in July 1918 embodying their proposals, popularly known as the 'Montford' Report. A Bill on the basis of this Report passed by both the Houses of the British Parliament, received Royal assent in December 1919 and became the Government of India Act, 1919.

The basic scheme of the Act embodied four general principles:

(a) Complete popular control, as far as possible, in the field of Local Government.

(b) The Provincial Governments to be in a large measure independent of the Government of India, and to be responsible in some measure to popular representatives.

(c) The Government of India, to remain responsible to Parliament; yet the Indian Legislative Council to be enlarged and popular representation and influence in it to be enhanced.

(d) The control of Parliament and the Secretary of State over the Government of India and the Provinces to be relaxed in proportion to the above changes.

As a preliminary to the transfer of more powers to the Provinces under the Act, it was thought desirable to standardize the Provinces themselves. Hitherto, there had been three categories of Provinces according as they were under Governors, Lieutenant-Governors or Chief-Commissioners. Of these, the Chief Commissioners were at the head of relatively small and less important Provinces. But Lieutenant-Governors were in charge of extensive areas. Under the new scheme, these were upgraded and placed on a par with the Governor's Provinces. The title of Lieutenant-Governor was abolished. The transfer of the Capital from Calcutta to Delhi prepared the way for the creation of this uniformity by distinguishing between the Central Capital and the Provincial Capital by locating them at different places. However, it must be pointed out that the Governors of the Presidencies of Madras, Bombay and Bengal still enjoyed certain privileges which were not given to the Governors of the newly created or upgraded Provinces. All the same, the standardization achieved was real.

We may now consider the extent of decentralization brought about by the Act. A term which was widely in use in those days, although in a loose way, to cover this aspect was 'Provincial Autonomy'. What did it mean? In the words of Sir Frederick Whyte, the first President of the Central Legislative Assembly:

> In current political controversy, it wrongly covers both the freedom of a Provincial Government from external control by the Government of India and the internal political conditions of representative and responsible government. The true meaning of the word lies in the former interpretation. A Province may enjoy provincial autonomy without what are commonly called free institutions. That is to say, in its true meaning provincial autonomy tells us nothing of the condition of the domestic Government prevailing in any particular Province or State.[2]

The whole tenor of the Act of 1919 supports this point of view.

The extent of independent powers conferred upon the Provinces can be divided into broad areas, namely, finance, legislation and administration. These had been carefully defined in what are called 'Devolution Rules', which were an integral part of the Reforms Scheme. The underlying principle of these Rules was to distinguish between the spheres of the Central and Provincial Governments. In practice, this meant a classification of the functions of Government into 'Central' and 'Provincial'.

The classification was made on the following basis: All subjects of all-India importance were brought under the category of 'Central'. Where a subject was of predominantly local interest, it was categorized as 'Provincial'. However, the division was not as rigid as that under a federal constitution. Moreover, the Central Legislature was not precluded from dealing with provincial subjects.

Financial Devolution

The subject of financial devolution may be considered under two heads:

(*a*) Provincial contribution to the Government of India.

(*b*) Relaxation of control over the Provinces.

The first step towards minimizing central control over provincial contributions was taken by a complete separation of the central and the provincial sources of revenue. According to this, land revenue, excise, irrigation and stamps were made exclusively provincial items. The resultant loss of income to the Central Government was made good by the method of provincial contributions to the Central Government.[3]

Before the Reforms, the provincial budgets were included in the budget of the Government of India. But the Act provided for almost complete freedom to the Provinces in this matter. The Central Government wanted thereafter only certain information with regard to the financial position of the Provinces. Further, the taxation powers of the Provincial Council were enlarged by doing away with the requirement of the previous sanction of the Governor-General.

Legislative Devolution

As has already been pointed out, legislative devolution was brought about by drawing up separate items of legislation for the Centre and the Provinces. The old requirement of previous sanction from the Governor-General to initiate legislation was removed in the case of those items which were classified as Provincial. These covered a fairly wide range of subjects under which the peculiar social and local problems of every Province could be dealt with. The Provincial Legislatures were also empowered to make laws for the 'peace and good government' of the Provinces.

The central control over provincial legislation that still remained was two-fold. First, an authentic copy of every Act to which the Governor had given his assent, had to be sent to the Governor-General who might or might not give his assent to it. If the Governor-General gave his assent, then a copy of the Act had to be sent to the Secretary of State who, again, might or might not give his assent to it.

Administrative Devolution

Administrative devolution was natural by-product of financial and legislative devolution. Numerous orders were passed, mostly of a technical character, which had the effect of giving the Provincial Government substantial power in the field of administration.

With this background of the devolution of powers we may now examine the structural changes the Reforms introduced in the Provinces.

The Provincial Executive: Dyarchy

The new structure of the Provincial Executive was designed to meet two conditions: responsibility to popular representatives, and the political backwardness of the people and the administrative inexperience of their leaders. These are patently conflicting in nature. And yet they were provided for in the device of Dyarchy, a device by which the functions of the Provincial Government were divided between those which were to be given to popular control and those which must continue to remain in official hands. The former were called 'Transferred Subjects' and the latter 'Reserved Subjects'. The Governor-in-Council was in charge of the Reserved Subjects, and the Governor acting with the Ministers of the Transferred Subjects. The guiding principle of this division was to include within the Transferred List those departments which afforded most opportunities for local knowledge and social service, those in which Indians had shown themselves to be keenly interested, those in which mistakes that might occur, though serious would not be irremediable, and those which stood most in need of development. But departments primarily concerned with law and order, land-revenue or tenant rights were not to be transferred.

The administration of the Reserved Subjects was entrusted to members of the Governor's Executive Council, appointed by the Crown for a period of five years and receiving a fixed pay. They were not responsible to the Provincial Legislature.

The Transferred Subjects were entrusted to Ministers who were to be nominated by the Governor from among the elected members of the Provincial Council and were to hold office during his pleasure. Their salary was to depend on the vote of the Legislature. In practice, the Provinces of Bengal, Bombay and Madras had four Executive Councillors and three Ministers; in Bihar and Orissa three Executive Councillors and two Ministers and in the remaining Provinces two Councillors and two Ministers were appointed.

The Governor's role as the link between the two halves of the Executive was not only pivotal but also complex. He was to lead the two wings of the Government which were operating in two distinctly separate fields and responsible to two masters. As such, he was obliged not only to yoke the Councillors and the Ministers to the chariot of Provincial Administration but also to drive it. To what extent was this difficult operation successful will be examined presently.

The Legislature: The Provincial Councils[4]

While the Minto-Morley Reforms envisaged the principle of 'association' of the people in the Provincial Government, the ten years that preceded the Monford Reforms constituted a kind of probation for the new principle which it envisaged, namely, responsible government, however rudimentary it was. The Legislative Councils, therefore, had to be reformed with regard to their constitution and functions, in conformity with that principle. These changes can be briefly examined under the following heads:

1. Numbers

Whereas the Act of 1909 laid down the maximum number, the Act of 1919 specified the minimum. Further, this minimum itself was substantially bigger than the maximum under the previous Act. For example, as against a maximum of 50 in the major Provinces, the new Councils had a minimum of over 100

(Madras 118, Bombay 111 and Bengal 125). In most cases, the reconstituted Councils had more members than the prescribed minimum.

2. *Proportion of officials and non-officials*

In the new councils at least seventy per cent of the members were to be elected, and not more than twenty per cent could be officials. The Governor's powers to nominate non-officials was thus restricted to ten per cent.

3. *The method of selection*

Uniform constituencies based upon territory was considered unsuited to Indian conditions. Hence, the constituencies were designed to represent particular communities or special interests such as the Universities, Landholders, Chambers of Commerce, etc. Thus communal (religious) representation became an integral part of the Indian political system.

4. *Qualifications for voters*

The right to vote even in a general constituency depended on a number of qualifications such as, *(i)* residence in that constituency for a minimum period of time; *(ii)* ownership or occupation of a house which had a minimum rental value; *(iii)* payment of a minimum municipal tax or income tax or some other tax or the receipt of a military pension. Owing to these qualifications, the number of eligible voters was extremely small.

5. *Duration of the Council*

The Act fixed the normal life of the Council as three years. But it could be dissolved earlier by the Governor. If the Council was dissolved, a new Council was to be elected within six months after the dissolution.

6. *Functions of the councils*

(a) Interrogatory: **The members had the right to ask questions and supplementaries on a variety of subjects.**

(b) **Deliberative:** The members could move resolutions to ventilate popular grievances. They could also move for adjournment for discussing matters of urgent public interest.

(c) **Legislative:** Although there were a number of restrictions,

Table 1. Composition of the Provincial Councils under the Act of 1919

Province	Elected members											Nominated members		Total
	General electorates		Communal electorates						Special electorates					
	Non-Moh-omme-dans (Rural)	Non-Moh-omme-dans (Urban)	Moh-ommed-ans (Rural)	Moh-ommed-ans (Urban)	Euro-peans	Anglo-Indians	Indian Chris-tians	Sikhs	Uni-versity	Land-holders	Com-merce and Indus-try	Offi-cials (nomi-nated and ex-of-ficio)	Non-offi-cials	
Madras	56	9	11	2	1	1	5	..	1	6	6	23	6	127
Bombay	35	11	22	5	2	..	..	..	1	3	7	20	5	111
Bengal	35	11	33	6	5	2	..	..	1	5	15	20	6	139
Urrited - Provinces	52	8	25	4	1	..	..	..	1	6	3	18	5	123
Punjab	13	7	27	5	..	..	..	12	1	4	2	16	6	93
Bihar and Orissa	42	6	15	3	1	..	..	..	1	5	3	20	7	103
Central - Provinces	31	9	6	1	..	..	..	..	1	3	3	10	6	70
Assam	20	1	12	..	..	..	..	..	..	..	6	9	5	53

the Councils had a certain measure of power to take up consideration of bills dealing with a variety of subjects.

(d) **Financial:** The financial powers of the Councils were limited. Nevertheless, they were considerably more than what they enjoyed under the Act of 1909. They had the power of general discussion as well as voting on demands for grants, although the latter was confined to a small number of items.

The essential weakness of the Councils, in spite of all these enhanced powers, lay in the special powers of the Governor with regard to both legislation and the budget. In the field of legislation, his powers were both positive and negative and had reference to both essential and non-essential legislation. In the matter of the budget, he had the power to authorize such expenditure as might in his opinion be necessary for the safety or tranquility of the Province. Further, in the case of a grant refused or reduced by the Council, the Governor could restore it by certifying the demand as essential to the discharge of his responsibility for the subject. Thus, despite the acceptance of the principle of responsible government, the Act of 1919 in actual operation did not bring that principle into practice.

The Pattern of the Central Government

The Central Government had not undergone any change in its basic principles. The Government of India was still responsible to the British Parliament through the Secretary of State. From a popular point of view, it was still an unrepresentative government. Nevertheless, there were certain changes brought about by the Act, which should be noted.

Hitherto, the strength of the Executive Council of the Governor-General had been fixed at seven, six ordinary members and one extraordinary. The Reforms removed this rigidity giving the Council greater elasticity both in the size and the distribution of Indians in the Council from two to three. A detailed scheme for redistributing the departments of the Government of India was adopted by Lord Chelmsford himself and was implemented by April 1923 by his successor Lord Reading. According to this, there were nine departments, *i.e.* Foreign and Political, Railways and Commerce, Industries and Labour, Education, Health and

Lands, Army, Home, Legislative, Finance and Ecclesiastical. The Viceroy was directly in charge of the Foreign and Political Department. The Ecclesiastical Department, and Railways and Commerce were placed under the charge of one member. Each of the remaining six departments was entrusted to one member. Thus, there was a total of seven members in addition to the Viceroy in the Executive Council.

The Legislature

Under the Reforms, a bicameral legislature—the Indian Legislative Assembly and the Council of State—was established. The Council had a maximum of sixty members of whom not more than twenty could be officials, and not less than thirty were to be elected. The Assembly had a minimum strength of 140 memebrs.[5] At least five-sevenths of these were to be elected and at least one-third of the remaining (nominated) were to be non-officials.

The method of indirect election to the Indian Legislative Council which had been prevalent under the Act of 1909 was abolished and, for the first time, direct election was introduced to fill a large majority of the seats in the Assembly. The election, however, recognized the principle of communal representation. Similarly, industry and commerce and landholders were also given special representation.

The composition of the Council of State was complex.[6] A variety of special interests were given representation. The diversity of composition was secured also by keeping the franchise fairly high to secure the representation of the hereditary aristocracy and the mercantile aristocracy. The franchise was also bestowed for special personal qualifications such as past or present membership of a legislative body or local authority, being Fellow of a University, etc.

Just as in the case of the Provincial Legislatures, the Indian Legislature too had four different types of functions; *(i)* Interrogatory, *(ii)* Legislative, *(iii)* Financial and (iv) Deliberative. With regard to the first and the last, the powers of the Central Legislature were similar to those of the Provincial Legislature. There were, however, important differences between the two with respect to legislation and the budget.

In the legislative field, the powers of the Council of State were co-ordinate with those of the Assembly. Since the Government could always depend on a majority of the Council to support its measures, the popular majority of the Assembly could not force its will against the Government in any matter of legislation. With respect to the budget, a large number of items were categorized as non-votable; the Legislature was not even allowed to discuss them. Discussion was allowed on the remaining items but even here, the Council dominated by officials could flout the will of the Assembly.

On top of all these were the special powers of the Governor-General in the fields of legislation and supplies. When he found himself in conflict with the Indian Legislature, he had at his disposal a number of devices to flout the legislative will. He could refuse leave to introduce certain bills where such leave in advance was necessary. Even if the Legislature rejected a bill recommended by him, he could certify that it was essential for the safety, tranquillity and interests of British India and it would become an Act on the signification of his assent or when he signed it. The only check upon this unqualified power of the Governor-General lay in the hands of the British Parliament before which every such Act had to be laid at least eight days before receiving Royal assent.

Governor-General could also refuse his assent to bills passed by the Legislature, whenever he considered it necessary. In the financial sphere too, the Governor-General had absolute powers to restore, if necessary, any grant that had been reduced or rejected by the Assembly. In practice, the Governor-General had been liberally making use of these overriding powers in the face of a hostile Assembly. On the whole, the Reforms proved totally inadequate to satisfy the popular demand for responsible government at the central level and, that being so, the popularly elected Indian representatives in the Assembly were almost invariably hostile to the Government in all the discussions. In the words of C.R. Das, the Swarajists[7] who went into the Assembly were there not to work it but to wreck it from within.

The Failure of Dyarchy

In its operation, Dyarchy proved to be a failure. An official committee headed by Sir Alexander Muddiman made a thorough

Table 2: Statement showing the Constitution of the Legislative Assembly under the Act of 1919 (excluding the President)

	Nominated Members			*Elected Members*							
	Offi-cials	*Non-Offi-cials*	*Total*	*General*	*Muslim*	*Sikh*	*Land Owners*	*Euro-peans*	*Indian Com-merce*	*Total*	*Grand Total*
Government of India	12	..	12	..	..	..	..	..	..	..	12
Madras	2	2	4	10	3	..	1	1	1	16	20
Bombay	2	4	6	7	4	..	1	2	2	16	22
Bengal	2	3	5	6	6	..	1	3	1	17	22
United Provinces	2	1	3	8	6	..	1	1	..	16	19
Punjab	1	1	2	3	6	2	1	..	..	12	14
Bihar and Orissa	1	1	2	8	3	..	1	..	..	12	14
Central Provinces	1	..	1	3	1	..	1	..	..	5	6
Assam	1	..	1	2	1	..	..	1	..	4	5
Burma	1	..	1	3	..	..	..	1	..	4	5
Berar	..	2	2	..	..	..	..	..	..	..	2
Ajmer	..	1	1	..	..	..	..	..	..	..	1
Delhi	..	..	..	1	..	..	..	..	..	1	1
Total	25	15	40	51	30	2	7	9	4	103	143

Table 5. Statement showing the Constitution of the Council of State under the Act of 1919 (excluding the President)

	Nominated Members			*Elected Members*					
	Officials	*Non-Officials*	*Total*	*General*	*Muslim*	*Sikh*	*Europeans Commerce*	*Total*	*Grand Total*
Government of India	12	:	12	:	:	:	:	:	12
Madras	1	1	2	4	1	:	:	5	7
Bombay	1	1	2	3	2	:	1	6	8
Bengal	1	1	2	2	2	:	1	6	8
United Provinces	1	1	2	3	2	:	:	5	7
Punjab	1	2	3	1	1½	1	:	3½	6½
Bihar and Orissa	1	:	1	2½	1	:	:	3½	4½
Burma	:	:	:	1	:	:	1	2	2
Central Provinces	:	:	:	2	:	:	:	2	2
Assam	:	:	:	½	½	:	:	1	1
Delhi	1	:	1	:	:	:	:	:	1
Total	19	6	25	20	10	1	3	34	59

examination of the working of Dyarchy in the Provinces and came to the conclusion that it had failed. Although the committee had produced majority and minority reports, both were united on this point. They differed only in their specific allegations. The majority reported the following defects:

(*a*) The interference of the 'Reserved half' of the Government on the 'Transferred half' and *vice versa*.

(*b*) The failure to encourage joint deliberation between the two halves of the Government.

(*c*) The absence of joint responsibility of the Ministers.

(*d*) The lack of real authority in the Ministers as a result of interference from the Governor, the Government of India and the Secretary of State.

(*e*) The excessive control exercised by the Finance Department (a reserved subject) over the Transferred Departments.

(*f*) The failure on the part of the Indian Civil Service to cooperate with the Ministers.

Some of these defects deserve to be examined in more detail. The lack of clear demarcation of subjects between the two halves enhanced the possibility of mutual interference between the two halves of the Government. Whenever such conflicts arose, the Governor was to act as arbitrator and generally he sided with the Reserved half. The minority of the Commission regarded this as an inherent defect of Dyarchy. The majority, on the other hand, thought that the two halves would work more smoothly if the division of subjects between the two halves was based upon more scientific principles.

Joint deliberation of matters of policy and administration was not an obligatory part of the system. The initiative in this connection rested with the Governor. But only a few of the Governors encouraged this practice. The majority of the Muddiman Committee wanted this to be accepted as a principle in order to make the embryonic beginning of a cabinet system. But the minority thought that even if this were adopted as a principle, it would not remove the inherent defect of Dyarchy. 'We maintain', they said, 'that it is an inherent defect of the present Constitution that the Government should be divided into two halves.'

The principle of joint responsibility was not secured nor was it possible to secure it under the system. The Ministers were not selected on the basis of organized political parties in the Legislature, but on an individual basis. There was also no office of Chief Minister. In the absence of joint responsibility, each Minister's aim was to hold on to his position somehow. So long as he managed to be in the good books of the Governor, there was a good chance of his continuing in office. Such an attitude, instead of giving training to Indians in the science of responsible government, trained them only in the arts of flattery and sycophancy.

The Governor's powers in the distribution of subjects were absolute. Further, he appointed the Ministers in his discretion, consulted them individually, looked upon them as mere advisers and dismissed them as and when he liked. This struck at the very root of ministerial responsibility. The Governor was not a constitutional head with respect to the Transferred Subjects.

The practice of departmental secretaries having direct access to the Governor independent of the Ministers further undermined the Minister's position in the Government as well as his responsibility. The practice reinforced the suspicion of the Ministers that the permanent Civil Services were influencing the Governor behind the back and without the knowledge of the Ministers. Moreover, this privilege made the Services feel that they could afford even to ignore altogether the Ministers if they chose to do so.

The control exercised by the Finance Department over the Transferred Subjects was excessive. Further, the Finance Department was always in charge of a Member of the Executive Council and not of a Minister. This department was not merely satisfied with furnishing financial advice but it constantly tried to control the policy of the Ministers. Often, this control was irksome and sometimes even mischievous. As the Ministers held the charge of comparatively unimportant subjects (according to the objectives of a Police State), never were their requests for adequate funds for new schemes granted by the Finance Department.

Perhaps, the most unwholesome feature of Dyarchy was the position of the Permanent Services *vis-à-vis* the Ministers. The

Ministers had to implement their policies through the Services. To do this effectively, they depended on the dutiful support and co-operation of the Services. But since the top layer of the Services, particularly the members of the Indian Civil Service, were recruited by the Secretary of State and were responsible only to him they did not show any great loyalty to the Ministers. On the contrary, the Ministers were humiliated by members of the Indian Civil Service by their insubordinate and even defiant attitude in many matters.

In the Legislature too, the position of the Ministers was none too happy. The biggest and the most organized of all political parties was the Indian National Congress. In most of the Provincial Legislatures the Congress had either a clear majority or the leading position. But since the Congress was against the dyarchical system, their representatives refused to accept ministerships. Inevitably, the choice therefore fell upon representatives of the smaller parties or independents. Such Ministers never had a majority to back them in the Legislatures. Often, the possibility of a successful no-confidence motion against them hung above their heads. No Minister who held on to office in such circumstances could do anything substantially useful to the people. Hence ministerships under Dyarchy became a byeword for opportunism, or the patronage of the British Government.

Thus, Dyarchy failed. Even its staunch supporters soon found it uninspiring when once they were associated with its operation. The people of India, it became soon clear, would not be satisfied with this half-way house between autocracy and responsible government. In the words of Sir Courtney Ilbert, it was like one of those caravansarais which would be run up rapidly for an Indian Prince to meet a temporary need.[8] But even as a caravansarai it did not satisfy those for whom it was intended. When Lord Olivier, the Secretary of State for India in the first Labour Government, compared the Act to a sea-worthy vessel and observed that it should carry Indians across if only they would get into it and row, Pandit Motilal Nehru replied: 'It may be sea-worthy but what we want is not only a sea-worthy vessel but a vessel big enough for our cargo, big enough to accommodate the millions of passengers that have to cross over from servility to freedom.'[9] When put to the test of practice, it was found that the

Act had nothing to offer by way of substantial transfer of power to the representatives of the people. Even those optimists, like the Indian Liberals, who gave it a fair trial, found it wanting in many respects and were therefore terribly disappointed. The result was the emergence of a new spirit, a new unity and a new movement of the educated classes under the banner of the Indian National Congress. Mahatma Gandhi led the movement. He called it a 'non-violent, non-co-operation movement'. Soon, it gathered momentum and assumed the shape of a full-fledged agitation for complete transfer of power to Indian hands. Everyone felt the need of a constitution which would suit the conditions existing in India. The only difference of opinion was as to the nature of the constitution, particularly whether it should be federal or unitary in character. Thus, for the first time in the history of India, the possibility and the feasibility of an All India Federation became the most important subject for discussion among Indian and English political leaders.

NOTES

1. Published posthumously in 1917, it advocated a substantial measure of self-government.
2. *India: A Federation?*, pp. 36-7.
3. See the *Report of the Meston Committee* which went into this question in great detail.
4. See Table 1 on p. *78*.
5. See Table 2 on p. *81* for the composition of the Assembly.
6. See Table 3 on p. *83*.
7. Swarajists were those active members of the Indian National Congress who were in favour of contesting the elections under the Act of 1919 rather than boycotting it (as advocated by those led by Gandhi). C.R. Das and Motilal Nehru were the leaders of the Swarajists.
8. Ilbert and Meston, *The New Constitution of India*, p. 13.
9. *Debates in the Central Assembly*. 10 March 1924.

10

Constitutional Development from 1919 to 1935

The Reforms of 1919 were considered to be utterly inadequate by the Indians. The Indian National Congress at its annual session in 1919 condemned the Reforms as "inadequate, unsatisfactory and disappointing." While it asked the British Government to take early steps to establish full responsible government in India in accordance with the principle of self-determination, it resolved to work the Reforms "so far as may be possible" with a view to bring about the early establishment of responsible government in India.

The Indian were not in an uncompromising mood, but certain events spoiled the political atmosphere in the country. On the Report of a Committee presided over by Justice Rowlatt, Two bills were introduced in the imperial Legislature in February 1919 and passed into law by the official majority in spite of the opposition of the people. Mahatma Gandhi appealed to the people of India to offer *Satyagraha* against the oppressive laws. *Hartals* were held all over the country. Disturbances took place at various places. Martial Law was declared in the Punjab. On the *Baisakhi* day (13th April, 1919), there occurred the Jallianwala Bagh tragedy. General Dyer ordered the opening of fire on a peaceful crowd at Amritsar. 1650 rounds were fired, about 400 people were killed and 1200 were wounded. According to Dyer himself, his object was to create "a sufficient moral effect from a military point of view not only on those who were present, but more especially throughout the Punjab." The people were subjected to great humiliations. The crawling order was most resented. The people were required to pass through a street like four-footed animals. The Punjab leaders were jailed. At different places, Bombs were thrown on innocent persons. All this resulted in resentment against the British Government.

Certain events brought the Congress and the Muslims together. The Muslims of India protested against the hard terms imposed on Turkey after the first World War. Mahatma Gandhi joined hands with the Muslims and started his non-violent non-cooperation movement for the redress of the *Khilafat* and the wrongs of the Punjab and the establishment of *Swarajya* in India. The Calcutta session of Congress in September, 1920 endorsed the policy of Mahatma Gandhi and called upon the people to give up their titles and honorary offices and also boycott schools, law Courts, Legislative Councils and British goods. The movement was very strong for two years. However, the events of Chauri Chaura in the U. P. where 22 policemen were burnt to death by a mob, made Mahatma Gandhi suspend the movement. The Mahatma was himself arrested in March 1922 and the movement collapsed.

Although the Moderates were prepared to do everything in their power to make the new constitutions a success," they were themselves not satisfied with the Reforms. It was felt that the Reforms did not go far enough. On 23rd September 1921, a resolution was moved in the Assembly by Rai Jadunath Mojumdar Bahadur for the establishment of autonomy in the provinces and the introduction of responsibility in the Central Government. To that resolution, an amendment was moved by Mr. Jamnadas Dwarkadas in which he asked the Governor-General-in-Council "to appoint a committee consisting of officials and non-officials, including members of the Indian Legislature, to consider the best way of bringing about a provincial autonomy in all the Governor's Provinces and of introducing responsibility in the Central Government and to make recommendations." Sir William Vincent, the Home Member, suggested the following formula which was adopted by the Assembly: "That this Assembly recommends to the Governor-General-in-Council that he should convey to the Secretary of State for India the view of this Assembly that the progress made by India on the path of responsible government warrants a re-examination and revision of the Constitution at an earlier date than 1929."

The Government of India submitted a report of this debate to the Secretary of State for India. The latter was of the opinion that the possibilities the new constitution has not been exhausted. He maintained that progress was possible under the existing constitution. The merits and capabilities of the electorate had not been tested by time and experience. The new constitutional machinery had still to be tested in its working as a whole. The reply of the Secretary of state was followed by a resolution moved in the Assembly by Diwan Bahadur T. Rangachariar in February 1923 expressing extreme dissatisfaction with it. Another resolution was moved by Dr. Hari Singh Gour in July, 1923 which recommended to the Governor-General to move the Secretary of State to carry out his suggestion with regard to further reforms possible under the constitution.

At this stage, the Swarajists appeared on the scene. So far the Congress has followed a policy of non-cooperation. However, certain of its leaders led by C. R. Das and Motilal Nehru turned to a new method of embarrassing the Government. That method was "of wrecking the legislatures from within." The members of the Swarajist Party took the pledge of 'uniform, continuous and sustained obstruction with a view to making the Government through the Assembly and the Councils impossible," and they had a striking success in the elections.

In the new Assembly, Diwan Bahadur Ranagachariar moved a resolution recommending "to the Governor-General-in-Council that he be pleased to take at a very early date the necessary steps (including, if necessary, appointment of a Royal Commission) for revising the Government of India Act so as to secure for India full Self-Government Dominion Status within the British Empire and provincial autonomy in the provinces. The Government opposed the resolution but proposed to make a serious attempt to investigate justifiable complaints against the working of the scheme in practice; to assess the causes and to examine the remedies necessary." Neither the original resolution nor the proposal of the Government was acceptable to the Swarajist Party and consequently Pandit Motilal Nehru, leader of the Swarajist Party, moved the following amendment and the same was carried:

"This Assembly recommends to the Governor-General-in-Council to take steps to have the Government of India Act revised with a view to establish Full Responsible Government in India and for the said purpose—

(a) to summon at a early date a representative Round table Conference to recommend with due regard to the protection of the rights and interests of important minorities the scheme of a constitution for India; and

(b) after dissolving the Central Legislature to place the said scheme for approval before a newly elected Indian Legislature for its approval and submit the same to the British Parliament to be embodied in a statute."

Muddiman Committee Report

The Government of India did not accept the resolution of the Assembly, but set up a Committee under the Chairmanship of Sir Alexander Muddiman—

(1) to enquire into the difficulties arising from, or defects inherent in, the working of the Government of India Act and the Rules thereunder in regard to the Central Government and the Governments of Governor's Provinces; and

(2) to investigate the feasibility and desirability of securing remedies for such difficulties or defects, consistent with the structure, policy and purpose of the act,

  (a) by action taken under the Act ,

  (b) by such amendments of the Act as appear necessary to rectify any administrative imperfections."

The Muddiman Committee did not submit a unanimous report. *The majority view* was that the existing constitution was working in most provinces and was affording valuable political experience. As the new constitution had been in existence only for a short period, it was not possible to say definitely as to whether it would succeed ultimately or not. However, detailed recommendations were made for improving machinery of the Government. The *minority view* was that dyarch had absolutely failed and could not succeed at all in the future. It was only a fundamental change of the constitution which could bring about an improvement. To quote them, "It has been urged that an advance could be made by action under S. 19A of the Act and without any radical amendment of the Act itself. With all respect to those who maintain this view, we entirely differ from it:

"In the first place, it is obvious that under S. 19A the Secretary of State can only 'regular and restrict' the exercise of the powers of superintendence, direction and control vested in him.

"In the second place, such regulation and restriction of powers must be with a view to give effect to the purposes of the Government of India Act. These purposes are defined in the preāmble, and we think hat even if the Secretary of State felt so disposed, he could not, by the mere exercise of his powers under this section, abolish diarchy.

"In the third place, reading the second and third parts of Section 19A with the first part, it seems to us that the relaxation of the control contemplated by S. 19A can only be with regard to Provincial Government and cannot have any relation to the Central Governments. "We also think that the relaxation of control provided by this section cannot mean the same thing as divestment."

In September, 1925, the Report of the Muddiman Committee was discussed in the Central Assembly. The Government of India proposed to accept the principal underlying majority report and proceed with the consideration of its recommendations. Motilal Nehru moved the following amendment which was carried in the Assembly in spite of the opposition of the Government: "That immediate steps should be taken to move his Majesty's Government to make a declaration in Parliament embodying such fundamental changes in the constitution of India as would make government fully responsible; and that a Round Table Conference or Convention, representative of all interests, should be held to frame a detailed scheme which should be placed before the Legislative Assembly for approval, and afterwards submitted to the British Parliament to be embodied in a statue."

Appointment of Simon Commission

In November, 1927, was appointed the Simon Commission. Different views have been expressed as to why the Statutory

Commission was appointed earlier. According to some, the British Government was forced to appoint the Commission earlier on account of the agitation carried on in India. However, the real reason seems to have been different. In December 1925, Lord Birkenhead, Secretary of State for India in the Conservative Ministry, referred to the possibility of accelerating the Commission. The whole object of Lord Birkenhead and the Conservative Government was not to leave the Commission to be appointed by the Labour Government which it was felt would almost certainly come into power at the next general elections. Another object was to use the appointment of the Commission as a bargain-counter and to disintegrate the Swarajist Party.

In a private letter date 10th December 1925, Lord Birkenhead wrote thus to Lord Reading: " I always had it plainly in mind that we could not afford to run the slightest risk that the nomination of 1928 Commission should be in the hands of our successors. You can readily imagine what kind of a Commission in its personnel would have been appointed by Col. Wedgwood and his friends. I have, therefore, throughout been of the clear opinion that it would be necessary for us as a matter of elementary prudence to appoint a Commission not later than the summer of 1927. I should, therefore, like to receive your advice if any moment you discern an opportunity for making this a useful bargain counter, or for further disintegrating the Swarajist Party." Again: "I am sure that having regard to political contingencies in this country, we must keep the nomination of the personnel of the Commission in our own hands. In this matter, we cannot run the slightest risk. My present view, therefore, is-and I believe that the Prime Minister shares it–that we shall in any event, be playing for safety it we are driven to nominate the Commission in the middle of 1927. If such an acceleration affords you any bargaining value, use it to the full and with the knowledge that you will be supported by the Government."

The Statutory Commission consisted of seven members and was presided over by the late Sir John Simon. All of its members were Englishmen. The Commission was boycotted by the Indians on the ground that it had no Indian member. The excuse given for not appointing any Indian on the Commission was that the intention of the framers of the Act of 1919 was to confine the

Commission to members of Parliament. However, the Act did not lay down any such restriction. But even if the British Government wanted to restrict the nomination to members of Parliament, there were two Indian members at that time. Lord Sinha was a member of the House of Lords and Mr. Shapurji Saklatwala was in the House of Commons. Lord Sinha has been closely associated with the various stages of constitution reforms in India. His presence on the Commission would have been very valuable. The real reason seems to have been that the Conservative Government did not want any Indian to be on the Commission. According to Dr. A.B. Keith, an avoidable blunder was committed by the Indians by boycotting the Commission. Only a body external to India could properly decide whether the country was fit for a further step towards the goal of self-Government or not. As India was not independent, she could not investigate her own case.

The Simon Commission was appointed "for the purpose of inquiring into the working of system of Government, the growth of education and the development of representative institutions in British India and matters connected therewith" and reporting "as to whether and to what extent it is desirable to establish the principle of responsible Government, or to extend, modify, or restrict the degree of responsible Government then existing therein, including the question whether the establishment of second chambers of the local legislatures, is or is not desirable. As the inquiry was coming to a close, the Commissioners "were increasingly impressed by the impossibility of considering the constitutional problems of British India without taking into account the relation between British India and the Indian States." With the approval of the British Government, the Commission also considered the relations between British India and the Indian States.

In his letter dated 6th February 1928, Sir Johan Simon laid down the procedure to be followed by the Commission in these words: "instead of dealing with them–documents containing the material which the Government of India and the Local Governments had been preparing for the Commission—by ourselves, we wish to propose that they, and the evidence given in the explanation or amplification of them, should come before 'a Joint Free Conference,' over which I should preside, consisting of the seven British Commissioners and a corresponding body of representatives chosen by the Indian Legislatures (just as we ourselves have been chosen by the British Parliament.)

"We put forward the plan of a 'Joint Free Conference' not only because we should welcome the assistance of colleagues from the Indian Legislatures, but because we think it is only right and fair, and in the truest interests of India and Britain alike, that opportunity should be provided for such memoranda and testimony to be scrutinized and, if necessary, elucidated from the Indian side on free and equal terms. We suggest, therefore, that the two Houses of the Central Legislature should in due course be invited to choose from their non-official members a Joint Committee, which might conveniently be seen in numbers, and that each Local Legislative Council should be asked to constitute a similar body. The Indian side of the Conference would consist, when Central subjects were being dealt with, of those first named; in a Province, the Indian wing would primarily consist of the Provincial members but, in order that the Central Joint Committee may not have a partial view of the material put before it, we should be glad if arrangements could be arrived at which would enable its members, or some of them, to be present as an additional element and provincial sittings...

"We see no reason, however, why evidence from public and representative bodies, and from individuals, should not normally be given to the Conference as a whole, just as evidence presented by or on behalf of the various Governments would be. If a case arises when this general plan cannot be followed, I should make no secret of it, and should ask my colleagues in the Joint Free Conference . . . to accept from me such account of the matter as I can give them on behalf of the Commission, with due regard to the reason why the testimony has been separately received. I imagine that the Indian side may find occasions when they would think it well to act in the same way...

"Above all, I would urge that one of the merits of the method of Joint Free Conference is that, besides securing due recognition of equal status, it provides the opportunity for that free exchange of views and mutual influence which are best calculated to promote the largest measures of agreement that is possible...

"The Commission is, of course, bound to carry through its task in nay event and discharge to the full the duty cast upon it, but we are undertaking this duty only after having made it known that the method of collaboration on honourable and equal terms is open, and that we put it forward in all sincerity and good will."

The Simon Commission was boycotted not only by the Congress and other representative organisations, but also by other distinguished leaders of India. Resolutions were passed condemning the constitution of the Commission. To quote one, "We have come to a deliberate conclusion that the exclusion of Indians from the Commission is fundamentally wrong. The underlying principle of the scheme that Indians are to have no authoritative voice either in the collection of proper materials and evidence or in taking of decisions by way of recommendations of the Commission to Parliament is of such a character that India cannot, with any self-respect acquiesce in it. Unless a Commission on which British and Indian statesmen are invited to sit on equal terms is set up, we cannot conscientiously take any part or share in work of Commission as at present constituted."

The day on which the Commission landed in India, there was a Hartal all over the country. Wherever the members of the Commission went, they were greeted with black flags and cries of "Simon go back." The Central Assembly was invited to form a Committee to cooperate with the Commission, but it refused to do so. A large number of persons were arrested and prosecuted. However, prosecutions did not damp the enthusiasm of the people against the Commission.

The Nehru Report.

The Indians condemned the appointment of an all-white Simon Commission and Lord Birkenhead while justifying the exclusion of Indians from the Commission, challenged the latter to produce an agreed constitution and submit the same to the British Parliament for consideration. This challenge was accepted by the Indians and an all Parties Conference was held in Bombay on 19th May 1928. This conference was presided over by Dr. M.A. Ansari. The Conference appointed a Committee under the Chairmanship of Pandit Motilal Nehru to consider and determine the principles of a constitution for India. Sir Tej Bahadur

Sapru, Sir Ali Imam, Mr. M. S. Aney, Sardar Mangal Singh, Mr. Shuaib Quareshi, G. R. Pradhan and Subhash Chandre Bose were its members. The Committee produced a report which has gone down in history as the Nehru Report. According to Dr. Zacharias, the report is "a masterly and stamen like report," and according to another critic, "The Nehru Report deserves to be read and studied in all its details, as it sheds light on every subject it touches and displays a practical commonsense, which never loses itself in doctrinaire utopias, but which equally spurns to shelter itself behind the enunciation of mere platitudes. The recommendations of the report were unanimous except in regard to the basis of the constitution. While the majority favoured Dominion Status not merely as distant goal, but as "the next immediate step," it however, gave liberty of action to all those group and parties which made complete independence their goal.

Although the Report envisaged a future linking up of the Indian states with the rest of India in a federal policy, it confined itself to British India. The Report laid down generally that all treaties made between the East India Company and the Indian States and all such subsequent treaties so far as they were enforced, shall be binding on the Commonwealth of India and that the Commonwealth shall exercise the same right in relation to and discharge the same obligations towards the Indians States as the Government of India exercised and discharged previously. In regard to matters of justifiable character, in case of differences between Commonwealth and Indian States on any matter arising out of treaties, engagements, Sanads or similar other documents. The Governor-General-in-Council may with the consent of the state concerned, refer such matters to the Supreme Court for its decision.

As regards the communal question the report made many wise recommendations. It proposed joint electorates with reservation of seats for minorities on population basis with the right to contest additional seat. No seats were to be reserved for any community in Punjab and Bengal. Full protection was to be given to the religious and cultural interests of the Muslim community. New provinces on linguistic basis were to be created with a view to the "planning of Muslim-majority provinces against Hindu-majority provinces."

The Report enumerated 19 fundamental rights which were to be embodied in the statute. It was to be declared that all powers of the Government and all authority are derived from the people. No person shall be deprived of his liberty, nor shall his dwelling or property be entered, sequestered or confiscated, save in accordance with law. Freedom of conscience and free profession and practice of religions will be guaranteed to every person. The right of free expression of opinion and the right to assemble peacefully and without arms and to form associations or unions shall be guaranteed for purposes not opposed to public order or morality. All citizens shall have the right to free elementary education. All citizens shall be equal before law and possess equal civic rights. There shall be no penal law of a discriminative nature. No person shall be punished for any act which is not punishable under the law at the time it was committed. No corporal punishment or other punishment involving torture of any kind shall be lawful. Every citizen shall have the right to a writ of Habeas Corpus. There shall be no state religion for the Commonwealth of India or for any province, nor shall any state endow any religion or give preference to any religion. No person attending any school receiving state-aid or other public money shall be compelled to attend religious instruction that may be given in the school. No person shall by reason of his religion, caste or creed be prejudiced in any way in regard to public employment, office of power or honour and the exercise of any trade or calling. All citizens shall have an equal right of access to, and use of, public roads, public wells and all other places of public resort. Freedom of combination and association for maintenance and improvement of labour and economic conditions shall be guaranteed to every one and of all occupations. All agreements and measures tending to restrict or obstruct such freedom shall be illegal. No breach of contract of service or abetment shall be made a criminal offence. Parliament shall make suitable laws for the maintenance of health and fitness for work of all citizens, securing of a living wages for every worker, the protection of motherhood, welfare of children, and the economic consequences of old age, infirmity and unemployment. Every citizen shall have the right to keep and bear arms in accordance with the regulations made in that behalf. Man and woman shall have equal rights as citizens.

The report provided for a parliament of two houses, viz., Senate and House of Representatives, Governor-General was to be appointed by the British Government. He was to be paid out of the Indian revenues and his salary was not to be altered during his continuance in office. Senate was to consist of 200 members elected by provincial councils. The House of Representatives was to consist of 500 members. It was to be elected on an adult franchise basis. The life of the Senate was to be seven years and that of the House of Representatives 5 years.

The Governor-General was to act on the advice of the Executive Government. Prime Minister was to be appointed by the Governor-General and other Ministers were to be appointed on the advice of the Prime Minister. The Executive Government was to be collectively responsible to the Parliament. Governor-General-in-Council was to appoint High Commissioners and other foreign representatives similar to those appointed by Canada and other Dominions. He was also to appoint Auditor-General of India.

The Governor of every province was to be appointed by the King of England. He was to be paid out of the provincial revenues. Provision was also to be made for a Legislative Council elected on an adult-franchise basis. The Provincial Council was to sit for 5 years. However, it could be dissolved earlier by the Governor. The latter could also extend its life under special circumstances. Provision was made for a President and Vice-President of the Legislative Council.

The Governor was to act on the advice of the provincial Executive Council whose number was not to exceed 5. Governor-General was to select the Chief Minister and the other members of the Executive Council were to be appointed by him on the advice of the Chief Minister. Provision was to be made for a Supreme Court. It was to consist of a Lord President and other Justices. The members of the Supreme Court were to be appointed by the Governor-General-in-Council, but were not be removed from office except on an address from both houses of Parliament praying for such removal on the ground of misbehaviour or incapacity. The Supreme Court was to have both original and appellate jurisdiction. Provision was also to be made for taking of appeals to the King-in-Council under certain circumstances.

Governor-General-in Council was to appoint a Committee of Defence consisting of the Minister of Defence, Minister of Foreign Affairs, Commander-in-Chief, Commander of Air Forces, Commander of Naval Forces, Chief of the General Staff and two other experts. Prime Minister was to be the Chairman of the Committee. The functions of that Committee were to advise the government and the various departments concerned on questions of defence and general policy.

As regards the civil services, all officers of public services at the time of the establishment of Commonwealth, were to become officers of the Commonwealth. The Governor-General was to appoint a Public Services Commission. All officers of the Army Services were to retain all their existing rights regarding their salaries, allowances and pensions. They were also to get compensation, for any loss incurred by them.

The Nehru Report was submitted on 10th August, 1928 and the All Parties Conference met at Calcutta on 22nd December, 1928 to consider the Report. As regards the communal question, Mr. Jinnah on behalf of the All India Muslim League moved amendments to the Report. The first amendment was that one-third of the elected representatives of both the houses of the Central Legislature should be Muslims, but the amendment was rejected. The second amendment was that in the event of an adult franchise not being established in the Punjab and Bengal, there should be reservation of seats for the Muslims on a population basis for 10 years subject to re-examination after that period, but the Muslims should have no right to contest additional seats. This amendment was also lost. The third amendment moved by Mr. Jinnah was that residuary powers should vest in the provinces. This was also not accepted. Another amendment moved by him was that by amendment of the constitution should be made unless it was first passed both the houses of Parliament separately by a majority of four-fifths and was approved by a similar majority of both the Houses in joint session. This amendment was unanimously accepted. It is to be noted that Sir Tej Bahadur Sapru pressed the Conference to accept the amendment of Mr. Jinnah with a view to secure a settlement. While doing so, he remarked thus: "The simple position is that for the sake of settlement, you are invited by Mr. Jinnah however illogical and unreasonable to agree to this proposition, which I consider not inconsistent with the Nehru Report. Speaking for myself, I would like you, to picture Mr. Jinnah whom I have known intimately for 15 years, as a spoilt child. If he is a spoilt child, naughty child, I am prepared to say, give him what he wants and be finished with it. I am not going to ask him to be reasonable but we must, as practical statesmen, try to solve the problem and not be mislead by arithmetical figures. However, it is to be noted that Mr. M. R. Jaykar who represented the Hindu point of view, was opposed to the demands of Mr. Jinnah.

Congress Resolution of 1928

The Congress at its session on 31st December, 1928 passed the following resolution:— "This Congress, having considered the constitution recommended by the All-Parties Committee Report welcomes it as a great contribution towards the solution of India's political and Communal problems and congratulates the committee on the virtual unanimity of its recommendations and, whilst adhering to the resolution relating to complete independence passed at the Madras Congress, approves of the Constitution drawn up by the Committee as a great step in political advance, especially as it represents the largest measure of agreement attained among the important parties in the country.

"Subject to the exigencies of the political situation this Congress will adopt the constitution if it is accepted in its entirety by the British Parliament on or before December 31, 1929 but in the event of its non-acceptance by that date or its earlier rejection, the Congress will organise a campaign of non-violent non-cooperation by advising the country to refuse taxation and in such other manner as may be decided upon.

"Consistently with the above, nothing in this resolution shall interfere with the carrying on, in the name of Congress, of the propaganda for complete independence."

A session of the All-India Muslim League was convened in March 1929. The subjects Committee of the League Session which met on March 31, approved of the Nehru Report by a majority subject to certain specified safeguards which Jinnah had advocated at Calcutta Convention. At the open session of the League, this resolution was adopted by a majority.

Jinnah's Fourteen Points (1929)

Mr. Jinnah summoned a meeting of the All India Muslim League at Delhi in March 1929 and put forward his Fourteen points as the minimum Muslim demands for any political settlement. While rejecting the Nehru Report, the resolution of the League laid down us under:-

"That no scheme for the future constitution of the Government of India will be acceptable to the Musalmans of India until and unless the following basic principles are given effect to and provisions are embodied therein to safeguard their rights and interests:

1. "The form of the future constitution should be federal with the residuary powers vested in the provinces.
2. "A uniform measure of autonomy shall be granted to all provinces.
3. "All legislatures in the country and other elected bodies shall be constituted on the definite principle of adequate and effective representation of minorities in every province without reducing the majority in any province to a minority or even equality."
4. "In Central Legislature Muslim representation shall be one third.
5. "Representation of communal groups shall continue to be by separate electorates as at present provided; it shall be open to any community, at any time, to abandon its separate electorate in favour of joint electorates.
6. "Any territorial redistribution that might at any time be necessary shall not in any way affect the Muslim majority in the Punjab, Bengal and North-West Frontier Province.
7. "Full religious liberty *i. e.*, liberty of belief, worship and observance, propaganda, association and education shall be guaranteed to all communities.
8. "No bill or resolution or any part thereof shall be passed in any legislature or any elected body if three-fourths of the members of any community in that particular body oppose such a bill, resolution or part thereof on the ground that it would be injurious to the interests of that

community, or in the alternative such other method is devised as may be found possible and practicable to deal with such cases.

9. "Sind should be separated from the Bombay Presidency.
10. "Reforms should be introduced in the N.W.F. Province and Baluchistan on the same footing as in other provinces.
11. "Provision should be made in the constitution giving Muslims an adequate share along with the other Indians in all the services of the state and in local self-governing bodies having due regard to the requirements of efficiency.
12. "The constitution should embody adequate safeguards for the protection of Muslim culture and for the promotion of Muslim Education, language, religion, personal laws and Muslim charitable institutions and for their due share in the grants-in-aid given by the state and by the self-governing bodies.
13. "No Cabinet either central or provincial should be formed without there being a proportion of at least one-third Muslim Ministers.
14. "No change shall be made in the constitution of the Central Legislature except with the concurrence of the State constituting the Indian Federation."

There was a change of government in England. The Labour Party headed by Ramsay McDonald, came to power. High hopes were entertained regarding the future of India. While in the Opposition, Ramsay McDonald had always sympathised with the Indian aspirations and advocated their cause. No wonder, the Indians were hopeful about the future.

Lord Irwin got convinced that it was not possible to maintain an irresponsible Central Government continuously. He paid a hasty visit to England to confer with the new Labour Government and on his return issued the following statement on 31st October, 1929: "In view of the doubts which have been expressed both in Great Britain and India regarding the interpretation to be placed on the intentions of the British Government in enacting the Statute of 1919, I am authorised on behalf of his Majesty's Government to state clearly that in their judgment, it is implicit in the Declaration of 1917 that the natural issue of India's Constitutional progress as there contemplated is the attainment of the Dominion Status." He also stated that the Simon Commission had suggested to His Majesty's Government and the latter had accepted the suggestion that after the publication of their Report and before its examination by the Joint Parliamentary Committee, they should call together a conference "in which His Majesty's Government meet the representatives both of British India and of the States for the propose of seeking the greatest possible measure of agreement for the final proposals which it would latter be the duty of His Majesty's Government to submit to Parliament."

Critics point out that whatever may be thought about the statesmanship of this declaration, it should have not been made until the Commission had concluded its labours. It left that unfortunate body in the air, and at the same time stole its thunder. Moreover, the phrase "Dominion Status" was unhappily so ambiguous that it could be given various interpretations. The Government of India seem to have used the phrase in the sense in which it was employed in the Preamble to the Act of 1919 as applicable to the constitution of a dependency enjoying responsible Government. On the other hand, they gave to it the same meaning as was given to it by the Balfour Declaration of 1926. There Dominions were described as "autonomous communities within the British Empire, equivalent in status, in no way subordinate one to another in any aspect domestic or external affairs, though united by a common allegiance to the Crown and freely associated as members of the British Commonwealth of Nations." The Congress leaders also were not satisfied with the limited scope and purpose of the Round Table Conference. What the Indians demanded was the convening of a Constituent Assembly for the purpose of drafting a constitution for India. It is evident that the views of the people of India and the British Government radically differed from each other. However, an interview was arranged between Mahatma Gandhi and Lord Irwin, with a view to explore the possibilities of a compromise. The interview failed to achieve its purpose. The result was that when the Indian National Congress met at Lahore after a few days under the Presidentship of Pandit Jawaharlal Nehru, it passed resolutions boycotting the Round Table Conference, declaring the object of the Indian National Congress as the attainment of Swaraja or complete independence for India and authorising the All-India Congress Committee to start civil disobedience movement. 26th January was observed as India's Independence Day and the civil disobedience movement was started in March 1930. Mahatma Gandhi started his historic march to Dandi to violate the salt laws. Thousands of people all over the country deliberately violated certain laws of the country and courted arrest. There were *lathi* charges by the Police. Repression was in full swing. Ordinances were issued in quick succession by the Government to meet the situation. Editors and proprietors of newspapers and printing presses were arrested and fined. There seemed to be a complete breach between the Government and the nationalist movement in the country.

Simon Commission Report, 1930

The Report of the Simon Commission was published in May 1930. First of all, the report considered as to what should be the ultimate constitutional framework of all India and what should be the place of provinces in that. The Report declared that framework could not be of a unitary type. It must be federal, not merely in response to the growth of provincial loyalties but primarily because it must embrace all India and it was only in a Federation that the Indian states could be expected in course of time to unite with British India.

(1) According to the Report, dyarchy should be abolished in the provinces and the whole field of provincial administration should be entrusted to ministers responsible to their legislatures. "Each province should as for as possible be the mistress in her own house". It was pointed out that the retention of reserved subjects implied the continuance of control over that part of the provincial administration by the Central Government and the Secretary of State for India. That was not a desirable thing. In the new provincial set up, the ministries were not to be formed entirely on the British model. The Governor was to be allowed to select those ministers who commanded a majority in the legislature. He was not to appoint a ministry on the advice of Prime Minister or a Chief Minister. In all legislation and administration, ministers were to be free from interference by the Government or the Central Government except for such

stated vital reasons as the maintenance of the safety of the province or the protection of minorities. It was recommended that franchise should be extended and the legislature be enlarged.

(2) The Report recommended that the question of making Sindh and Orissa as separate provinces should be given further expert examination. However, it should be decided forthwith to separate Burma from the Government of India. The North-West Frontier province was considered to be ripe for the first step in constitutional advance. That province should be given a Legislative Council and its representation in the Central Legislature should be strengthened.

(3) With regard to the Centre, the Report made recommendations which aimed at preparing the way for an All-India federation. The Central Legislature was to be refashioned on the federal principle. The members of the Federal Assembly or the lower house were to be representatives not of sections of the people of India at large but of the provinces. They were to be elected by the Provincial Councils. The elections and nominations to the Councils of States were also to be on a provincial basis. The distribution of seats among the various provinces for the Assembly was to be roughly on population basis. Each province was to have 3 members in the Council of State.

(4) So far as the Central Executive was concerned, there was a note of "gradualness" in the Report. No substantial change was recommended. The whole Government was to continue as an official Government. There was to be no Government responsible to the Legislature. There was to be no dyarchy at the Centre. It was pointed out that there was the need of keeping the Centre strong and stable "while the Provincial Councils were learning by experience to bear the full weight of new and heavy responsibilities. The reason given for this was not the immediate need of the political situation in India, but the ultimate needs of the federation. It was stated that the provinces must find themselves before nature of their participation in a federal Government could be

determined. It is necessary to take a long view of the development of Indian self-Government... A Premature endeavor to introduce forms of responsible Government at the Centre before the conditions for its actual practice have emerged would in the end result not in advance but in retrogression."

(5) It was pointed out that an All-India Federation was to be set up in the distant future. The idea that "the federation of Greater India can be artificially hastened or that, when it comes, it will spring into being at a bound", was set aside. For the present, only one new step was recommended. In order to "foster the sense of need for further developments and bring more nearly within the range of realisation other steps which are as yet too distant and too dim to be entered upon and described", a Council for Greater India should be set up, representing both British India and the States, discuss in a consultative capacity all matters of common concern, a list of which should be drawn up and scheduled. The Preamble of the new Act should record the desire to bring about a closer association between the two parts of India.

(6) The Act of 1919 had provided for setting up of a Commission after 10 years for inquiring into the working of the reforms and making of recommendations for the future. The Report recommended that the method of periodical inquiry should be given up. The new constitution should be so elastically framed as to enable it to develop by itself. The provincial legislatures should have power to modify their own composition and procedure and self-Government should grow not by making laws but by usages and conventions.

According to P.E. Roberts, the Simon Commission Report "will always stand out as one of the greatest of India State papers. The impressive unanimity of the commissioners, who from their known party antecedents must clearly have sacrificed all but their deepest convictions to attain it, ought to have commended their sagacious and temperately worded conclusions to men of goodwill." (*British India*, p. 598). However, the Report was condemned by the Indians. The British Government itself had also partly forestalled it and ultimately side-tracked it, although some of its recommendations were ultimately embodied in the Act of 1935. According to Dr. A. B. Keith, "It was probably foolish of Indian opinion to repudiate the report out and out. If it had been accepted, the British Government could hardly have failed to work on it, and responsible government in the provinces would have been achieved much earlier than it could be under any latter scheme. Moreover, the pressure of such Governments on the centre would doubtless have operated strongly in the direction of inducing the British Government to aim at federation and the States to come to terms with Indian political leaders. It is noteworthy that the commission endeavored to suggest that responsible government in India need not follow rigidly existing models, a fact which at once rendered it suspect in the eyes of Indian politicians, whose views on these topics have throughout shown a remarkable lack of ingenuity and a determination slavishly to copy Western models hardly compatible with the national spirit by which they are animated (*Constitutional History of India*, pp. 293-94).

Round Table Conferences, (1930-31)

After the publication of the Simon Commission Report and its condemnation by the people of India, the British Government called the First Round Table Conference in London. The Conference met in November 1930. As the Congress leaders were in jail, the Government appointed safe men belonging to other parties, communities and interests to represent India. Representatives from the Indian States were also invited to participate in the deliberations and included men like Sir Mirza Ismail, Sir Akbar Hydari and the Maharaja of Bikaner. There were lengthy discussions of the question of the future form of the Government of India. Ultimately, three basic principles were settled and accepted by the British Government. The form of the new Government of India was to be an All-India Federation in which the British Indian Provinces and the Indian States were to join. Subject to such reservations and safeguards as might be considered necessary for the transitional period, the Federal Government was to be made responsible to the Federal Legislature. Provinces were to be given autonomy in their own affairs. At the end of the First round Table Conference, Ramsay

MacDonald made the following important statement: "The view of His Majesty's Government is that responsibility for the Government of India should be placed upon Legislatures, Central and provincial, with such provisions as may be considered necessary to guarantee, during a period of transition, the observance of certain obligations and to meet other special circumstances, and also with such guarantees as are required by minorities to protect their political liberties and rights. In such statutory safeguards as may be made for meeting the needs of the transitional period, it will be a primary concern of His Majesty's Government to see that the reserved powers are so framed and exercised as not to prejudice the advance of India through the new Constitution to full responsibility for her own Government. Pledge after pledge had been given to India that British Raj was there not for perpetual domination. Why did we put facilities for education at your disposal ? Why did we put in your hands text-books from which we draw political inspiration? If we meant that the people of India should for ever be silent and negative, subordinate to our rule, why have our queens and kings given you pledges? Why has our Parliament given you pledges? Finally, I hope, and I trust, and I pray that by our labours together India will come to possess the only thing which she now lacks, to give her the status of a Dominion amongst the British Commonwealth of Nations–what now lacks for that–the responsibilities and the cares, the burdens and difficulties, but the pride and the honour of responsible Self-Government."

As it was not considered advisable to proceed with the work of the final form of the future constitution of India in the absence of the representatives of the Indian National Congress, it was decided to call a Second Round Table Conference, and in the meanwhile efforts were to be made to bring about a reconciliation between the Congress and the Government. The efforts of Sir Tej Bahadur Sapru and Sir M. R. Jayakar were crowned with success and the famous Gandhi-Irwin Pact was signed in March 1931. The Government released all the political prisoners. Mahatma Gandhi withdrew the Civil Disobedience Movement. An atmosphere of good-will having been created, Mahatma Gandhi left for Landon to attend the Second Round Table Conference as the sole representative of the Congress. In spite of the magnetic personality of Mahatma Gandhi and his devotion to the work in hand, and communal tangle could not be solved. Mahatma Gandhi gave a Carta Balanche to Mr. M. A. Jinnah, but all efforts for a settlement failed on account of the uncompromising attitude of Mr. Jinnah and the part played by Sir Samuel Hoare, the Secretary of State for India. Realising the failure of his mission, Mahatma Gandhi left England in disgust and was arrested on his arrival in India.

It is true that as a result of the economic crisis in the world and especially in England, the Labour Government of Ramsay MacDonald had been replaced by a National Government. But somehow, Ramsay MacDonald managed to follow his previous policy with regard to India. At the second Round Table conference, many problems were considered, but the members could not come to any definite conclusion. Consequently, the work was referred to various committees which were required to submit detailed reports. As regards the question of communal representation, Ramsay MacDonald made it clear that if the various communities in India did not come to any definite settlement, the British Government will be forced to give its own Award regarding the same.

Communal Award, 1932

As the Indians could not arrive at any settlement, Ramsay MacDonald gave his famous "award" known as the Communal Award on 16th August, 1932. The scope of this Award was purposely confined to the arrangements to be made for the representation of British Indian communities in the provincial legislatures, consideration of representation to the Central Legislature being deferred for the time being as that involved a question of the representation of the Indian States which needed further discussion. The hope was expressed that once a pronouncement was made upon questions of the method and proportions of representation, the communities themselves may find it possible to arrive at a *modus vivendi* on the communal problem. If, before the passing of the new Government of India Act, the Government was satisfied that the communities concerned were mutually agreed upon an alternative scheme they would be prepared to recommend to Parliament the substitution of the alternative scheme for the Communal Award. "His Majesty's Government wish it to be most clearly understood that they themselves can be no parties to any negotiations which may be initiated with a view to revision of their decision and will not be prepared to give consideration to any representation aimed at securing modification of it which is not supported by all parties affected... If before the new Government of India Act has passed into law they are satisfied that the communities who are concerned are mutually agreed upon a practical alternative scheme either in respect of any one or more of Governor's provinces or in respect of the whole of British India, they will be prepared to recommend to Parliament that the alternative scheme should be adopted."

According to the Award, elections to the seats allotted to Muslim, European and Sikh constituencies will be by voters voting for separate communal electorates covering between them the whole area of a province. Special provisions were made for excluded areas. Provision was to be made in the new Constitution of India to allow the revision of electoral arrangements after the lapse of 10 years with the assent of the communities affected, for the ascertainment of which suitable means were to be devised.

All qualified voters who were not voters in Muslim, Sikh, Indian Christian, Anglo-Indian or European constituencies, were entitled to vote in a general constituency.

Seven seats were reserved for the Marathas in certain selected plural-member general constituencies in Bombay.

The members of the depressed classes who were qualified to vote were to vote in a general constituency. However, special seats were to be reserved for them. Those seats were to be filled up by election from special constituencies in which only the members of the depressed classes electorally qualified were to be entitled to vote. Any person voting in such a special constituency was also to be entitled to vote in a general constituency. These constituencies were to be formed in those selected areas where the depressed classes were most numerous, and except in Madras, they were not to cover the whole of the area of a province. In the case of Bengal, in some general constituencies, the majority of the voters belonged to the depressed classes. Consequently, no special number was to be fixed for their seats in that province. However, they were not to get less than 10 seats in Bengal. The maximum duration of the depressed-classes constituencies was to be 20 years, provided they were not abolished earlier.

The election of the Indian-Christians was to be by voters voting in separate communal constituencies. It was felt that practical difficulties will prevent the formation of the Indian-Christian constituencies covering the whole area of a province and consequently special Indian-Christian constituencies were to be formed in one or two selected areas in a province. The Indian-Christian voters in those areas were not to vote in a general constituency. Outside those areas, they were to vote in a general constituency. Special arrangements were to be made in Bihar and Orissa where a large number of the Indian-Christians belonged to the original tribes.

The Anglo-Indians were also to vote on communal lines. The intention was that the Anglo-Indian constituencies were to cover the whole area of a province and postal ballot was to be employed for that purpose.

Women were also given special representation on communal lines. The electors of a particular community were to elect their own quota.

Special seats were to be allotted to Commerce and Industry, Mining and Planting, to be filled up by election through the Chambers of Commerce and other associations. Their details were to be worked out later on.

Seats allotted to landholders were to be filled by land -holders constituencies.

It was stated that the work of the determination of the constituencies was to begin soon. The Government reserved to itself the right of making slight variations in the number of seats given to the various communities with a view to facilitate the work of the delimintation of constituencies. However, the proportion was not to be materially changed. The composition of the second chambers in the provinces was not to disturb in any essential the balance between the communities resulting from the composition of the lower house.

Poona Pact (1932)

Mahatma Gandhi in his letter written in March 1932, to Sir Samuel Hoare, Secretary of State for India, had warned him that he would resist with his life the grant of separate electorates to the depressed classes. When the Communal Award was published and it was found that the British Government was determined to give separate communal representation to the depressed classes, Mahatma Gandhi wrote to Ramsay MacDonald that the matter was "one of pure religion" with him and he asked: "Do you realise that , if your decision stands and the constitution comes into being, you arrest the marvellous growth of the work of the Hindu reformers who have dedicated themselves to the uplift of their suppressed brethren in every walk of life?" Mahatma Gandhi's letter had no effect on the Prime Minister of England who took the matter light-heartedly and would not have bothered if the Mahatma had died. When the British Government refused to move in the matter and the condition of Mahatma Gandhi became serious on account of his fast unto death, the Indian leaders made up their minds to get the Award modified by mutual agreement. Negotiations took place with Dr. Ambedkar and Rajah and ultimately the Poona Pact was signed in September 1932, and was accepted by the Government.

The Poona Pact reserved seats for depressed classes out the general electoral seats in provincial legislatures as follows:- Madras 30, Bombay with Sindh 15, Punjab 8, Bihar and Orissa 18, C. P. 20, Assam 7, Bengal 30, and U. P. 20. The total of the reserved seats for the depressed classes was 148.

As regards the procedure for elections to these seats by joint electorates, all members of the depressed classes registered in the general electoral roll in a constituency were to form an electoral college which was to elect a panel of 4 candidates belonging to the depressed classes for each of the reserved seats by the method of single vote. The four persons setting the highest number of votes in the primary election were to be candidates for election by the general electorate.

The depressed classes were to have representation in the Central Legislature on the principle of joint electorates and seats were to be reserved for them in the same way as in the case of the provinces. 18% of the generai seats for British India were to be reserved for the depressed classes.

The system of primary elections to a panel of candidates for election to Central and Provincial Legislatures was to be abolished after 10 years or earlier, if an agreement to that effect was made.

The depressed classes were to be given fair representation in the local bodies and the public services subject to educational qualifications.

In every educational grant in the provincial budget, an adequate sum was to be earmarked for the education of the depressed classes. The procedure to be adopted for election of the representatives of the depressed classes to the Central Legislature was postponed as that involved the whole system of representation to the Centre.

Criticism of the Communal Award.

1. It is true that the Indian National Congress passed a resolution by which it neither accepted nor rejected the Award, but the fact remains that there were many defects in the Award for which it was condemned by the Indians. It has been pointed out that the Award was unjust to the Hindus and the Sikhs. It maintained the weightage given to the Muslims in the legislatures in those provinces where the Muslims were in a minority. Instead of giving similar weightage to the Hindus in Bengal, the Award gave them only 32 per cent of the seats when they constituted 44.8 per cent of the total population. It gave 10% of seats to the Europeans who were only 0.01 per cent of the total population. It is true that the Award cut down the representation of the Muslims also, but the cut in the case of the Hindus was greater than that of the Muslims. In the case of the Punjab also, the Hindus instead of getting weightage as a minority, had their representation cut down to give some weightage to the Sikhs. The Sikhs also failed to get the weightage that the Musalmans got in other provinces. No wonder, the Award was opposed by the Hindus and the Sikhs.
2. The British Government had stated hat they were entirely disinterested in the matter of the communal settlement, but the critics point out that it was the British disinterestedness which penalised the Hindus everywhere. Instead of getting weightage in the provinces where they were in a minority, their representation was cut down. The Europeans were given 2,50,000 times weightage in Bengal.

3. According to Attlee, the Award was weighted on behalf of the Muslims and against the Hindus.
4. According to Mehta and Patwardhan, " The electorate in 1919 was broken up in 10 parts; now it is fragmented into 17 unequal bits. Separates electorates were thrust, against their wishes, on women and Indian-Christians. The Hindu community was further weakened by giving separate representation to the scheduled classes. Divisions on the basis of religion, occupation and service were made. Every possible cross-division was introduced." (The Communal Triangle, P. 72)
5. Lord Zetland criticised the Communal Award in these works: " It is one thing to concede separate communal electorates for the purpose of giving minorities reasonable representation in the various legislatures; it is an entirely different thing to employ the system for the purpose of conferring upon a majority community in any particular province a permanent majority in the legislature unalterable by any appeal to the electorate. Such a course has never hitherto been adopted. It was considered and rejected by the Statutory Commission, who declared that a claim submitted to them which in Bengal and Punjab would give to the Muslim Community a fixed and unalterable majority in the general constituency seats, was one which they could not entertain; it would be unfair, they wrote, " the Mohammedans should retain the very considerable weightage they now enjoy in the 6 provinces and that there should at the same time be imposed, in the face of Hindu and Sikh opposition, definite majority in the Punjab and in Bengal unalterable by an appeal to the electorate."
6. Dr. Rajendra Prasad has made the following observations on the Communal Award: "The distribution of seats among the various communities was no less remarkable. In all discussions about the communal problem, Bengal an the Punjab presented difficulties. In both these Provinces, the Musalmans are in a majority; but the majority is a small one about 55 p.c. In both these provinces it was demanded on behalf on the Musalmans

that there should be both separate electorates and reservation of seats for them although they happened to be in a majority. In Bengal the position was complicated by the desire of the British government to give a very heavy weightage to the Europeans, while in the Punjab the non-Mohammedans were divided into Hindus and Sikhs. The Sikhs insisted that, if there were to be separate electorates and reservations of seats they as an important community should be given weightage as Musalmans had got in other Provinces where they were in a minority. The Communal Award maintained with a small variation the proportion of seats given to Musalmans by the Montagu-Chelmsford Reforms in all the Provinces except Bengal and the Punjab. In Bengal, the Hindus were in the minority of 44.8 per cent. Of the total population. They were given only 80 out of 250 seats, i.e., only 32 per cent of the total. The Musalmans who were 54.8 per cent of the population were given 119 seats, i.e., 47.6 per cent of the total. The Europeans who were .01 per cent of the population were given 25 seats, *i.e.*, 10 per cent of the total number of seats. It will thus appear that the Musalmans who were in a majority were reduced to a minority in the representation and the Hindus who were in a minority were deprived even of their due proportion – in order to give a very heavy weightage of 2,50,000 times to the Europeans. What is noteworthy is that although the representation of both Muslims and Hindus was reduced, the cut was greater in the Hindus representation. In other words, unlike other Provinces weightage was given to the smallest community not out of the majority community alone but out of another minority which was required not only to give up any weightage which it might feel entitled to as a minority but also to make a greater sacrifice proportionately that the majority community. In the Punjab also to give weightage to the Sikhs, the Hindus were required to give up a portion of their representation, although they were in a minority and would be entitled to weightage according to ordinary canons of fairness and justice. It may also be noted that in both these Provinces, the Award reduced the Muslim representation to such an extent as to make it a minority of the total, although they still constituted the largest group in the Legislative Assembly and had those seats reserved for them, to be filled through separate electorates. No wonder the Award was assailed with great vehemence by the Hindus who were required to make sacrifices in the Provinces where they were in a majority and also in the Provinces where they were in a minority, and in Bengal the scarifies that was imposed was proportionately much greater – nearly double – than that required of the majority community" (India Divided, pp. 129-30).

7. In his Presidential Address to the Congress Nationalist Party Conference held at Calcutta in August, 1934, Pandit Madan Mohan Malaviya remarked thus: " At present, we are living under one government, of course a foreign government, but what shall we get by means of this communal electorate? Not a Government by the people, for the people, and of the people, but a Government of one community over another. In the Punjab, it will be a Government by Muslims of Hindus, and in the United Provinces it will be a Government by Hindus of Muslims. It will not be democracy. It will be a special kind of despotic Government. It will be tyranny of one community over another and it is this despotism which the Communal Award seeks to instal.

Defects of Communal Representation.

(1) It may be desirable to point out some of the defects of communal representation. This system allowed arbitrary, invidious, humiliating and unjust distinctions to be made between the Muslims and Hindus in the matter of electorates, franchise and qualifications of candidates.

(2) Communal electorates were opposed to the history of all self-governing countries and involved a divided allegiance between the State and community which no state could admit.

(3) They perpetuated class-divisions and thus retarded the growth of the citizen spirit which transcends the communal or the religious spirit.

(4) Communal representation accentuated and perpetuated those differences of castes and creeds which were lessening their importance with the growth of a national sentiment under the unifying influence of western education and the Reformist movements among the Hindus and Muslims.

(5) Communal representation was viewed with universal suspicion as a Machiavellian device intended to widen existing lines of cleavage, to check the growing sense of nationality and to secure the position of the Government by the application of the maxim of "divide and rule."

(6) The principal of communal electorates was extended to the Local Boards and Municipalities. Communal tension increased everywhere. Communal riots became the order of the day. Ultimately, it resulted in the establishment of Pakistan.

(7) Communal representation led to the demand to fill Government posts and reserve admissions in schools and colleges in the ratio of the communities and the caliber of the Legislative Councils and the Government services suffered.

(8) Critics pointed out that no civilized Government had recognised religious differences by creating separate electorates of Protestants. Catholics or Jews in Europe, of Germans, English, French, and Italians in the U.S.A., of Christian, Muslims, Buddhists, and the followers of Confucius in China and Japan. There seemed to be no justification in employing such a novel system in the case of India.

(9) The system of communal representation encouraged communities to settle down into a feeling of satisfied security and gave no stimulus in emulation and improvement.

(10) The authors of the Nehru Report remarked thus: "It is admitted by most people now that separate electorates are thoroughly bad and must be done away with. We find however that there has been a tendency amongst the Muslims to consider them as a "valued privilege",

although a considerable section are prepared to give them up in consideration for some other things. Everybody knows that separate electorates are bad for the growth of a national spirit, but everybody perhaps does not realise equally well that separate electorates are still worse for a minority community. They make the majority wholly independent of the minority and its votes are usually hostile to it. Under separate electorates therefore the chances are that the minority will always have to face a hostile majority, which can always, by sheer force of numbers, override the wishes of the minority. This effect of having separate electorates has already become obvious, although the presence of the third party confuses the issues. Separates electorates thus benefit the majority community. Extreme Communalists flourish thereunder and the majority community, far from suffering, actually benefits by them. Separate electorates must therefore be discarded completely as a condition precedent to any rational system of representation. We can only have joint or mixed electorates."

Third Round Table Conference

To Take up the story of the Round Table Conferences, a Third Round Table Conference was called by the British Government rather reluctantly as it was of the opinion that the rest of the work could be done in India. The result was that the session of the Third Round Table Conference lasted from 17th November to 24th December 1932. The Labour Party did not cooperate in the deliberations and the Indian National Congress was unrepresented. The delegates to the Conference merely discussed the reports of the various committees appointed by the Second Round Table Conference and decided a few more points.

The White Paper, (1933)

When the whole scheme regarding the future constitution of India was thrashed out, the British Government issued in March 1933, a small document known as the While Paper. It gave in detail the working basis of the new Indian Constitution with a dyarchy at the Centre and a responsible Government in the Provinces. As was to be expected, the White Paper was condemned by the Indian public opinion. However, in spite of the opposition and criticism, the British Government went on with its programme.

In April 1933, a Joint Select Committee was appointed to examine and report on the Government proposals as contained in the White Paper. The Committee consisted of 16 members each from the Houses of Commons and the House of Lords and its Chairman was Lord Linlithgow. The committee invited representatives from British India and the Indian States. After examining many witnesses and going through the Memoranda received from the Indian Association, the British Indian Delegations, Sir Tej Bahadur Sapru, M.R. Jayakar and other prominent individuals, the Joint Select Committee submitted its report on 22nd November, 1934. Although it did not alter the fundamentals as given in the White Paper, it recommended many changes in the structure of the Provincial and Federal legislatures and other matters also.

When the reforms scheme was thoroughly discussed and given final shape by the Joint Select Committee, a Bill was drafted on those lines and introduced in the House of Commons on 5th February, 1935. Sir Samuel Hoare, the Secretary of State for India, was in charge of the Bill, which was severely criticised by the Labour Party for its limited scope. The Labour members tried to amend the Bill in such a way as to recognise explicitly India's right to Dominion Status. The diehards led by Winston Churchill tried to introduce reactionary elements into the Bill. However, the Government went on with its own scheme which was passed by the House of Commons on 4th June, 1935. The Bill was introduced in the House of Lords on 6th June, 1935, and was passed in July 1935. Here also the efforts of the Labour members to liberalise the Bill failed. As the Government had made some amendments in the Bill at this stage, the Bill had to be sent back to the House of Commons which accepted the proposed amendments. The Bill received the Royal Assent on 2nd August, 1935 as Government of India Act, 1935.

11

The Government of India Act, 1935

(1) The Government of India Act of 1935 was a very lengthy and complicated Statute. That was partly due to the fact that the Act dealt with a highly complex type of a Federal Constitution and also because it sought to provide legal safeguards against misbehaviour on the part of the Indian Ministers and the legislators.

(2) The Act provided for an All-India Federation. The question of Indian federation presented a peculiar problem on account of the disparity between the Indian States and the Provinces of British India with regard to their legal status and their internal political structure. The Indian States were under the complete control of the Political Department of the Government of India. The Provinces, on the other hand, had some sort of a democratic Government. According to the Act of 1935, all the provinces were to join the Indian Federation automatically. Entry into the Federation was to be a purely voluntary action on the part of each State, however small and insignificant that State may be. At the time of joining the Federation, the ruler of the State was to execute an Instrument of Accession in favour of the Crown. On acceptance of that Instrument, the State was to become a unit of the Federation. The Crown was forbidden to accept an Instrument of Accession if its terms appeared to be inconsistent with the scheme of the Federation. While the provinces were to be alike in respect of the position

of the quantum of Legislative and Executive powers in the Federation, the States were to differ regarding the extent of their powers in the Federation. The scope of the federal jurisdiction in the States was to depend solely upon the transfers made by their respective rulers through their Instruments of Accession. The Instrument was to authorise the various Federal authorities to exercise their respective function under the Act in relation to that particular State. It was to be the duty of the ruler to see that due effect was given within his State to the provisions of the Act in so far as those provisions were made applicable by virtue of the Instrument. The ruler was authorised to extend the functions of the Federal authority in respect of his State by a subsidiary Instrument, but no subsequent Instrument could decrease the scope of the authority of the Federation as provided by the original Instrument of Accession.

The Indian States were to send 125 members to the Federal Assembly and 104 members to the Council of States. The provinces were to send 250 members to the Federal Assembly and 156 members to the Council of States. The members from the Indian States were to be nominated by the rulers, but those from the provinces were to be elected on communal lines.

The functions of the Crown with regard to the Indian States were to be performed in India by his representative who in fact was the Viceroy himself.

The Indian Federation as provided by the Act of 1935 was different from the other federal systems. There was no simple division of powers between the Centre and the units. The Act provided for three Lists: Federal List, Provincial List and the Concurrent List. The Federal Government was authorised to pass laws on the subjects given in the Federal List. The subjects given in the Provincial List were within the exclusive jurisdiction of the Provincial Legislature. As regards the Concurrent List, both the Federal Legislature and the Provincial Legislatures could pass laws on the subjects given in that List. However, if a law was passed by the Federal

Legislature on any subject given in the Concurrent List, the Provincial Legislature could not make law on the same subject afterwards. As regards the residuary power, the Governor-General in his discretion was given the power to decide as to which of the three Lists a particular subject was to be allotted.

(3) The Act of 1935, also provided for dyarchy at the Centre. That dyarchy which was abolished by the Act of 1935, was introduced at the Centre. Certain Federal subjects were reserved in the hands of the Governor-General to be administered by him with the assistance of not more than 3 Counsellors to be appointed by him. Those subjects were Defence, External Affairs, Ecclesiastical Affairs and the administration of Tribal Areas. In the administration of the other Federal subjects, the Governor-General was to be aided and advised by a Council of Ministers whose number was not to exceed 10. The Federal Ministry was to administer all the Federal Departments except the above-mentioned reserved Departments. The Federal Ministry was to be formed on the usual cabinet lines except that it was to include the representatives of the States who were the nominees of their rulers and the representatives of the important minorities. It is true that the inclusion of these elements was not obligatory under the Act, but the Governor-General was instructed by means of an Instrument of Instructions to secure such representation to the best of his ability. In spite of the composite character of the Ministry, their responsibility was to be collective. The Ministry was to be responsible to the Federal Legislature.

The critics pointed out to the weakness of the position of the Ministers an account of the large number of powers given to the Governor-General and to be exercised by him in his individual judgement and in his discretion. According to Prof. K.T. Shah, "The position assigned under the new Constitution to the Council of Federal Ministers is ornamental, without being useful, onerous without ever being helpful to the people they are supposed to represent, responsibility without power, position without authority, name without any real influence" (Federal Structure, p. 223). To quote the same author again, "It seems extremely doubtful if the popular ministers of the Federation of India will have any real opportunity to inaugurate constructive schemes of economic betterment or social reconstruction. . . . The necessary Funds are either unavailable because earmarked already for non-productive expenditure and lavish scale of over-head charges; or difficult to find in the absence of new taxation proposals for which the Governor-General may not always view with favour. Additional burdens are especially difficult in a Federation to propose and particularly unwelcome in popular Governments ....If the communal curb upon ministerial enthusiasm does not prove quite effective, there are the enormous powers of the Governor-General, as protector and champion of the vested interests and imperialist exploitation, which are bound to be employed to impede or frustrate too enthusiastic ministers. There are specific provisions in the Constitution as those relating to any discrimination against British vested interests . . . which will hamper the work of the ministers in their work. The ministers' own internal difficulties—want of solidarity, *etc.*—may prevent them from achieving anything beneficial to the people." (Ibib., pp. 249-50).

(4) The Federal Legislature was to be bicameral, consisting of the Federal Assembly and the Council of States. The Federal Assembly was to have a life of 5 years from the date of its first meeting. On the expiry of the period, it was to automatically dissolved. However, the Governor-General was given the power to extend its life. The Council of States was to be a permanent body of which one-third members were to retire after every 3 years. The members from the States were to be nominated by the rulers. The representatives from British India were to be elected. The Hindu, Muslim and Sikh members were to be elected on communal lines.

(5) The powers of the Indian Legislatures were severely restricted. There were certain subjects on which neither

the Federal Legislatures nor the Provincial Legislatures could legislate. The Indian Legislatures were debarred from making any law affecting the Sovereign or the Royal Family or the succession to the throne or suzerainty of the Crown or any part of India, or the law of British nationality, or the Army act, the Air Force Act, or the law of Prize Courts. The Indian Legislatures could not make any law amending any of the provisions of the Act of 1935, or any Order-in-Council made under it, or only rules made thereunder by the Secretary of State or by the Governor-General or a Governor in his discretion or in the exercise of his individual judgement. They could not make any law affecting the prerogative right of the Crown to grant special leave to appeal to the Privy Council except in so far as that was expressly permitted by the Act. They could not pass any legislation which discriminated against the British interests in commercial and other spheres. Moreover, there was a large number of subjects of vital importance on which initiation of legislation required previous sanction of the Governor-General in respect of Federal Legislation, of the Governor-General and the Governor in respect of Provincial legislation.

There were many non-votable items in the budget over which the Federal legislature was given absolutely no control. These non-votable items constituted about 80% of the Federal budget. If any item of the budget was rejected by the Federal Assembly, the same could be put before the Council of States if the Governor-General so directed. If the two Houses of the Federal Legislature differed with respect to any demand, the Governor-General was required to summon a joint sitting for voting on that demand and the decision of the majority was to prevail.

The Governor-General was empowered to summon a joint sitting of the two Houses of the Federal Legislature when a Bill passed by one chamber was rejected by the other, or was amended in a form to which the first chamber was not agreeable. After a Bill was passed by both the chambers of the Federal Legislature, the Governor-

General, in his discretion, might assent to it, or veto it or send it back for re-consideration or reserve it for His Majesty's consideration. The Act assented to by the Governor-General could be disallowed within a year by the King-in-Council.

(6) The Act provided for the establishment of a Federal Court with jurisdiction over the States and the Provinces. The Court was to consist of a Chief Justice and two puisne Judges. It was given both original and appellate powers. It was the duty of the Federal Court to interpret the Constitution and to see that the provinces and the Federal Council acted only within those spheres which were reserved for them by the Constitution. However, the last word in this matter was to be said by the Privy Council sitting in London.

(7) The Act of 1935, abolished the India Council of the Secretary of State. The Secretary of State was given advisers who may or may not be consulted, or whose advice may or may not be followed, except in regard to their advice in respect of the Services. This change was made because there was a lot of agitation in India against the continuation of the India Council on account of its anti-Indian attitude.

(8) In the exercise of powers in their individual judgement and in their discretion, the Governors, through the Governor-General and the Governor-General himself, were made strictly responsible to the Secretary of State. However, it is to be noted that the control of the Home Government over Indian affairs was lessened. This was partly due to the introduction of provincial autonomy in the provinces and responsible Government at the Centre. There was no control from London when the Governor-General and the Governors acted according to the advice and consent of their ministers.

(9) Another important feature of the Act was the provision of elaborate safeguards. These safeguards were vital subtractions from the principle of responsible Government as well as of self-Government. These safeguards were to two kinds. In the first place, there was a denial of

legislative powers to the Indian Legislatures in regard to a large number of subjects. Secondly, there was the grant of powers to the Governor-General or the Governors to over-ride their ministers and legislators in certain circumstances including the assumption of absolute dictatorial powers in the event of the breakdown of the constitution. Critics pointed out that the provisions regarding safeguards were against the territorial integrity of the country. In the words of Dr. Keith, "With the safeguarding of minorities, the essence of responsible Government is seriously, if not fully, compromised."

(10) The Constitution of 1935, was rigid. The British Government alone was given the authority to amend the Constitution. According to S.M. Bose, "The Indian Legislatures have only been given powers to express by resolution to His Majesty's Government their intention of a constitutional change in respect of the matters specified in this section. But the actual power of modifying the Act has been placed by the Act in the hands of His Majesty's Government by the Order-in-Council laid in draft before both Houses as provided in Section 309. In other words, no amending legislation by Parliament will be required. In respect of those other matters specifically mentioned in the Act, variations may be made by Order-in-Council."

(11) But the most important characteristic of the Act of 1935, was the provision for provincial autonomy. This was in accordance with the August Declaration of 1917. The Act of 1919, had given a little control in the provincial field into the hands of the Indian ministers. The Act of 1935 was a definite improvement on the Act of 1919, in as much as there were no reserved subjects with the Governor. However, this does not mean that the Act of 1935, established a full-fledged responsible Government in the provinces. That could not be so on account of the fact that the Governor was given many powers which he was to exercise in his discretion and in his individual judgement.

The Home Government.

The Office of the Secretary of State for India was created by the Act of 1858, when the Board of Control and the Court of Directors were abolished after the Mutiny. The latter was a member of the British Parliament and also a member of the British Cabinet. Up to 1919, he was paid out of the Indian revenues but the Act of 1919 provided that in future he was to be paid from the British Treasury. He was assisted in his work by a Parliamentary Under-Secretary, a Permanent Under-Secretary, an Advisory Body and the India Office.

Under the Act of 1919, the Secretary of State enjoyed numerous powers. He was authorized to superintend, direct and control the affairs of the Government of India. Both the Governor-General and the Governors were required to pay due obedience to his orders. The Act of 1935, changed the position to a considerable extent. It granted what is known as provincial autonomy. As the Indian ministers came to have a lot of control over provincial administration, the control of the Secretary of State diminished over the provinces. Likewise, the establishment of dyarchy at the Centre by the Act of 1935, also lessened the control of the Secretary of State over the Government of India. The control of the Secretary of State came in only when the Governors or the Governor-General acted in their discretion. Similarly, when the Governors and the Governor-General acted in their individual judgement and decided to do things against the advice of the ministers, the control of the Secretary of State appeared again. As the discretionary powers of the Governor-General and the Governors were very large, the control of the Secretary of State also remained substantial. The Secretary of State exercised control over the Reserved Departments of Defence, External Affairs, Tribal Areas, and Ecclesiastical Affairs, and the Federal Railway Authority, and the Reserve Bank of India. He could control the whole administrative machinery of India by giving appropriate directions to the Central and Provincial administrations.

He had many powers with regard to the services. He appointed officers belonging to the Indian Civil Service, Indian Police Service and the Irrigation Service. He determined the conditions of service of all such persons. He was the constitutional advisor of the Crown with regard to the Indian affairs. He advised the King in the exercise of all his powers of appointment and the vetoing of any Bill which may have been reserved by the Governor-General for the consideration of His Majesty or which may have been even assented to by the Governor-General.

The Secretary of State was required to submit all the draft Instruments of Instructions to be issued to the Governor-General and the Governors, before Parliament for its approval. He was also to submit before Parliament all Orders-in-Council to be issued by His Majesty under the powers granted by the Act. He was the agent of Parliament and was also responsible to Parliament for the Indian affairs. It was his duty to supply the British Parliament all the information regarding Indian affairs and also to answer all questions regarding the same.

Prof. K.T. Shah describes the position of the Secretary of State in these words: "On a general review of all these varied and substantial powers, the Secretary of State still stands out unmistakably as the most dominating authority in the Indian Constitution. His powers may not be so imposing in appearance as those of the Governor-General or the Provincial Governors. But these are merely his creatures, obedient to every nod from the Jupiter of Whitehall, amenable to every hint from this juggler of Charles Street. His powers extend not merely to matters of fundamental policy; to the protection of British vested interests; to the safeguarding of Britain's imperial domination. They comprise even matters of routine administration, the more important doings of the Indian Legislature, and even the appointments, payment or superannuation of certain officers in the various Indian Services or Governments. He has, in fact all the powers and authority in the governance of India, with little or none of its responsibility."

Advisors

The Secretary of State was assisted by an Advisory Body. This Advisory Body was formerly known as the India Council and was set up by the Act of 1858, to assist the Secretary of State for India in the discharge of his duties. Under the Act of 1919, the India Council consisted of not less than 8 and not more than 12 members, appointed by the Secretary of State. The Secretary of State-in-Council was a corporate body which could sue and be sued and conducted business in the United Kingdom in relation to the Government of India. Ordinarily, the Secretary of State was not bound by the advice of the of India, Council, but in matters relating to grants from the revenues of India, making of contracts, and rules and regulations connected with the Civil Service, he was bound by the majority view of the India Council.

This India Council was abolished by the Act of 1935. According to the new Act, the Secretary of State was to appoint not less than 3 and not more than 6 advisors. At least half of these persons were to be those who had held office in India for at least 10 years and who had not left India for more than 2 years at the time of their appointment. They were to hold office for 5 years only. They could not sit in Parliament. Their function was merely advisory and as a rule the Secretary of State was not bound by their advice. However, in matters relating to rules and regulations concerning the Civil Services, the Secretary of State was required to secure the concurrence of at least one-half of the advisors. The Act provided that "It shall be in the discretion of the Secretary of State whether or not he consults his advisors on any matter, and if so, whether he consults them individually and whether or not he acts in accordance with any advice given to him by them."

High Commissioner for India

The Government of India Act of 1919, provided for the appointment of a High Commissioner for India in the United Kingdom. His pay, pension, powers, duties and conditions of employment were to be determined by an Order-in-Council. The office of the High Commissioner was created in 1920, by an Order-in-Council. The Governor-General-in-Council was authorized to appoint from time to time a High Commissioner and also remove or suspend the same, He was to hold office for five-years and was eligible for re-appointment, His salary of £3,000/- was to be paid out of the Indian revenues, although he was not entitled to any pension. He was to enjoy "the same status as his Dominion colleagues." He was to be under the control and direction of the Governor-General-in-Council. His duties were to act as the agent of the Governor-General-in-Council in the United Kingdom, act on behalf of the local Governments in India for such purposes, and in such cases as the Governor-General-in-Council may prescribe, and conduct such business relating to the Government of India hitherto conducted in the office of the Secretary of State-in-Council as may be assigned by the Secretary of State. He was empowered to make and sign contracts in the name and on behalf of the Secretary of State-in-Council. In 1920, the Stores Department, the India Students Department and certain other minor matters were transferred to the High Commissioner. He was to arrange for the probationary training of the officers of the All-India Services and their passage to India, payment of leave-allowances and pensions. He was to make arrangements for civil officers sent to Europe for special study. He was to supervise the work of the Indians participating in Imperial International Exhibitions. The Act of 1935, did not make any substantial change in the office of the High Commissioner for India.

Federal Government

Under the Act of 1935, the Governor-General was the corner-stone of the entire constitution of India. It was he who gave unity and direction to its various, diverse and often conflicting elements. It was he who was expected to keep the ship of the State on an even keel and to protect the British vested interests in India. It is desirable to discuss his position under the Act of 1935.

Appointed by the King on the advice of the British Prime Minister, the Governor-General acted in three different capacities. Ordinarily, he was to act according to the advice of his Council of Ministers. When he did that, he acted as a constitutional head like the King of England or the Governor-General of Canada. But he did not always act according to the advice of the Ministers. In certain cases, he acted in his individual judgment. While doing so, he was to consult his Ministers, but may or may not act upon their advice. This he did when he preformed the special responsibilities of the Governor-General. The following were the special responsibilities of the Governor-General :—

(1) Safeguarding the financial stability and the credit of India.

(2) The prevention of any grave menace to the peace or tranquility of India or any part of India.

(3) Safeguarding of the legitimate interests of the minorities.

(4) Safeguarding of the legitimate rights of the public servants and their dependents.

(5) The prevention of commercial discrimination.

(6) Prevention of discriminatory taxation against goods of British origin or Burmese origin.

(7) Safeguarding of the interests of the Indian States and the dignity of their rulers.

(8) The securing of the due discharge of his discretionary powers.

While acting in his discretion, the Governor-General did not even consult the ministers. He acted in his discretion in the following matters :—

(1) He was in-charge of the reserved Departments of Defence, External Affairs, Ecclesiastical Affairs and Tribal Areas and he appointed three Counsellors to help him in his work.

(2) He could appoint and dismiss the Council of Ministers and also could preside over their meetings.

(3) He could issue two kinds of ordinances. One type of ordinance he could issue at any time and that lasted for 6 months. The other kind of ordinance was issued when the Legislature was not sitting. The Governor-General was also given the power to issue what were known as Governor-General's Acts. But these Acts had to be forwarded to the Secretary of State.

(4) The previous sanction of the Governor-General was required for the introduction of certain bills in the Federal Legislature and the Provincial Legislatures. He was authorized to stop the discussion of any Bill at any time by the Legislature. He could withhold his assent to a Bill passed by the Legislature or send the same back for reconsideration or reserve the same for the consideration of His Majesty.

(5) He was given control over about 80% of the Federal Budget. The non-votable items of the budget formed a major part of the budget.

(6) The Governor-General could in his discretion send any instructions to the Governors and it was the special responsibility of the latter to carry them out.

(7) The Governor-General could suspend the Constitution.

(8) He was given the authority to summon, prorogue or dissolve the Federal Assembly. He could summon both houses for a joint sitting. He could address the Legislatures or send messages regarding a certain bill.

It is not possible to exhaust the discretionary powers given to the Governor-General under the Act of 1935.

Under the Act of 1935, the Governor-General was to be assisted by a Council of Ministers. Their position has already been discussed above.

As regards the Federal Legislature, its composition and powers have been discussed above.

Government of the Provinces

The position of the Governors under the Act of 1935, resembled that of the Governor-General although it differed a little on account of the introduction of Provincial Autonomy. A Governor was appointed by the King by a Commission under the Royal Sign Manual. His office was constituted by Letter's Patent. His salary was fixed by the Act. The job of a Governor was the prize post which usually went to those members of the Indian Civil Service who had brilliant record of service.

Like the Governor-General, the Governors also acted in three different capacities. Ordinarily, they were to act according to the advice of the ministers. When they did so, they acted as constitutional heads and their position could be compared to the Lt.-Governor of a Canadian Province.

They were also authorised to act in their individual judgement. While doing so, they had to listen to the advice of the ministers but they may or may not act upon their advice. The Governors acted in individual judgement while performing their special responsibilities which were as follows :—

(1) Prevention of any grave menace to the peace or tranquility of the Province or any part of the Province.

(2) Safeguarding of the rights and legitimate interests of the public servants and their dependents.

(3) Safeguarding of the rights and interests of the Indian

States and the dignity of their rulers.

(4) Safeguarding of the legitimate interests of the minorities.

(5) Administration of partially-excluded areas.

(6) Prevention of commercial discrimination against Englishmen and their goods.

(7) Execution of the orders and directions of the Governor-General issued by him in his discretion.

(8) It was the duty of the Governor of C.P. to see that a reasonable share of the provincial revenues was spent for the benefit of the people of Berar.

(9) It was the duty of the Governor of Sind to secure the proper administration of the Lloyd Barrage and Canals' Scheme.

The Governors acted in their discretion in the following cases:—

(1) They could appoint and dismiss ministers. This power was very substantial. In the case of Bengal and the North-West Frontier Province, this power was used by the Governors to exclude a certain party and keep the other party in power.

They presided over the meetings of the Council of Ministers. By doing so, they could influence the deliberations and conclusions of the Ministers. Their great administrative experience must have been an asset to them.

(2) They could issue two kinds of ordinances. One type of ordinance could be issued by them at any time and that lasted for six months. The other kind of ordinance was issued only when the Legislature was not sitting. They could issue what were known as Governor's Acts. In certain cases, their previous sanction was required for the introduction of certain bills in the Provincial Legislature. They could stop the discussion of any bill in the Legislature at any time. Even when the Bill was passed, the Governors could veto the same or send the same back for reconsideration by the Legislature. They could reserve the same bill for the assent of the Governor-General.

(3) They appointed members of the Provincial Public Service Commission. They were given large powers regarding the Police Force and also the authority to suppress terrorists.

(4) It is the Governors who decided what items of expenditure were to be regarded as "expenditure charged upon revenues of the province." These items were taken out of the control of the Legislature. The non-votable items formed about 40% of the budget. If the whole or any part of the budget was rejected, Governors were authorised to restore the same.

(5) Under Section 93 of the Act, the Governors were given the authority to suspend the Constitution and take over the administrating their own hands.

It is to be noted that under the Act of 1935, the Governors enjoyed substantial powers. The powers given to them were not merely kept in theory. They were intended to be exercised and were actually exercised. However, the extent to which these powers were exercised depended upon the character of the individual Governor and also the position and prestige enjoyed by the Provincial Ministry.

Provincial Ministers

The position of the Provincial Ministers under the Act of 1935, was certainly superior to those of the Ministers under the Act of 1919. There were certainly no reserved Departments. All the Departments were to be under the charge of the ministers. The Governor was expected to carry on the administration of the province according to the advice of the Ministers.

It was laid down in the Instrument of Instructions that the Governor was to summon that person to form the Ministry who could be expected to command a majority in the Provincial Legislature. The other Ministers were to be appointed by the Governor on the advice of the Chief Minister. It was the duty of the Governor to see that minorities were given representation in the Ministry. If a person was not a member of the Legislature at the time of his appointment, he was to get himself elected within six months of his appointment. The Governors were instructed to encourage collective responsibility amongst the Ministers. They were allowed to preside over the meetings of the Council of Ministers.

However, it is to be noted that the powers of the Ministers were to be limited. They did not enjoy complete autonomy in the provincial field. The enormous powers of the Governor were responsible for the weakness of the position of the Ministers. The Governor had many legislative powers and it is these powers which restricted the legislative control of the Ministers. The Governor may not allow a particular bill to be introduced in the Legislature. He may veto a bill which has been passed by the Legislature on the itiniative of the Ministry. He may stop the discussion of the bill at any time. The issuing of ordinances and the Governor's Acts also limited the legislative scope of the Ministers. The same could be said about finance. The Ministers had not a free hand in the matter of proposing new taxes. The Governor may not give his sanction to a bill for that purpose. The Ministers had not complete control over the budget, 40% of which was non-votable.

The Governors could dismiss their Ministers and this was actually done in many cases. Fazl-ul-Haq, the Chief Minister of Bengal, was unceremoniously dismissed by the Governor in 1943. Alla Bux, the Chief Minister of Sind, was dismissed because he gave up the title of Khan Bahadur. The Governor of the Punjab dismissed Shaukat Hayat Khan.

Different views were expressed regarding the position of Ministers under the Act of 1935. According to Lord Zetland, "Let it not be supposed that the field of Government is to be divided into two parts, in which the Governor and the Ministry operate separately at the risk of clashes between them. The essence of the new Constitution is that the initiative and responsibility for the whole of the Government of province, though in form vesting in the Governor, passes to the Ministry as soon as it takes office." According to Sir Maurice Hallet, the Governor of U.P., "After all, the relations of a Governor with his Ministers were not those of a master and his servant; rather they are partners in a common enterprise—the good Government of the province." However, it is to be noted the actual position of the Ministry depended upon its party strength in the Legislature and the personality of the members who constituted the Ministry. In the last analysis, much depends upon the personal equation.

The Nature and Working of Provincial Autonomy

It cannot be denied that Provincial Autonomy as set up by the Act of 1935, was a definite improvement on the system set up by the Act of 1919. But it was wrong to suppose that Provincial Autonomy was intended to establish a full-fledged responsible Government in the Provinces. Had that been the intention, the authors of the Act of 1935, would have stated the same in so many words. There was no necessity for coining a new term. The truth is that the British Government did not intend to give full responsible Government in the provinces. It is clear from the large number of discretionary powers given to the Governors. The same intention becomes evident when we consider the nature and extent of the special responsibilities of the Governors. If the Governor was expected to play the role of the guardian of the British interests and the other vested interests, that was bound to affect adversely the position of the Ministers. A study of the various statements made by the persons who were intimately connected with the framing and passing of the Act of 1935, shows that Provincial Autonomy was expected to work under many restrictions.

According to Lord Zetland who was the Secretary of State for India in 1937, "The Parliament of this country reserved to itself a potential measure of control in a certain limited and clearly defined sphere—the special responsibilities of the Governors. Since the Governors when acting in respect of special responsibilities, were responsible both fro acts of commission and omission, to the Parliament of this country, he would naturally be prepared to answer any question bearing upon the discharge by the Governors of their duties within their sphere." This clearly points out to the limitations of provincial autonomy.

On the occasion of the Second Round Table Conference, Ramsay MacDonald remarked thus: "We are all agreed that the Governors' Provinces of the future are to be responsibly governed units, enjoying the greatest possible measure of control from outside interference and dictation in carrying out their own policies in their own sphere."

According to the Joint Select Committee, Provincial Autonomy is a scheme "whereby each of the Governors' provinces will possess an Executive and a Legislature . . . broadly free from control by the Central Government and Legislature. This we conceive to be the essence of provincial autonomy, though no doubt there is room for wide differences of opinion with regard to the manner in which that exclusive authority is to be exercised.... the Central Government and Legislature would, generally speaking, cease to possess in the Governors' Provinces any legal power or authority with respect to any matter falling within the exclusive Provincial sphere, though, as we shall explain later, the Governor-General in virtue of the power of supervising the Governors will have authority to secure compliance in certain respects with directions which he may find it necessary to give."

It is rightly stated that "there is a world of difference between the real significance of the world "Autonomy" and the so-called "Autonomy" as given by the British Parliament to India." "Provincial Autonomy is a mere farce and far from living reality." "The Provincial Autonomy according to the Government of India Act is merely a sham."

As regards the *working of provincial autonomy*, it is to be noted that the first general elections under the Act of 1935, were held in 1937. The Congress got a majority in six provinces and consequently the Congress party was invited to form Ministries in those Provinces. However, the Congress High Command refused to form the Ministries unless an assurance was given by the Governors that they would not interfere in the day-to-day administration of the provinces. The Governors refused to give such an assurance and the Congress kept itself aloof. On 21st June, 1937, Lord Linlithgow, Governor-General and Viceroy of India gave the following assurance : "There is no foundation for any suggestion that a Governor is free, or is entitled or would have the power to interfere with the day-to-day administration of a province outside the limited range of the responsibilities resting on him. These special responsibilities are restricted in scope to the narrowest limits possible. Even so limited as they are, a Governor will at all times be concerned to carry his Ministers with him, while in other spheres in the field of their ministerial responsibilities, it is *mandatory* on a Governor to be guided by the advice of his Ministers, even though for whatever reasons he may not himself be wholly satisfied that that advice is in the circumstances necessarily and decisively the right advice." On this assurance, the Congress Committee resolved to allow the

Congressmen to take office but made it clear that "office is to be accepted and utilised for the purpose of working in accordance with the lines laid down in the Congress Manifesto" and "to further in every possible way the Congress policy of combating the New Act on the one hand and of prosecuting the constructive programme on the other." In July 1937, Congress Ministers were formed in six provinces.

The Congress Ministries remained in office for two years. They did a lot of useful work during that period. It is true that there were many limitations on their powers, but they managed to accomplish a lot on account of the earnestness and the devotion which they brought to their work. They brought a new approach to work with themselves. They considered themselves to be the servants of the people and their sympathetic approach was responsible for relieving the distress of the people. The Congress Ministers could be proud of their record. They concentrated on the nation-building activities.

The Congress ministries resigned in October 1939, on the issue of war. The Congress leaders remained in jail during the Second World War. The Congress formed ministries again in 1946 is seven Provinces.

Defects in the Act of 1935

(1) It seems desirable to state the important points of criticism levelled against the Act of 1935. According to Pandit Nehru, the new Indian constitution was a "machine with strong brake's and no engine." According to another critic, "the India Act of 1935, tests to the full Indian capacity for administration and government exactly as a man's capacity for swimming is tested to the full by throwing him into a river with his hands and feet tied." "To call the new Indian constitution an edific of self-Government is a grim joke which the joker may enjoy, but not those at whose expense it is cracked." Remember, the new Federal structure has got to be fought tooth and nail. It is difficult to find suitable language to characterise this. It is disgusting, poisoning and offensive." According to Pandit M.M. Malaviya, "The new Act has been thrust upon us. It has a somewhat democratic appearance outwardly, but it is absolutely hollow from inside."

According to C. Rajgopalachariar, "The new constitutions is worse than dyarchy." According to Mr. M.A. Jinnah, the scheme of 1925, was "thoroughly rotten, fundamentally bad and totally unacceptable." Dr. Keith denounced the proposed Federation as "bastard Federalism."

(2) The Indians were not given control over the Government of their country. They could not change or amend their constitution. The Whitehall framed the policy which was followed by the Government of India. The Indians detested the control from London.

(3) Indians detested the dyarchical form of Government at the Centre. It was pointed out that the evils of dyarchy which were found in the provinces under the Act of 1919, were bound to be repeated at the centre also.

(4) The inauguration of the All-India Federation depended upon the condition that a specified number of States joined the Federation. However, the Act gave the Indian States the choice to join or not to join the Federation. This was a serious drawback.

(5) The Indian States were given a privileged position under the constitution. The representation given to them both in the Council of State and the Federal Assembly was more than what was due to them on the basis of their territory, population or the contributions to be made by them to the revenues of the Federal Government. While the numbers from British India were to be elected by the people, the Indian princes were allowed to nominate their quota. The critics pointed out that as the India princes were absolutely under the control of the Political Department of the Government of India and did what they were directed to do, the representatives from the Indian States will be under the control of the British Government. They dare not vote against their masters. The nominees from the Indian States could be used by the British Government in India to serve their own interest and stop the progress of the country.

(6) The Indians protested against the indirect elections to the Federal Assembly. It was contended that indirect elections

were against the very canons of democracy. They were against the spirit of the times.

(7) The Indians protested against the control which was to be exercised by the Secretary for State of India over the Indian Civil Service, the Indian Police Service and other All-India Services.

(8) The Indian Army got the lion's share out of the Indian budget, but the Indians were given absolutely no control over it as Defence was made a reserved subject. The Indians also protested against the pace at which the Indianisation of the Army was going on.

(9) The seats in the Legislatures were to be filled on the basis of the Communal Award. The result was that the constitution was communalism-ridden. The Communal Award cut at the very root of Indian nationalism and solidarity and was consequently the most dangerous. It was pointed out that longer the period for which the Communal Award worked, he greater will be the difficulty in keeping the unity of the country.

(10) According to Sir Shanmukham Chetty, "It is indeed a far cry between the Government Act and Dominion Status. The principle of Dominion Status asserts that the Dominion should have the right to the same measure of autonomy in external affairs as in internal matters and that it is the duty of the British Government to give effect to the doctrine accepted. But India has neither control in the internal nor in the external affairs. The internal administration shall be under the guidance of the Governor-General and the Governors who are vested with tremendous powers; the external affairs shall be under the guidance of Parliament, the Crown and the Secretary of State. Indians shall not be able to work out their own destiny. The safeguards, reservations, special powers of the Governor-General and the Governors, the weakness of the Indian Legislatures, and the Ministers in the Federal and the Provincial Governments with no Central responsibility and weak provincial autonomy, the Communal Award, the States representation bought at the expense of British Indians, the financial and other

economic drawbacks, half measures of the Indianisation of the Army with no control over the Defence—all these things show that Indians shall not be having Dominion Status."

(11) According to Sir Shafat Ahmed Khan, "Though a number of important subjects have been transferred and placed in charge of Ministers who are to be responsible to the Federal Legislature, they are elaborately fenced round by safeguards and other ingenious devices that it will be difficult for a Minister to move freely and safely through this labyrinth and formulate a policy that will offer opportunities for the free and unhampered exercise of our national ability and energy. Ministers can be checked and controlled at almost every turn and their cherished plans might be thwarted by . . . a stubborn Counsellor or a financial advisor steeped in theory and vanity. The special responsibility of the Governor-General will pervade every Department of Government and no subject will be free from it. It is not a special Department concerned exclusively with the legislation or administration of a specific subject, but a power of faculty whereby the Governor-General is empowered to put his fiat on any matter which trenches either directly or indirectly upon his authority as specified in the Act.

"Again, the Legislature is so curiously composed and its procedure is ingeniously contrived that it will find it difficult to function freely and independently. It will be destitute of organic unity, will let the momentum of a common allegiance and national solidarity, and may resolve itself into congeries of inconsistent and even destructive sections, lacking the rudiments of leadership and team work, and exhibiting all the characteristic features of the Federal Parliament of Austria-Hungary before the War. It will not be a National Assembly but a Confederation of Indian States and Provinces, a miniature League of Nations." (*The Indian Federation*)."

(12) According to Fazl-ul-Huq, Premier of Bengal, under the Act of 1935, there was to be neither Hindu Raj nor Muslim Raj but the British Raj (*The Indian Annual Register*, 1937, vol. 2, p. 411).

(13) Commenting on the Government of India Bill, 1935, Mr. Attlee remarked thus: "The keynote of the Bill is mistrust."

The Indian National Congress condemned the federal scheme on many grounds. It was pointed out that the scheme did not envisage any real transfer of power into the hands of the Indians. Moreover, the federal legislature was saddled with an element of conservatism in the form of the nominated representatives of the States. It was contended that the constitutional advancement of India would always be vetoed by the Indian States.

(14) The rulers of the Indian States criticised the federal scheme on the ground that it did not give them any power or authority to leave the federation if once they joined it. The federation had great power of coercing them. The representatives from British India were bound to predominate the Federal Legislature and federal executive and thereby influence the viceroy to take steps which might impair their sovereignty.

(15) The discretionary powers of the Governors reduced provincial autonomy to a farce. Those powers and responsibilities "Combine, crib and confine" the powers of the provincial legislature and executive. Some of these powers and responsibilities were so vaguely defined that those could be interpreted to mean anything according to the exigencies of the moment. The Governor was made the sole judge to decide whether any particular matter fell within his discretionary scheme or affected any of his special responsibilities. The Governor could become a virtual dictator of the province within the letter of the law.

(16) The powers of the Provincial Legislatures were very much restricted. The upper chambers were deliberately made reactionary bodies.

12

Constitutional Development from 1937 to 1950

Although the Government of India Act was passed in 1935, only the part relating to the provinces came into force in 1937. No attempt was made to enforce the Federal part of the Act. It has already been pointed out that although the Congress got majority in six provinces, it refused to shoulder responsibility unless the Governors gave an assurance that they would not interfere in the day-to-day administration. Ultimately, the Governor-General of India gave such an assurance and the Congress Ministries came to power. These Ministries remained in power for about two years.

When the World War II broke out in September 1939, India was immediately declared a belligerent country by the British Government without consulting the people of India. The Congress Working Committee strongly protested against this action of the British Government. They called upon the British Government to declare their war aims in clear-cut terms. They asked whether the war aims of the Government included "the treatment of India as a free nation whose policy will be guided in accordance with the wishes of the people." They firmly declared that "the Committee cannot associate themselves or offer any co-operation in a war which is conducted on imperialistic lines and which is meant to consolidate imperialism in India and elsewhere."

That British Government refused to give the assurance demanded by the Congress. It made merely vague promises to the effect that at the end of the war the British Government would be wiling to consult the various interests in India to make such modifications in the Act of 1935, as might seem desirabie. The result was that the Congress decided to non-co-operate with the British Government. The Congress High Command called the Congress Ministries in eight provinces to resign and they did resign accordingly in October 1939. The administration of those eight provinces was taken over by the Governors. Only the three non-Congress Ministries of Sind, Punjab and Bengal remained in office.

There was a lot of discontentment in the country. To meet that discontentment, Lord Linlithgow declared in January, 1940 that "Dominion Status of the Westminster variety as soon as possible after the war" was the goal of British policy in India. However, there was no response from the side of the Congress.

The **August Offer, (1940)**

On the eve of the Battle of Britain a new Declaration of British policy known as the "August Offer" was published on August 8, 1940. The August Offer was in the form of a statement made by the Viceroy on behalf of the British Government. The following is the summary of the so-called Offer :—

(1) Though the differences which prevented national unity remained unbridged in India, the expansion of the Executive Council of the Governor-General and the establishment of an Advisory War Council should no longer be postponed.

(2) In view of the doubts as to whether the position of minorities would be sufficiently safeguarded in any future constitutional change, the British Government reaffirmed its desire that full weight should be given to minority opinion. "It goes without saying that they could not contemplate transfer of their present responsibilities for the peace and welfare of India to any system of Government whose authorities directly denied by large and powerful elements in India's national life. Nor could they be parties to the coercion of such elements into submission to such a Government." This clearly indicated that the British Government was prepared to allow the Muslim League to have her own way in the matter of the partition of the country.

(3) Subject to the fulfilment of their obligations—an allusion to such questions as defence, minority rights, the treaties with the States, and the position of the Secretary of State Services—the British Government concurred in the Indian desire that the framing of the new constitution should be "primarily the responsibility of Indians themselves, and should originate from Indian conceptions of the social, economic and political structure of the Indian life."

(4) Constitutional issues could not be decided at "a moment when the national life is engaged in a struggle for existence," but after the war a representative Indian body should be set up to formulate new constitution, and meantime the British Government would welcome and assist any efforts to reach agreement as to the form and operation of this constitution-making body and as to the principles of the constitution.

(5) In the interval, the British Government hoped that all parties and communities in India would co-operate in India's war-effort, and by thus working together pave the way for India's attainment of free and equal partnership in the British Commonwealth of Nations.

It was pointed out that the August Offer registered an advance of first-rate importance in the method of handling the constitutional problem. It was clearly stated that the Indians were to be primarily responsible for making the new constitution of India. It followed that if the Indians agreed to the kind of constitution they wanted and if that constitution provided for the due discharge of British obligations, it would be virtually impossible for the British Parliament to reject that constitution. In other words, the Indians were invited to determine their own constitutional future in the same way as the Canadians had done in 1864-67. Australians in 1891-1900 and South Africans in 1908-9. It was declared that the establishment of Dominion Status in India was the goal of the British Government. Mr. Amery stated thus: "The status of a Dominion—or of this country for that matter, for our status in the Commonwealth, although not perhaps our stature, is the same as theirs—is one not inferior to that of nations that perforce stand alone, but superior. . . There is no higher status in the world."

It was pointed out by the critics of the August Offer that the British Government missed the last chance of bringing the Congress into the war. Although the Congress Working Committee had shown its willingness to repudiate the stand of Mahatma Gandhi on the question of war, the British Government did not respond whole-heartedly. The Congress President, Maulana Azad, rejected the August Offer. According to Mahatma Gandhi the August Offer widened the gulf between India as represented by the Congress and England. Pandit Nehru declared that the whole conception of Dominion Status for India was "as dead as a door-nail." The Congress Working Committee passed a Resolution rejecting the British Offer.

The response of the Muslim League to the August Offer was different. The Working Committee of the Muslim League welcomed that part of the Offer which was condemned by the Congress. According to them, the Offer met the League's demand "for a clear assurance to the effect that no future constitution, interim or final, should be adopted by the British Government without their approval and consent." It was declared that "the partition of India was the only solution of the most difficult problem of India's future constitution." But in spite of this, the Muslim League neither accepted nor rejected the Offer.

The Liberals of India asked for a further clarification of the policy of the British Government. They demanded that the enjoyment of Dominion Status must be quite unqualified and a time-limit for its attainment must be fixed. That must not be delayed on account of the attitude of any minority in India. It was also pointed out that the Indian members of the Executive Council of the Governor-General must be party leaders and they should also be in a majority.

Nothing came out of this August Offer on account of the attitude of the Congress. The Offer was not accepted. Mr. Amery commented upon the attitude of the Congress in these words: "Inspired by an ardent national patriotism, they have striven to make that organisation national and all-embracing. If only they had succeeded, if Congress could in fact speak, as it professes to speak, for all the main elements in India's national life, then however advanced their demands, our problem might have been very different and in many respects far easier than it is today."

Again, "The constitutional deadlock today is not between a consentient Indian national movement asking for freedom and a British Government reluctant to surrender its authority but between the main elements of India's own national life."

The Cripps Mission (1942)

The deadlock in Indian politics continued. While the British Government refused to come to terms with the Congress, the latter refused to co-operate with the former. During this period, the Second World War was proceeding. The international situation began to deteriorate. In December 1941, Japan joined the war against the U.S.A. and Great Britain. The Japanese armies advanced swiftly all over the North-East Asian countries. The tide of their conquest rolled at a tremendous pace towards Burma and India. When Singapore fell in February 1942, the security of India was threatened. Rangoon fell on March 7. Colombo was bombarded. Some bombs fell on the eastern coast of India. Calcutta was threatened and refugees began to leave that great city.

But in spite of this threatening situation, the attitude of the Indian leaders did not change. The Congress was as hostile as ever. It was not prepared to help the British against anybody. It could help only if India was given independence. The Muslim League was more concerned with the partition of India than its immediate salvation from the Japanese conquest.

However, the situation demanded a new approach. Everybody insisted that the new move should come from the British Government. Sir Tej Bahadur Sapru stated the same when he sent a cable to Mr. Churchill, the Prime Minister of England. On March 11, 1942, Mr. Churchill announced that the War Cabinet had come to a unanimous decision on Indian policy and that in order to explain it and "to satisfy himself upon the spot by personal consultation, that the conclusions, upon which we all agreed and which we believe represent a just and final solution, will achieve their purpose." Sir Stafford Cripps, the leader of the House Commons, would proceed as soon as possible to India. Mr. Churchill also declared that "the crisis in the affairs of India arising out of the Japanese advance has made Britain wish to really all the forces of Indian life to guard their land from the menace of the invader".

The following is the text of the speech of Churchill in the House of Commons : "The crisis in the affairs of India arising out of the Japanese advance, has made us wish to rally all the forces of Indian life, to guard their land from the menace of the invader. In August 1940, a full statement was made about the aims and policy we are pursuing in India. This amounted in short to a promise that as soon as possible after the war, India should attain Dominion Status in full freedom and equality with this country and other Dominions under a constitution to be framed by Indians, by agreement among themselves and acceptable to the main elements in the Indian national life. This was, of course, subject to the fulfilment of out obligations for the protection of minorities, including the depressed classes, and of our treaty obligations to the Indian States, and to the settlement of certain lesser matter arising out of our long association with the fortunes of the Indian sub-continent.

"However, Sir, in order to clothe these general declarations with precision and to convince all classes, races and creeds in India of our sincere resolve, the War Cabinet have agreed unitedly upon conclusions for present and future action which if accepted by India as a whole, would avoid the alternative dangers either that the resistance of a powerful minority might impose an indefinite veto upon the wishes of the majority or that a majority decision might be taken which would be resisted to a point destructive of internal harmony or fatal to the setting up of a new constitution. We had thought of immediately setting for the terms of this attempt, by a constructive British contribution, to aid India in the realization of full self-government; we are, however, apprehensive that to make a public announcement at such a moment as this might do more harm than good. We must first assure ourselves that our scheme would win a reasonable and practical measure of acceptance, and thus promote the concentration of all Indian thought and energies upon the defence of the native soil. We should ill-serve the common cause if we made a declaration which would be rejected by essential elements in the Indian world and which provoked fierce constitutional and communal disputes at a moment when the enemy is at the gates of India.

"Accordingly we propose to send a member of the War Cabinet to India, to satisfy himself upon the spot, by personal consultation that the conclusions upon which we are agreed and which we believe represent a just and final solution, will achieve their purpose. My Rt. Hon'ble friend, the Lord Privy Seal and Leader of the House has volunteered to undertake this task. He carries with him the full confidence of His Majesty's Government and he will strive in their name to procure the necessary measure of assent, nor from the Hindu majority, but also from those great minorities, amongst which the Muslims are the most numerous and on many grounds, prominent.

"The Lord Privy Seal will, at the same time, consult with the Viceroy and the Commander-in-Chief upon the Military situation bearing always in mind the paramount responsibility of His Majesty's Government by every means in their power to shield the peoples of India from the perils which now beset them. We must remember that India has a great part to play in the world's struggle for freedom and that her helping hand must be extended in loyal comradeship, to the valiant Chinese people, who have fought alone so long. We must remember also that India is one of the bases from which the strongest counter-blows must be struck at the advance of tyranny and aggression.

"My Rt. Hon'ble friend will set out as soon as convenient and suitable arrangements can be made. I am sure he will command in his task the heart felt good wishes of all parts of the House and that, meanwhile, no word will be spoken or debates be held here or in India which would add to the burden he has assumed in his mission or lessen the prospect of good result. During my Rt. Hon'ble and learned friend's absence from this House, his duties as Leader will be discharged by My Rt. Hon'ble friend, the Foreign Secretary."

Soon after his arrival in India, Cripps communicated the contents of the Draft Declaration to the members of the Executive Council on March 23, 1942. The same was communicated to the Indian leaders on March 25. On March 29, he made public his proposal at a press conference. The negotiations started on March 25, and ended unsuccessfully on April 10, 1942. Cripps had to go back empty-handed. During his stay in India, Cripps had to work against heavy odds. The Japanese army was progressing towards India. The news from the front grew steadily worse. Not much could be expected from the atmosphere that prevailed in the country and the previous relations of the Congress and the British Government. Mahatma Gandhi called the Declaration as "a post-dated cheque on a bank that was obviously failing."

Draft Declaration.

The following is the text of the Draft Declaration of the British Government brought by Cripps to India :-

"*(a)* Immediately upon cessation of hostilities, steps shall be taken to set up in India, in the manner described hereafter, an elected body charged with the task of framing a new constitution for India.

"*(b)* Provision shall be made, as set out below, for participation of Indian States in the constitution-making body.

"*(c)* His Majesty's Government undertake to accept and implement forthwith the constitution so framed subject only to:

(i) The right of any province of British India that is not prepared to accept the new constitution to retain its present constitutional position, provision being made for its subsequent accession if it so decides.

"With such non-acceding provinces, should they so desire, His Majesty's Government will be prepared to agree upon a new constitution giving them the same full status as the Indian Union and arrived at by a procedure analogous to that here laid down.

(ii) The signing of a treaty which shall be negotiated between His Majesty's Government and the constitution-making body. This treaty will cover all necessary matters arising out of the complete transfer of responsibility from British to Indian hands; it will make provision, in accordance with undertakings given by His Majesty's Government, for the protection of racial and religious minorities, but will not impose any restriction on the power of the Indian Union to decide in future its relationship to other member-States of the British Commonwealth.

"Whether or not an Indian State elects to adhere to the constitution, it will be necessary to negotiate a revision of its treaty arrangements so far as this may be required in the new situation.

"*(d)* The constitution-making body shall be composed as follows, unless the leaders of Indian opinion in the principal communities agree upon some other form before the end of hostilities :

"Immediately upon the result being known of provincial elections which will be necessary at the end of hostilities, the entire membership of the Lower Houses of Provincial Legislatures shall as a single electoral college proceed to the election of the constitution-making body by the system of proportional representation. This new body shall be in number about 1/10th of the number of the electoral college.

"Indian States shall be invited to appoint representatives in the same proportion to their total population as in the case of representatives of British India as a whole and with the same powers as British Indian members.

"*(e)* During the critical period which now faces India and until the new constitution can be framed, His Majesty's Government must inevitably bear the responsibility for and retain the control and direction of the defence of India as part of their world was effort but the task of organizing to the full the military, moral and material resources of India must be the responsibility of the Government of India with the co-operation of the people of India. His Majesty's Government desire and invite the immediate and effective participation of the leaders of the principal sections of the Indian people in the councils of their country, of the Commonwealth and of the United Nations. Thus they will be enabled to give their active and constructive help in the discharge of a task which is vital and essential for the future freedom of India."

Sir Staffords' Broadcast

In his broadcast from Delhi on March 30, 1942, Sir Stafford declared that he wanted to make it quite clear and "beyond any possibility of doubt or question that the British Government and the British people desire the Indian peoples to have full self-government, with a status as free in every respect as our own in Great Britain or as of any of the great Dominion members of the British Commonwealth of Nations." Regarding the principles on which his proposals were based, he stated that the new constitution of India was to be framed by the elected representatives of the Indian people themselves. Immediately after the cessation of the hostilities, a constitution-making body was to be set up consisting of elected representatives from British India and the Indian States if the latter wished to become a part of the new Indian Union. In the meanwhile, the British Government were to do their utmost for the defence of India and appeal for co-operation from the Indians. He referred to the difficulties arising out of the conflicting interests of the various communities in India. "There are those who claim that India should form a single united country. There are others who say it should be divided up into two, three or more separate countries. There are those who claim that provincial autonomy should be very wide with but few Centrally controlled federal services; others stress the need for centralisation in view of the growing complexity of economic development.

"These and many other and various ideas are worthy to be explored and debated, but it is for the Indian peoples, and not for any outside authority, to decide under which of these forms India will in the future govern herself.

"If the Indian people ask our help, it will, of course, be gladly given, but it is for you, the Indian peoples, to discuss and decide upon your future constitution. We should look on with deep interest and hope that your wisdom will guide you truly in this great adventure."

Regarding the position of the provinces in the future set-up, Cripps stated that they were to be invited to come for deliberations. They were to stay in the Indian Union if they decided in its favour or to leave the same. There was to be no compulsion. "Come together to frame a common constitution—if you find after all your discussion and all the give and take of a constitution-making Assembly that you cannot overcome your differences and some provinces are still not satisfied with the constitution, then such provinces can go out and remain out if they wish and just the same degree of self-government and freedom will be available for them as for the Union itself, *i.e.*, to say complete self-government. We hope to see an Indian Union strong and united because it is founded upon the free consent of all its peoples, but it is not for us, Britishers, to dictate to you, the Indian peoples. . . . . You will work out and decide that problem for yourself."

Regarding the interim changes to be introduced in the Government of India, Cripps declared that except the responsibility for defence the rest of the Departments were to be transferred into the hands of the Indian members of the Executive Council of the Governor-General, "This reservation does not mean that the Governor-General and his Executive Council will or indeed could be excluded from taking an effective part in the counsels for the defence of India. In this wide-flung war, defence cannot be localized in a single country and its proportion must permeate the activities of every Department of Government and must demand from every Department the fullest co-operation. If His Majesty's Government are to take full responsibility for the conduct of the naval, military or air defence of India, as it is their duty to do, then the defence of India most be dealt with by them as part of the world war effort in which they are now engaged, and the direction of that defence must vest in the hands of the Commander-in-Chief under the War Cabinet and their highest staff officers." In order that India might have her full voice in the control of strategy not only in India, but in all the theatres of war, a representative of India was to be appointed to the War Cabinet and the Pacific Council of the United Nations. After the close of the war, India was to appoint her own representatives to the Peace Conference.

Defence

It is to be noted that the proposals of the British Government did not include the subject of defence. Cripps declared in his first Press Conference at Delhi that the Department of Defence could not be transferred into the hands of the Indians even if all the parties in the country made a united demand. The result was that the Working Committee of the Congress decided to reject the proposal. When Cripps came to know of it, he asked the Congress

President not to publish the decision of the Working Committee. Earlier, Cripps had told the Congress President :

> "The Viceroy would be prepared to consult with Indian leaders on this basis to see whether it were possible to designate an Indian to some office connected with the Government of India's defence responsibilities without in any way impugning upon the functions and duties of the Commander-in-Chief either in his capacity as Supreme Commander of the Armed Forces in India or as the Member of the Executive Council in Charge of Defence."

There were interviews between the Congress President, Jawaharlal Nehru, Commander-in-Chief and Cripps, but the negotiations did not bring forth any result. It was then that Col. Johnson arrived in India on 3rd April, 1942. It cannot be denied that Col. Johnson took a prominent part in the discussions on defence fro about a week. It is pointed out that the centre of gravity shifted from Sir Stafford to Johnson, from London to New York and from Churchill to Roosevelt. Col. Johnson requested Pandit Nehru to see him at his residence on 7th April, 1942. As a result of the negotiations Cripps put forward a new formula on 7th April, 1942. According to it, the Commander-in-Chief was to retain his seat in the Executive Council of the Viceroy as a War Member. He was to retain his full control over all the war activities. However, an Indian member was to be added and he was to be in charge of defence. He was to deal with demobilization, post-war reconstruction, petroleum, representation on the Eastern Group Supply Council, amenities for troops, canteen organisation and certain non-technical educational institutions, stationery, printing of forms for the army, social arrangements for all foreign missions and officers, evacuation of threatened areas, signals of co-ordination and economic welfare.

When even this offer was rejected by the Congress, Col. Johnson intervened with a letter containing the following proposals :—

"*(a)* The Defence Department shall be placed in charge of a representative Indian member with the exception of functions to be exercised by the Commander-in-Chief as War Member of the Executive Council.

"*(b)* A War Department will be constituted which will take over such functions of the Defence Department as are not retained by the Defence Member.

However, the Working Committee made certain alternations in the formula. On 10th April, 1942, the defence formula was finally rejected by the Congress.

Regarding the immediate arrangements, Cripps said: "The intention of this paragraph is to indicate to the Governor-General who is responsible for the formation of the Government of India, the broad lines upon which in accordance with the scheme that Government may be formed. All the details of that Government are for the Governor-General to decide and we have not attempted and should not attempt to take that responsibility out of his hands." Again, "Nothing was obligatory on the Governor-General, but he could Indianise the Executive Council. The general direction was laid down in the paragraph. The object was to give fullest measure of Government to the Indian people at the present time consistent with the possibilities of the present constitution which could not be changed till the end of the war. But there might be some small changes made with regard to the position of the Executive Council, particularly the condition that there should be three service members of ten years' standing." "The intention of the document, as far as possible, subject to the reservation of defence, is to put power in the hands of the Indian Legislatures." Regarding the defence, Cripps declared : "The defence of India will not be in Indian hands, even if all the parties want it. It would be the worst thing for the defence of India: it would disorganise the whole defence arrangements, and such disorganization would be fatal."

Cripps Answers Questions

Cripps answered a large number of questions which were put to him at his press conferences and some of them are given below.

Q. Will the Indian union be entitled to disown its allegiance to the Crown?

A. Yes. In order that there shall be no possibility of doubt, we have inserted in the last sentence of paragraph (c) (ii) "but (the proposed treaty) will not impose any restriction on the power of the Indian Union to decide in future its relationship to other member-States of the British Commonwealth." The Union would be completely free to remain within or to go without the Commonwealth.

Q. Will the Indian Union have the right to enter into a treaty with any other nation in the world?

A. Yes.

Q. Can the Union join any contiguous foreign country?

A. There is nothing to prevent it.

Q. Exactly at what stage does the British Government propose to leave the country?

A. As soon as the constitution-making body has framed a new constitution to take the place of the old, the British Government undertake to accept and implement the new one and the moment the new constitution comes into operation, the change-over takes place.

Q. What happens to the Indian Army?

A. So far as the New India is concerned, they can have the whole of the Indian Army and everything else. As soon as the constitution is settled, everything will be transferred to India. (This last sentence is interpreted by Prof. Coupland "to cover the services at present controlled by the Secretary of State.")

Sir, Stafford made it clear that the scheme was to be accepted or rejected as a whole.

Criticism

(1) It has been pointed out that the Draft Declaration was an advance on the August Offer in four respects. It conceded to the projected Indian Union the liberty to secede from the British Commonwealth. Cripps emphasized this point at the Press Conference. The Indian Union was to be free to decide as to whether she was to remain within the British Commonwealth or to go out of it. *(2)* The framing of the new constitution was to rest not merely primarily, but solely in Indian hands. However, its acceptance was made subject to the fulfilment of British obligations. If

the Indians could not become free as a single unit, they could become free as two or more units. Disagreement amongst the Indians was not to give the British Government an excuse to perpetuate their rule in India. *(3)* The August Offer had invited the Indian leaders to start discussing the principles of the new constitution and the method of framing it. The Draft Declaration proposed a plan for a constitution-making body to be adopted if no Indian plan was agreed upon before the cessation of hostilities. *(4)* The Draft Declaration went further than the August Offer as regards the character of the interim system of Government. The Offer had provided for the inclusion of a certain number of representative Indians into the Executive Council. The Declaration invited the leaders of the principal sections of the Indian people to participate in the counsels of India, the Commonwealth and the United Nations.

(2) However, the Cripps proposals were criticised by all the interested parties in India. Each party criticised the proposals from its own point of view. The Congress objection was not so much to the long-term arrangement as to interim arrangements. The Congress acted on the principle that one bird in hand was better than two in the bush. Cripps had given an understanding to the Congress that with the exception of the Defence Department, other departments would be completely in the hands of the Indians, and the Governor-General will act as a constitutional head. However, at a later stage, he withdrew that statement. This made the Congress suspicious regarding the honesty of the British Government. The Congress wanted the Executive Council of the Governor-General to work as a Cabinet. This the British Government was not prepared to concede.

(3) It has been pointed out that the objections to the composition of the post-war Constituent Assembly, settlement on the question of Pakistan on the lines suggested in the Declaration and the division of powers under Defence etc., were not pressed. *The issue which proved fatal was the veto of Viceroy*. There were obvious

objections to the Executive Council being installed as an irremovable and irresponsible body with powers of a dictator and therefore the veto power could not be done away with altogether, but probably it would not have been difficult to set up a convention agreeing to act in an advisory capacity in the day-to-day administration but retaining the reserve of veto power for special reasons only.

(4) The Congress was opposed to the acceptance of the novel principle of non-accession of the provinces. To them it appeared that that implied the acceptance of the principle of Pakistan which would be a severe blow to Indian unity.

(5) The Hindu Mahasabha opposed the Cripps proposals on two grounds. It was opposed to the freedom given to the provinces to leave the Indian Union and set up a separate Government of their own. The Sabha also objected to the elections on the basis of Communal Award which was anti-national and undemocratic.

(6) According to Sir Tej Bahadur Sapru and M. R. Jayakar, "The creation of more than one Union, howsoever consistent in theory with the principle of self-determination, will be disastrous to the lasting interests of the country and its integrity and security." An effort should be made to obtain before the end of the war an inter-communal agreement for the maintenance of Indian unity on a federal basis. If that failed, and provinces should manifest over-whelming wishes in partition, then the proposed experiment might be tried, provided that no decision for non-adherence should be valid without a 65 per cent majority in the Provincial Legislature concerned."

(7) The Sikhs also opposed the provisions relating to the non-accession of the provinces. They stated that "we shall resist by all possible means separation of the Punjab from all-India Union."

(8) The Depressed Classes denounced the proposals on the ground that the necessary safeguards were not provided for their interests.

(9) The Muslim League opposed the creation of a single Indian Union. It was feared that if one single Union was created, the creation of another may become impossible. It also opposed the system of election by a single electoral college by proportional representation. This was not in accordance with the system of communal representation which enabled the Muslims to send their own representatives. The League also objected to the method and procedure for the non-accession of Indian provinces. Their contention was that the provinces of India were created for administrative convenience and not on any logical basis. They demanded the redistribution of the provinces. They opposed the plebiscite by the whole of the adult population of India. They demanded the inherent right of self-determination for the Muslims alone. In short, the scheme was not acceptable to the League because Pakistan was not conceded unequivocally and the right of Muslim self-determination was denied, although the recognition given to the principle of partition was much appreciated.

(10) This scheme failed because it was to be accepted or rejected as a whole. There was no scope for any negotiation or adjustment.

(11) Critics pointed to two snags in the proposals. One was the repetition of the August Offer of 1940 and the addition of the explanation that "the present declaration is intended—not to supersede, but to clothe these general declarations with precision and to convince people in India of the War Cabinet's sincere resolve." This created suspicion in the minds of the people. It indicated a necessity on the part of the British Government to safeguard its prestige. The second snag was that there was no indication in the proposals that the British Government was prepared to part with power.

(12) It is stated that Mahatma Gandhi was not at all impressed by the proposals brought by Cripps. He is stated to have told him thus : "Why did you come if this is what you have to offer? If this is your entire proposal to India, I would advise you to take the next plane home." Sir Stafford's reply was : "I will consider that."

(13) A friend of Cripps remarked thus : "It is sad beyond measure that a man like Sir Stafford Cripps should allow himself to become the devil's advocate."

(14) According to Dr. Pattabhi Sitaramayya, the Cripps proposals were a cheap but attractive bromide enlargement of the August Offer; or to vary the simile, they were really the still-born child of the Cabinet. All that Sir Stafford did in Delhi during the period of twenty days was to restore breath and life to this still-born baby by a process of artificial respiration and by incubation. Strenuous attempts were made in this behalf but they failed although from time to time there appeared to be a sign of the respiratory muscles acting or the cardiac muscles beating but the child was declared dead by the Working Committee so early as on the 31st March, 1942, *i.e.*, on the morrow of the publication of the proposals. Only Sir Stafford's request that the rejection should not be published stayed the hand of the Working Committee from its publication. This was followed by concessions of a halting and limiting character which was more an insult added to injury than an honest attempt to repair the wrong. These held the field till the 8th April by which time, they were again rejected and thereafter all hopes of recovery were given up. But then came the new American Doctor, Colonel Johnson, with his own recipe and with whom the former Doctor, Sir Stafford Cripps, held a consultation. The Colonel's prescription also failed and on the 11th morning the babe was buried seven fathom deep.

(15) Prof. Laski gave his verdict on Cripps's proposals in these words: "The one bright spot in the whole record was the mission of Sir Stafford Cripps for the preparation of which, let it be said with emphasis, Mr. Attlee deserves very great credit. But the Cripps Mission came too late: It looked more like a counter-move against Japan than a recognition of Indian claims, at any rate to many important Indians. It was carried out far too hurriedly; frankly, it was more important for Sir Stafford Cripps to go on working for unity in India than to announce the

routine of business in the House of Commons. And it had about it, if I may say so without irreverence, something of that British habit which Mr. Kingsley Martin has well described as art of forgiving generously those we have grievously wronged. It was psychologically disastrous for Sir Stafford to go to India in a 'take it or leave it' mood, and, on his return, practically announce that we washed our hands of the offer. That was bound to make it look as though our real thought was less the achievement of Indian freedom than of a *coup de main* in the propagandist's art among our allies who contrasted American relations with the Philippines against British relations with India."

(16) According to Dr. A.K. Ghoshal, the method of forming the constitution-making body was vitiated by sectionalism and Communalism. The existing provinces were taken as units for sending representatives to the Constituent Assembly on the assumption that they were constituted on correct principles. However, that presumption was not well-founded. The provinces were created haphazardly from considerations of administrative expediency. The distribution of seats in the provincial legislatures was not made on any just and equitable principles. In the constitution-making body, the same wrong principles were sought to be introduced. A body constituted on the principles of separate electorates, narrow franchise and communal reservations could hardly be expected to reflect the true and higher interests of the Indian nation as opposed to sectional and communal jealousies. One could not be sure of a good constitution coming out of such a Constituent Assembly. Moreover, the nominated representatives of the Indian States were to form a solid bloc of reactionary forces. They could join hands with other reactionary forces in the Constituent Assembly. The non-acceding provisions were the most obnoxious feature of the scheme. They were a "severe blow to the conception of Indian unity." They were liable to create not only one or more Ulsters in British India, but many Ulsters among the Indian States. The possibility of India being broken up into a congeries of small states was implicit in the

Scheme. Moreover, the procedure for determining whether the State wanted to accede to the Union or not was not stated either in the document brought by Cripps or other explanations given by him.

The procedure to determine whether a province wanted to accede to the Union or not was not clearly defined. It appears that the decision was to be taken by the members of the provincial legislature. According to Cripps, if the majority in favour of secession was less than 60% of the legislature, the minority was entitled to demand a plebiscite of the adult male population. In the plebiscite, the decision was to be by simple majority. In the case of Bengal, the Muslim and Hindu population was 54.7 p.c. and 45 p.c. respectively. In the provincial legislature, they were in the proportion of about 45 p.c. and 32 p.c. If the Hindus had representation corresponding to their population, even when the weightage to which they were entitled in Bengal as a minority, was refused, they could perhaps secure a majority in favour of accession in combination with some others of the same way of thinking. But as the things stood, they had very little chance of securing the necessary majority of at least 60 p.c. Even if they succeeded in securing a majority between 51 p.c. to 59 p.c. the Muslim could demand the right of plebiscite. As their population was 54.7 p.c. of the whole, they would have no difficulty in carrying a non-accession decision by a simple majority. The same was the case in the Punjab.

(17) Moreover, the acceptance by the British Government of a constitution framed by the constitution-making body was to be subject to the signing of a treaty covering "all necessary matters arising out of a complete transfer of responsibility from British to Indian hands." It was not stated as to who was to guarantee the enforcement of the terms of the treaty. If the British Government was to be the sole judge in the case of any dispute regarding the interpretation of the treaty, the independence of India was to have no meaning. The whole plan of Cripps was conceived less in the spirit of a sincere attempt to solve

the Indian problem than as a sop offered to party leaders to bring all sections of Indian population actively into a war.

The Cripps Mission is usually regarded to be a failure. But it is pointed out that although India rejected it in the belief that it was a post-dated cheque on a crashing bank, the British Government announced that they would consider themselves bound by it. As is well-known, the war was brought to a successful close, the bank did not crash and the cheque was ultimately honoured.

The August Resolution, (1942)

After the failure of the Cripps Mission, there was a lot of discontentment in the country. The Congress leaders got convinced that they could not expect anything from the British Government in the near future. Consequently, the All India Congress Committee passed the famous "Quit India" Resolution on August 8, 1942 This Resolution emphasized the necessity of immediate ending of the British rule in India and announced "the starting of a mass struggle on non-violent lines of the widest possible scale." The Government of India arrested all the members of the Working Committee and Mahatma Gandhi. The people of India hit back. In various parts of India, the Government machinery was completely thrown out of gear. The Government used all possible means to crush the revolt. Thousands of people were either mercilessly killed or put behind the bars. The political life of India was completely suspended. During this hour of India's trial, the Communist Party of India helped the Government in the prosecution of war. The deadlock continued up to 1944 when Mahatma Gandhi was released.

Rajagopalachariar Formula, March, 1944

In March, 1944, C. Rajagopalachariar put forward his formula to solve the deadlock prevailing in the country. On the 8th April, 1944, he wrote to M.A. Jinnah that the "basis for settlement" had the "full approval" of Mahatma Gandhi.

The following was the basis for terms of settlement between the Congress and the Muslim League:

"(1) Subject to the terms set outbelow as regards the

constitution for Free India, the Muslim League endorses the Indian demand for independence and will co-operate with the Congress in the formation of a provisional Interim Government for the transitional period.

"(2) After the termination of the war, a commission shall be appointed for demarcating contiguous districts in the north-west and east of India, wherein the Muslim population is in absolute majority. In the areas thus demarcated, a plebiscite of all the inhabitants held on the basis of adult suffrage or other practicable franchise shall ultimately decide the issue of separation from Hindustan. If the majority decide in favour of forming a sovereign state separate from Hindustan, such decision shall be given effect to, without prejudice to the right of districts on the border to chose to join either state.

"(3) It will be open to all parties to advocate their points of view before the plebiscite is held.

"(4) In the event of separation, mutual agreements shall be entered into for safeguarding defence, and commerce and communications and for other essential purposes.

"(5) Any transfer of population shall only be on an absolutely voluntary basis.

"(6) These terms shall be binding only in case of transfer by Britain of full power and responsibility of the governance of India."

In his letter, dated 18th September, 1944, Mr. M.A. Jinnah asked for certain clarifications from Mahatma Gandhi. He inquired as to who was to frame the constitution referred to in the scheme. He also wanted to know the basis or the lines on which the interim government was to be set up or constituted. He also wanted to know as to who was to appoint the Commission whose duty was to demarcate the contiguous areas where the Muslims had an absolute majority. The plebiscite was to be taken district-wise or on some other basis, if it was to be based on adult franchise or some other franchise. He also inquired as to who was to give effect to the verdict of the Commission, and to whom the power was to be transferred, and through what machinery and when.

Mahatma Gandhi wrote back to Jinnah that the Constitution was to be framed by the Provisional Government contemplated in the formula or an authority specially set up by it after the British power was withdrawn. The Provisional Government was to be set up on the basis of an agreement between the Congress and the League. The Commission was to be appointed by the Provisional Government. The form of plebiscite could be agreed upon between the League and the Congress. The power was to be transferred to the nation, that is, the Provisional Government by the British Government in a peaceful manner.

Mahatma Gandhi pointed out that the Lahore Resolution of the Muslim League was indefinite and Rajaji had taken from that the substance and had given it a shape. To this, Jinnah gave the following reply : "I cannot agree that Rajaji has taken from it as substance and given it shape. On the contrary, he has not only put it out of shape but mutilated it. . . ."

Mahatma Gandhi explained the process in these words : "We reach by joint effort independence for India as it stands. India become free will proceed to demarcation, plebiscite and partition if the people concerned vote for partition."

In his letter, dated 15th September, 1944, to Jinnah, Mahatma Gandhi pointed out that he found "no parellel in history for a body of converts and their descendants claiming to be a nation apart from the parent stock. If India was one nation before the advent of Islam, it must remain one in spite of the change of faith of a very large body of her children. . . . You do not claim to be a nation by right of conquest but by reason of acceptance of Islam. Will the two nations become one if the whole of India accepted Islam, . . . , ... The only real though awful test of one nationhood arises out of our common political subjection." To this, Jinnah gave the following reply : "We maintain and hold that *Muslims and Hindus are two major nations by any definition and test of a action*. We are a nation of a hundred million, and what is more, we are a nation with our own distinctive culture and civilisation, language and literature, art and architecture, names and nomenclature, sense of values and proportion, legal laws and moral codes, customs and calendar, history and traditions, aptitudes and ambitions, in short, we have our own distinctive outlook on life and of life."

"Jinnah's contention was that the Muslims of India as a nation had the right of self-determination and the *Muslim alone* were to be entitled to vote and not the non-Muslims. He also pointed out that "there cannot be defence and similar matter of Common Concern, when it is accepted that Pakistan and Hindustan will be two separate independent sovereign States." Mahatma Gandhi refused to accept the Muslims of India as a nation distinct from the rest of the inhabitants of India. Mere assertion was no proof.

In his letter, dated 24th September, 1944, Mahatma Gandhi suggested that "the areas should be demarcated by a Commission approved by the Congress and the League. The wishes of the inhabitants of the areas demarcated should be ascertained through the votes of the adult population of the areas or through some equivalent method.

> "If the vote is in favour of separation, it shall be agreed that these areas shall form a separate State as soon as possible after India is free from foreign domination and can therefore be constituted into two sovereign independent states. There shall be a treaty of separation which should also provide for the efficient and satisfactory administration of foreign affairs, defence, internal communications, customs, commerce, and the like, which must necessarily continue to be matters of common concern between the contracting parties.
>
> The treaty shall also contain terms for safeguarding the rights of the minorities in the two states.
>
> Immediately on the acceptance of this agreement by the Congress and the League the two shall decide upon a common course of action for the attainment of independence of India.
>
> The League will, however, be free to remain out of any direct action to which the Congress may resort and in which the League may not be willing to co-operate."

The negotiations were bound to fail. There was a fundamental difference of approach towards the main question. The main object of the Congress was to win over the League with a view to achieving the independence of the country, and for that purpose, it was prepared to pay some reasonable price. The Congress was not prepared to accept all the demands of the League. On the other hand, the League was not bothered about the independence of the country. It was anxious to secure the assent of the Congress to the establishment of Pakistan. Morever, the League was not prepared to ignore its patron, the British bureaucracy in India, who had consistently helped it in all difficult situations.

Desai-Liaqat Formula, 1945

Although the negotiations between Mahatma Gandhi and M.A. Jinnah failed on the basis of the Rajagopalachariar formula efforts were made by Bhulabhai Desai, leader of the Congress Party in the Central Legislative Assembly to solve the deadlock. The ultimately resulted in the Desai-Liaquat formula of January, 1945.

The genesis was described by Liaqat Ali Khan, General Secretary of the All-India Muslim League, in these words: "Mr. Desai met me after the last autumn session of the Central Legislative Assembly (1944) and we informally discussed the prevailing distressing conditions in the country, economic and otherwise, and the terrible hardships and plight of the people due to the situation that was created on account of the war. The war in Europe was reneging in the full fury and there was no indication as to when it would end, and it was the opinion of everyone that it would take at least two years after the termination of hostilities in Europe to bring the war to a successful conclusion against Japan. India was to be the main base of the Allies for military operations in the East against Japan, which meant greater sacrifices by the people of India and much greater hardships and privations than what they had been facing in the past.

> "It was recognised all-round that the Government of India, with its present composition, was incapable of dealing effectively with the various problems which had arisen and were bound to arise in the future.
>
> Mr. Desai, during the course of the conversations, asked me about the attitude of the Muslim League with regard to some interim arrangemnt at the Centre and temporary reconstitution of the Governor-General's Executive Council in a manner which would secure for it the confidence of all the peoples, so that it may be able to help them in their present plight and deal more effectively than what had been done in the past with the serious situation that was bound to arise in the future on account of the prolongation of the war. I

explained to him the position in the light of the resolutions that were passed from time to time by the Muslim League in this connection and told him that my personal view was that if any proposals were made to ease the situation, the Muslim League was bound to give its very careful consideration to them, as it had always done in the past, because the Muyslim League had always been anxious to come to the rescue of the people and assist them in their sad plight and help the country in tiding over the difficult period ahead. Mr. Desai saw me again in Delhi in the beginning of January this year just as I was leaving on a tour of the Madras Presidency and showed me some proposals which had been drafted for the formation of an interim Government at the Centre, a copy of which he was good enough to give me and which was to be treated as strictly private and confidential, and on the basis of which he told me he was going to make an effort to bring about a change in the composition of the Government of India.

"He told me his plan was to met the Viceroy and Mr. Jinnah in this connection. I told him that in my personal opinion the proposals were such that they could be made a basis for discussion, but I did not see any prospect of his making any headway unless he could either get Mr. Gandhi to move in the matter personally or get his definite approval and open support for the move that he was making, as Mr. Gandhi was the only person who could deliver the goods on behalf of the Congress in the absence of the Working Committee. During my talks with Mr. Desai, which were purely of a personal nature, I made it absolutely clear to him that whatever I had said was my individual view and I was not speaking either on behalf of the Muslim League or any one else. If and when Mr. Desai felt that he could speak with authority on behalf of the Congress, he would have to approach the President of the All-India Muslim League, who was the proper authority to entertain any proposals on behalf of the Muslim League."

The following is the text of the proposals for the formation of the Interim Government at the Centre:

"The Congress and League agree that they will join in forming an interim Government in the Centre. The composition of such Government will be on the following lines :

(a) "Equal number of persons nominated by the Congress and the League in the Central Executive. Persons nominated need not be members of the Central Legislature.

(b) Representative of minorities (in particular Scheduled Castes and the Sikhs).

(c) The Commander-in-Chief.

The Government will be formed and function within the framework of the existing Government of India Act. It is, however, understood that if the Cabinet cannot get a particular measure passed by the Legislative Assembly, they will not enforce the same by resort to any of the reserve powers of the Governor-General or the Viceroy. This will make them sufficiently independent of the Governor-General.

It is agreed between the Congress and the League that if such interim Government is formed, their first step would be to release the Working Committee members of the Congress.

The steps by which efforts would be made to achieve this end are at present indicated to take the following course. On the basis of the above understanding, some way should be found to get the Governor-General to make a proposal or a suggestion that he desires an interim Government to be formed in the Centre on the agreement between the Congress and the League and, when the Governor-General invites Mr. Jinnah and Mr. Desai either jointly or separately, the above proposals would be made, desiring that they are prepared to join in the forming of the Government.

The next step would be to get the withdrawal of Section 93 in the Provinces and to form as soon as possible Provincial Governments on the lines of a coalition."

However, in spite of the honest efforts of Desai and Liaqat Ali, no settlement could be secured between the Congress and the Muslim League, and the deadlock continued till the surrender of Germany on 5th May, 1945.

Wavell Plan, 1945

On 14th June, 1945, Lord Wavell, Governor-General and Viceroy of India, gave a broadcast to the people of India. On the same day, L.S. Amery, Secretary of State for India, made a similar statement in the House of Commons. The thoughts and sentiments in both were practically the same. The *modus operandi* consisted in calling a conference of representatives chosen by the Viceroy for the purpose of obtaining from the leaders of various parties a joint list or separate lists of worthy persons in order to constitute a new Executive Council of the Viceroy. Lord Wavell pleaded for men of influence and ability to be recommended by the various parties who would be prepared to take decision and responsibility of administration of all the portfolios including External Affairs," except the conduct of war which was to be under the Commander-in-Chief. There was to be an equal number of Muslims and Hindus other than the Scheduled Castes. The control of the Secretary of State for India and the Governor-General was to continue as provided under the Act of 1919. The veto of the Viceroy was to continue, although the same was not to be used unreasonably. It was to be used not in the interest of England but in the interest of India. The proposals were to affect only British India and not the Indian States. To quote Wavell, "In regard to the Indian States, while recognising that during the interim period the powers of the Crown representative will continue, it is clear that the National Government will have to deal with many matters which overlap and have concern with the states, *e.g.*, trade, industry, labour etc. Further the barriers between the States people and the princes and members of the National Government and other associates should be removed so as to help in mutual discussion, consultation and consideration of common problems and their solution."

Wavell pointed out that "if the meeting is successful I hope that we shall be able to agree on the formation of the new Executive Council at the Centre and that provincial ministries in Section 93 provinces would resume office and that these would be coalitions." However, "if the meeting should unfortunately fail, we must carry on as at present until parties come together."

Amery pointed out that while His Majesty's Government were at all times most anxious to do their utmost to assist the Indians in the working out of a new constitutional settlement, it would be a contradiction in terms to speak of imposition by this country of self-governing instiutions upon an unwilling India. Such a thing was not possible, nor could we accept the responsibility of enforcing such institutions at the very time when we were, by its parties, withdrawing from all control of British Indian affairs.

> "The main constitutional position remains therefore as it was. The offer of March 1942, stands in its entirety without change or qualification. His Majesty's Government still hope that the political leaders of India will be able to come to an agreement as to the procedure whereby India's permanent future form of Government can be determined."

The British Government had considered whether there was something which they could suggest in the interim period pending the formulation by Indians of their future constitutional arrangements, which would enable the Indians to co-operate with the British Government. It was clearly stated that

> "it is not the intention of His Majesty's Government to introduce any change contrary to the wishes of the major Indian communities. But they are willing to make possible some step forward during the interim period if the leaders of the principal Indian parties are prepared to agree to their suggestions and to co-operate in the successful conclusion of the war against Japan as well as in the reconstruction in India which must follow the final victory. To this end they would be prepared to see an important change in the composition of the Viceroy's Executive. It is proposed that the Executive Council should be re-constituted and that the Viceroy should in future make his selection for nomination to the Crown for appointment to his Executive from amongst leaders of Indian political life at the Centre and in the Provinces, in proportions which would give a balanced representation of the main communities, including equal proportions of Muslims and Caste Hindus."

The members of the Working Committee of the Congress were released from jail and high hopes were raised on all sides. Invitations were issued to the leaders including Mahatma Gandhi and Jinnah for the proposed conference to be held at Simla. The conference met on 27th June, 1945. After three days of deliberations, it was adjourned. On 11th July, 1945, Jinnah had a short interview extending over 15 minutes with the Viceroy. He seems to have made it clear that he would not agree to the inclusion of non-Leaguers in the list of the Viceroy on the ground that the League was the sole representative of the Muslims of India. The Viceroy did not accept his point of view. Shortly after that, Mahatma Gandhi met the Viceroy. On 12th July, 1945, Maulana Azad, President of the Congress, was invited by the Viceroy to see him. He was merely informed that Jinnah was not agreeable to the Muslim representatives in the list prepared by the Viceroy himself. However, the Viceroy did not reveal the contents of the list. On 14th July, 1945, Lord Wavell declared that the conference had failed. In a statement, Lord Wavell remarked thus : "The conference has . . . . . failed. Nobody can regret this more that I do myself. I wish to make it clear that the responsibility for the failure is mine. The main idea underlying the Conference was mine. If it had succeeded, its success could have been attributed to me and I cannot place the blame for its failure upon any of the parties."

At a Press conference on 14th July, 1945, Jinnah remarked thus:

> "On a final examination and analysis of the Wavell plan, we found that it was a snare. There was the combination consisting of Gandhi Hindu Congress, who stand for India's Hindu national independence as one India, and the latest exponent of geographical unity, Lord Wavell, and Glancy-Khizr, who are bent upon creating disruption among the Mussalmans in the Punjab, and we were sought to be pushed into this arrangement, by which, if we had agreed to, as proposed by Lord Wavell, we would have signed our death warrant."

Jinnah continued :

> "Next, in the proposed Executive we would be reduced to a minority of one-third. All the other minorities, such as the Scheduled Castes, Sikhs and Christians, have the same goal as the Congress. They have their grievances as minorities, but their goal and ideology is and cannot be different from or otherwise than that of United India. Ethnically and culturally they are very closely knitted to the Hindu society. I am not against full justice being done to all the minorities and they should be fully safeguarded and protected as such, wherever they may be, but in the actual working and practice, invariably their vote will be against us and there is no

safeguard for us except the Viceroy's veto, which, it is well known to any constitutionalist, cannot be exercised lightly as every day business against majority decisions with regard to the policy and the principles that will have to be laid down and measures adopted, both administrative and legislative.

On the top of this came the last straw on the camel's back, that even about the five members of the Muslim bloc which were allotted to us communal-wise, which is the essence of the Wavell proposals, we were told that the Muslim League was not entitled to nominate all the Muslim representatives as our chosen spokesmen and there were two claimants—the Congress which claimed two,.and Galancy-Khizr on behalf of the Punjab claimed one. This move on the part of these two went at the very root and the very existence of the Muslim League regarding its position, character and status. But finally we broke as Lord Wavell insisted upon his having one non-Leaguer, a nominee of Malik Khizr Hyat Khan, representing the Punjab Muslims."

Maulana Azad also made a statement on the same day at Simla. He declared that the Congress was prepared to accommodate the Muslim League consistently with its national policy. Failure of the Conference was due to the uncompromising attitude of the League. To quote him, "Two points arise out of the present position; the first is that the attitude of the Muslim League is responsible for the failure of the Conference and the second point which emerges from the situation is that after the refusal of the Muslim League the question naturally came before the Viceroy whether a forward step should be taken or not. The Viceroy decided not to take it for the present." Again, "With a faltering step and wavering mind, we cannot cover our destination. It is good to think twice before taking a step forward. But when the step has already been taken, hesitation is not virtue but weakness. If the British Government wish to give shape to things, they should have realised the communal condition. They should have been prepared not to surrender the right of veto to any group and thus block the path of progress."

Comments

It is pointed out that the procedure followed by Lord Wavell was not proper. He should have taken the leaders of the other parties into confidence and revealed to them the contents of his own list of the members of the Executive Council. It is possible that the Working Committee of the Congress might have agreed to accept his list, with or without minor alternations. He should not have allowed the League to sabotage the whole scheme. The responsibility for the failure must be shared by the Muslim League and the British Government. The latter should have acted firmly and fearlessly.

Critics also point out to a close analogy between the Cripps Mission and the Wavell Plan. Cripps came to India in the midst of beating of drums and fanfare of trumpets. He raised high hopes and made extravagant off-the-record promises to the Congress President and later denied the same. In the case of the Wavell Plan, the Viceroy definitely stated at Simla that there was no question of his veto being eliminated. To that extent, he was frank unlike Cripps. It is stated that when Cripps came to Delhi and invited Mahatma Gandhi to meet him, the Mahatma was so badly impressed by his proposals that he expressed the surprise that of all the people, Cripps should have made himself a messenger of Britain with those proposals. In the case of the Wavell Plan, Mahatma Gandhi felt that the Plan was sincere in spirit and contained the seeds of independence. When Cripps came to India, Mahatma Gandhi did not ask for the summoning of the Working Committee of the Congress at Delhi to consider his proposals. However, in 1945, he asked for the summoning of the Working Committee to consider the Wavell Plan. Moreover, Cripps came to India at a time when the British people seriously feared a Japanese invasion of India. When the threat of invasion passed away, the Cripps Mission came to an abrupt end. Likewise, the Wavell Plan came to light when the Labour Party threatened the Conservative Party in the elections that were held in July 1945. The elections passed and the Wavell Plan also came to an unexpected end. It is pointed out that the Simla Conference was due to the Russian pressure as the Cripps Mission was due to the American pressure. In 1945, it was the Congress that broke the Cripps Mission. In 1945, it was the Muslim League that broke the Wavell Plan, although Lord Wavell took the blame on himself. Lord Wavell had assured the Congress President that "no party to the Conference would be allowed to obstruct settlement out of willfulness." In spite of this, the hand of Lord Wavell was stayed at the last moment as was the case with Cripps. The Cripps Proposals failed virtually on the third day of the deliberations of the Working. Committee which met on 29th March, 1945. The decision of the Working Committee was not made public on account of the special request of Cripps. In 1945 also, the Simla Conference failed on the third day of its meeting *i.e.*, 29th June, 1945.

The failure of the Simla Conference convinced the Congress that nothing could be expected from the British Government so long as the Conservative Party remained in office. The British bureaucracy in India had allowed Jinnah to have his own way.

The Labour Party came to power on 10th July, 1945 and Lord Pethick-Lawrence, an old friend of India, became the Secretary of State for India in Mr. Attlee's Cabinet. In his speech to the new Parliament, the King referred to the Indian affairs in these words: "In accordance with the promises already made to my Indian peoples, my Government will do their utmost to promote in conjunction with the leaders of Indian opinion, early realisation of full self-government in India". The war with Japan ended officially on the midnight of 14th August, 1945. Lord Wavell was summoned to London for consultations and he reached there on 25th August. Before his return, fresh elections were announced in India both to the Central and Provincial Legislatures.

Wavell's Broadcast, (Sept. 1945)

Lord Wavell came to India on 18th September, 1945 and gave the following broadcast speech on 19th September, 1945 :—

> "After my recent discussion with His Majesty's Government in London, they authorised me to make the following announcement:
>
> As stated in the gracious speech from the Throne at the opening of Parliament, His Majesty's Government are determined to do their utmost to promote, in conjunction with the leaders of Indian opinion, the early realisation of full self-government in India. During my visit to London they have discussed with me the steps to be taken.
>
> An announcement has already been made that elections to the Central and Provincial Legislatures, so long postponed owing to the war, are to be held during the coming cold

weather. Thereafter, His Majesty's Government earnestly hope that Ministerial responsibility will be accepted by political leaders in all provinces.

It is the intention of His Majesty's Government to convene as soon as possible a constitution-making body and, as a preliminary step, they have authorised me to undertake, immediately after the elections, discussions with representatives of the Legislative Assemblies in the provinces, to ascertain whether the proposals contained in the 1942 Declaration are acceptable or whether some alternative or modified scheme is preferable.

Discussions will also be undertaken with the representatives of the Indian States with a view to ascertaining in what way they can best take their part in the constitution-making body.

His Majesty's Government are proceeding to the consideration of the treaty which will require to be concluded between Great Britain and India.

During these preparatory stages the Government of India must be carried on and urgent economic and social problems must be dealt with. Furthermore, India has to play her full part in working out the new world order. His Majesty's Government have therefore further authorised me as soon as the results of the provincial elections are published, to take steps to bring into being an Executive Council which will have the support of the main Indian parties.

That is the end of the announcement which His Majesty's Government have authorised me to make. It means a great deal. It means that His Majesty's Government are determined to go ahead with the task of bringing India to self-government at the earliest possible date. They have, as you can well imagine, a great number of most important and urgent problems on their hands: but despite all their pre-occupations, they have taken time, almost in their first days of office, to give attention to the Indian problem, as one of the first and most important. That fact is a measure of the earnest resolve of His Majesty's Government to help India to achieve early self-government.

The task of making and implementing a new constitution for India is a complex and difficult one, which will-require good will, co-operation and patience on the part of all concerned. We must first hold elections so that the will of the Indian electorate may be known. It is not possible to undertake any major alteration of the franchise system. This would delay matters for at least two years. But we are doing our best to revise existing electoral rolls efficiently. After the election. I propose to hold discussions with representatives of those elected and of the Indian States to determine the form which the constitution-making body should take, its powers and procedures.

The Draft Declaration of 1942 proposed a method of setting up a constitution-making body, but His Majesty's Government recognised that, in view of the great issues involved and the delicacy of the minority problems, consultation with the people's representatives is necessary before the form of the constitution-making body is finally determined.

The above procedure seems to His Majesty's Government and myself the best way open to us to give India the opportunity of deciding her destiny. We are well aware of the difficulties to be overcome, but are determined to overcome them. I can certainly assure you that the Government and all sections of the British people are anxious to help India which has given us so much help in winning this war. I for my part will do my best in the service of the people of India to help them to arrive at their goal, and I firmly believe that it can be done.

It is now for Indians to show that they have the wisdom, faith and courage to determine in what way they can best reconcile their differences and how their country can be governed by Indians for Indians."

Mr. Attlee's Broadcast, (Sept. 1945)

Mr. Clement Attlee, the British Prime Minister, announced on the same date that the offer of 1942 "stands in all its fullness and purpose." The following is the full text of his broadcast :

"The King's speech at the opening of the new Parliament contained this passage : 'In accordance with the promises already made to my Indian people, my Government will do their utmost to promote in conjunction with leaders of Indian opinion early realization of full self-government in India.'

"Immediately after assuming office, the Government turned its attention to Indian affairs and invited the Viceroy to come in order to review with him the whole situation, economic and political. These discussions have now concluded and the Viceroy has returned to India and has made an announcement of policy.

You will remember that in 1942 the Coalition Government made a Draft Declaration for discussion with Indian leaders, commonly known as the Cripps Offer.

It was proposed that immediately upon cessation of hostilities steps should be taken to set up in India an elected body charged with the task of framing a new Constitution for India. Sir Stafford Cripps took that offer to India, but it was unfortunately not accepted by leaders of Indian political parties; The Government is, however, acting in accordance with its spirit and intention.

The first step necessary is to get as soon as may be as democratic a representation of the Indian peoples as possible. War has in India, as in this country, prevented elections being held for a long time and the Central and Provincial Legislatures must now be renewed. Therefore, as has already been announced, elections will be held in India in the coming cold weather. Electoral rolls are being revised as completely as time permits and everything possible will be done to ensure free and fair election.

The Viceroy has today made known our intention to follow the election by positive steps to set up a constituent assembly of Indian elected representatives, charged with the task of framing a new Constitution. Government has authorised Lord Wavell to undertake preliminary discussions with representatives of new Provincial Legislatures, as soon as they are elected to ascertain whether the proposals of the Cripps Offer are acceptable as they stand, or whether some alternative or modified scheme should be preferable. Discussions will also take place with representatives of Indian States.

Government has further authorised the Viceroy as an interim measure to take steps after the elections to bring into being an Executive Council, having the support of the main Indian parties, in order that India may deal herself with her own social and economic problems and may take her full part in the working out of a new world order.

The broad definition of British policy towards India, contained in the Declaration of 1942, which had the support of all parties in this country, stands in all its fullness and purpose. This declaration envisaged the negotiation of a treaty between the British Government and the constitution-making body. Government is giving immediate consideration to the contents of such a Treaty. It can be said here that in that treaty we shall not seek to provide for anything incompatible with the interests of India. No one having any acquaintance with Indian affairs will underestimate the difficulty which will have to be surmounted in the setting up and smooth operation of a constitution making body. Still greater is the difficulty which will face the elected representatives of the Indian people in seeking to frame a constitution for a great continent containing more than 400,000,000 human beings.

During the war, Indian fighting men have in Europe, Africa and Asia played a splendid part in defeating the forces of tyranny and aggression. Indig has shared to the full with the rest of the United Nations the task of saving Freedom and Democracy. Victory came through unity and through the readiness of all to sink their differences in order to attain the supreme object, Victory. I would ask all Indians to follow this great example and to join together in a united effort to work out a Constitution which the majority and minority communities will accept as a just and fair Constitution, in which both the States and Provinces can find their places. The British Government will do their utmost to give every assistance in their power, and India can be assured of the sympathy of the British people."

Statement of 4th December, 1945

On 4th December, 1945, Lord Pethick-Lawrence made the following statement in the House of Lords : "The statement made by the Viceroy after his return to India contemplates steps which His Majesty's Government propose should be taken to promote early realisation of full self-government in India.

"The full significance of these proposals does not seem to have been properly appreciated in India.

Since it is the firm conviction of His Majesty's Government that it is by, and in consultation with directly elected representastives of the Indian people that decisions as to the future of the Government of British India should be taken, it was necessary that preliminary elections should be held to the Provincial Legislatures and the Central Assembly in India.

It was announced that after the elections in India, preparatory discussions would be held with the elected representatives of British India and with the Indian States in order to secure the widest measure of agreement as to the method of framing the constitution.

Pethick-Lawrence added:

Unjustified suggestions have gained wide currency in India that these discussions would be a fruitful source of delay. I desire to make it plain that His Majesty's Government regard the setting up of a constitution-making body by which Indians will decide their own future, and also other proposals embodied in the announcement as a matter of the greatest urgency.

This misunderstanding has led His Majesty's Government to consider whether opportunities of personal contact between this country and India which have been greatly interrupted during recent years cannot now be increased.

They regard it as a matter of importance that members of our own Parliament should have an opportunity to meet leading political Indian personalities to learn their own views at first hand.

They would also be able to convey in person the general wish and desire of the people of this country that India should speedily attain her full and rightful position as an Independent Partner State in the British Commonwealth and the desire of Parliament to do everything within our power to promote speedy attainment of that objective.

His Majesty's Government are therefore arranging for a Parliamentary Delegation to go to India under the auspices of the Empire Parliamentary Association.

The intention is that this party should leave this country as soon as possible. In view of the difficulties of transport, it will be limited in size. The Delegation will be selected by the Association in consultation with parliamentary representatives of the chief political parties in this country.

During the transition towards complete self-government, India will be passing through difficult times. No greater disservice could be done to future Indian Government and to the cause of Democracy than to permit the foundations of the State to be weakened and the loyalty of its servants to those who are in authority to be undermined before that new Government comes into being.

Therefore the Government of India cannot divest itself of the responsibility which rests upon it and upon all Provincial Governments in preserving law and order and of resisting any attempt to resolve constitutional issue by force.

The realisation of full Self-Government can only come by orderly and peaceful transfer of control of the machinery of State to purely Indian authority.

His Majesty's Government could not permit any attempt to be made to break the loyalty of the administrative services or of the Indian Armed Forces, and they will give full support to the Government of India securing that their servants are protected in the performance of their duty and that the future constitution of India shall not be called into being by force or threat of force.

In addition, the great need of India, whatever Governments are in power, is to raise the standards of life, of education and of health of the masses of people.

Boldly conceived plans to meet this are already in being and His Majesty's Government are giving every encouragement to proceed with them so that improving of social conditions may go forward simultaneously with the institution of self-government."

Address of Wavell, (10th December, 1945)

Addressing the annual function of the Associated Chamber of Commerce, Lord Wavell remarked thus on 10th December, 1945 :

"I can assure you unreservedly that the British Governemnt and the British people honestly and sincerely wish the Indian people to have their political freedom and a Governemnt or Governments, of their own choice. But there are certain elements of the problem which we must recognize. It is not a simple problem; it cannot and will not be solved by repeating a pass-word or a formula.

'Quit India' will not act as the magic 'Sesame' which opened Ali Baba's cave. It cannot and will not be solved by violence. Disorder and violence are in fact the one thing that may check the pace of India's progress. There are various parties to the settlement who must somehow or other reach a measure of agreement amongst themselves—Congress, the largest political party in India; the minorities, of whom the Muslims are the most numerous and most important; the Rulers of Indian States; and the British Government.

The objective of all is the same—the freedom and welfare of India. I do not believe an agreed solution between the parties is impossible: I do not believe it would even be very difficult, given good will, common sense and patience on all sides. And yet we stand on the edge of a tragedy. For it will be a grim tragedy for India and for the world, if an atmosphere of racial and communal hatred is allowed to prejudice the discussions which are to take place next year; and if violence results from that atmosphere.

I can assure you that His Majesty's Government, and I as their agent, will do our best to secure agreement, to help India to frame a constitution, and to secure the support of the principal parties in the Central Government so as to enable them to bear a full share of responsibility for administering the country during interval before the change of constitution can be made. His Majesty's Government has recently said so clearly, has emphasized the urgency it attaches to a solution; and means what it says. But it must have help and co-operation in securing a satisfactory solution and no solution will be satisfactory which will result in chaos and bloodshed, interference with trade and industry, and perhaps famine and general misery.

I am an old soldier, perhaps know better than you the horrors and wastefulness of bloodshed and strife, particularly civil strife. We have to avoid this; we can avoid it. We have to agree between ourselves; we can agree, if we are really determined to do so. Hindus and Muslims have to live together in this great land; they surely can arrange the terms on which they will do so.

The Indian States, which include so large a part of India and its peoples have to be accommodated within the Indian Union, if that is to prosper; they represent a very important element in the life of India, and often a very progressive one. Finally, there is the British Government and the British people.

I repeat that it is our earnest wish and endeavour to give India freedom; but we cannot and will not abandon our responsibilities without bringing about some reasonable settlement.

I do appeal most solemnly and earnestly at this critical moment of Indian history for goodwill on the part of all leaders. We are going through a very difficult and testing time, and it will need coolness and wisdom if we are to avoid calamity. In so far as I can help by personal contact, I am always prepared to do so.

The welfare of the people, the greatness and prosperity of a nation depend on the efficiency and devotion of the Civil Services, the Police, the Armed Forces.....who must be servants of the Government, not of a political party. There could be no greater disservice to the future of India than to endeavour to undermine the confidence of the Services or to draw them into the political arena. I can assure the Services, as His Majesty's Government has just done, that they will receive all support in the proper fulfilment of their duty."

Statement Of Secretary Of State, (Feb., 1946)

On 19th February, 1946, Lord Pethick Lawrence made a momentous declaration in the House of Lords in which he announced the decision of the British Government to send a special mission of Cabinet Ministers to resolve the constitutional deadlock in the country. The full text of his announcement reads:

"The House will recall that on 19th September, 1945, on his return to India after discussions with the British Government, the Viceroy made a statement of policy in the course of which he outlined the positive steps to be taken immediately after the Central and Provincial elections, to promote, in conjunction with leaders of Indian opinion, early realisation of full self-government in India.

Those steps include: first, preparatory discussions with elected representatives of British India and with Indian States in order to secure the widest measure of agreement as to the method of framing a constitution.

Second, the setting up of constitution-making body and third, the bringing into being of an executive Council having the support of the main Indian parties.

Elections at the Centre were held at the end of last year and in some of the Provinces they are also over and responsible governments are in the process of formation.

In other Provinces, polling dates are spread over the next few weeks. With the approach of the end of the electoral campaign, the British Government have been considering the most fruitful method of giving effect to the programme to which I have referred.

In view of the paramount importance not only to India and to the British Commonwealth but to the peace of the world of a successful outcome of discussions with leaders of Indian opinion, the British Government have decided, with the approval of His Majesty the King, to send out to India a special mission of Cabinet Ministers, consisting of the Secretary of State for India (Lord Pethick-Lawrence), the President of the Board of Trade (Sir Stafford Cripps) and the First Lord of Admiralty (Mr. A.V. Alexander), to act in association with the Viceroy in this matter.

This decision has the full concurrence of Lord Wavell.

I feel sure that the House will give its support and good-will to the Ministers and the Viceroy in carrying out a task in which the future of 400,00,000 people and crucial issues both for India and the world will be at stake.

During the absence of these Ministers, the Prime Minister will himself assume responsibility for Admiralty business and the Lord President (Mr. Herbert Morrison) will be in charge of the Board of Trade.

So far as India and Burma Offices are concerned, the Parliamentary Under-Secretary of State (Major Arthur Henderson) will be in charge during my own absence but he will be able to rely upon the personal advice of the Prime Minister whenever it is required and he will refer important issues to him, particularly those affecting Burma where the Government will not, like the Viceroy, be in personal touch with myself."

Mr. Clement Attlee made a similar statement in the House of Commons and added that the Mission would go to India towards the end of March, 1946.

The Cabinet Mission Scheme

The Mission reached Delhi on March 24, 1946. Prolonged discussions took place between the members of the Mission and the leaders of the Congress and the Muslim League. However, the two main parties could not come to any mutual understanding. The result was that the members of the Mission had to put forward their own formula for solving the constitutional problem. This formula was embodied in a joint statement issued by the Cabinet Mission and Lord Wavell on May 16, 1946.

After pointing out the impracticability of the Pakistan scheme, the statement of May 16 recommended that the new constitution of India should take the following basic form:

"(1) There should be a Union of India, embracing both British India and the States which should deal with the following subjects : Foreign Affairs, Defence, and Communications; and should have the powers necessary to raise the finances required for the above subjects.

(2) The Union should have an Executive and a Legislature constituted from British India and States representatives. Any question raising a major communal issue in the Legislature should require for its decision a majority of the representatives present and voting of each of the two

major communities as well as a majority of all the members present and voting.

(3) All subjects other than the Union subjects and all residuary powers should vest in the Provinces.

(4) The States will retain all subjects and powers other than those ceded to the Union.

(5) Provinces should be free to form Groups with executives and legislatures, and each Group could determine the Provincial subjects to be taken in common.

(6) The constitutions of the Union and of the Groups should contain a provision whereby any Province could, by a majority vote of its Legislative Assembly, call for a reconsideration of the terms of the constitution after an initial period of 10 years and at 10 yearly intervals thereafter."

As regards the constitution-making machinery, it was provided that the Legislative Assemblies of the provinces would elect the members of that body on the basis of one representative for one million of the population. The Sikh and Muslim legislators were to elect the quota of their communities determined on the population basis. Others were to elect the representatives for the rest of the population. The representatives from the provinces were to divide themselves into three sections A, B and C. Section C was to consist of the representatives of Bengal and Assam, Section B of the Punjab, Sind and North-West Frontier Province and Section A of the rest of the provinces of India. "These Sections shall proceed to settle the Provincial Constitution for the Provinces included in each Section, and shall also decide whether any Group Constitution shall be set up for these provinces and, if so, with what provincial subjects the Group should deal." The representatives of the Sections of the Indian States were then to re-assemble and settle the Union constitution.

The Provinces of India were given the power to opt out of the Groups by a decision of their Legislatures after the general elections under the new Constitution.

The Resolutions of the Union Constituent Assembly regarding major communal issues were to require a majority of the representatives present and voting of each of the two major communities. The Chairman of the Constituent Assembly was to decide which resolution raised major communal issues and was to consult the Federal Court before giving his decision.

Table of Representation

Section A

Provinces	*General*	*Muslim*	*Total*
Madras	45	4	49
Bombay	19	2	21
United Provinces	47	8	55
Bihar	31	5	36
Central Provinces	16	1	17
Orissa	9	0	9
Total ..	167	20	187

Section B

Provinces	*General*	*Muslim*	*Sikh*	*Total*
Punjab	8	16	4	28
N.W. Frontier Province	0	3	0	3
Sind	1	3	0	4
Total ..	9	22	4	35

Section C

Provinces	*General*	*Muslim*	*Total*
Bengal	27	33	60
Assam	7	3	10
Total ..	34	36	70
Total for British India			292
Maximum for States ..			93
Total ..			385

A plan for the Interim Government was also envisaged in the Scheme of May 16, 1946.

The Cabinet Mission declared on May 12, 1946 that the British Government could not and would not in any circumstances transfer paramountey to an Indian Government. However, it was made clear that when a new self-governing Government or Governments came into being in British India, it would not be possible for the British Government to carry out the obligations of Paramountey. In that case, all the rights surrendered by the States to the paramout power were to return to the Indian States. "Political arrangements between the States on the one side and the British Crown and British India on the other will thus be brought to an end. The void will have to be filled either by the States entering into a federal relationship with the successor Government or Governments in British India, or failing this, entering into particular political arrangements with it or them." This policy has been described as "a political scorched-earth policy."

Merits

The Cabinet Mission Scheme had both its merits and demerits:

(1) Its greatest merit was that the Constituent Assembly was to be constituted on the democratic principle of population strength. The principle of weightage was discarded altogether.

(2) The democratic method of the decision of issues by simple majority was adopted in the case of communal issues. However, safeguards were provided for minorities.

(3) The proposals also provided for an Indian union of Provinces and States, and rejected the idea of Pakistan completely. This was the last attempt made by British statesmen to save the country from division and disaster. Some of the anomalies of the Scheme were also due to the desire of the members of the Cabinet Mission to save Indian unity at any cost.

(4) The Scheme required that all the members of the Constituent Assembly were to be Indians. Neither the British Government nor the non-official Europeans in India were to be given any representation in the Constituent Assembly. The European members of the Provincial Assemblies were to absent themselves from voting.

(5) It was subsequently provided that there was to be no interference with the work of the Constituent Assembly either by the British Government or by its officials in India. Within the frame-work of the Scheme the Constituent Assembly was to be its own master.

Demerits

However, there were also certain defects in the Cabinet Mission Scheme.

(1) Although the rights of the Muslim minority were protected, the same was not done with regard to the other minorities like the Sikhs in the Punjab.

(2) The proposals of the Cabinet Mission with regard to the grouping of the provinces were not clear. Both the Congress and the Muslim League interpreted the provisions differently. The Muslims regarded the compulsory grouping of the provinces as one of the corner-stones of the Cabinet Mission proposals and were not prepared to come to a compromise on that question. The Congress stand was that the making of groups was optional for the provinces. The latter were free to join or not to join any group. As a matter of fact, Mahatma Gandhi asked the people of Assam not to join the group if they did not approve of the same. They were asked not to care for the consequences. To solve this difficulty, it was suggested that the provinces may join provisionally, but later on freedom may be given to them to leave it if they so desired. The Congress suggested that the matter might be referred to the Federal Court for decision. However, the British Government gave its verdict in favour of the compulsory grouping of the provinces. The Muslim League won and the Congress lost its point.

(3) Another defect of the Scheme was the order in which the Union and Sectional Assemblies were to meet and work and draft their constitutions. It looked ridiculous first to form the constitutions of the groups and the provinces and then to frame the constitution of the Centre or the Union. It was like putting the cart before the horse. This

practical difficulty would have been experienced if the whole scheme had been worked out in actual practice.

It is desirable to trace the events that followed after the publication of the statement of May 16, 1946. The All-India Muslim League passed a resolution on June 6, 1946 by which it accepted the Scheme in its entirety. On the other hand, the Working Committee of the Congress passed a resolution of June 26, 1946 by which it accepted the Scheme partially. The Congress accepted only that part of the Scheme which dealt with the constitution-making of the country. The view of the Committee was that the grouping of the provinces was not to be compulsory. However, the Congress rejected the interim Government scheme on the ground that the clarifications given to them on the subject were not acceptable. The resolution of the Working Committee of the Congress was ratified by the All-India Congress Committee.

The Sikhs rejected the Scheme completely on the ground that the compulsory grouping of the provinces as contemplated by the Scheme was suicidal to their interests.

Before the members of the Cabinet Mission left India, they issued a statement along with Lord Wavell, in which they expressed their satisfaction that the work of the making of the constitution would proceed with the consent of the major parties in India. They regretted that an interim Government consisting of the various parties could not be formed on account of certain difficulties. It was hoped that after the elections to the Constituent Assembly were over, negotiations would be started for the formation of an interim Government consisting of representatives of the various parties.

Jinnah who had accepted the Scheme in its entirety was annoyed at the British Government's decision to postpone the formation of the interim Government. He accused Lord Wavell for his having gone back on his promise. He was so very angry that the Muslim League under his leadership passed another resolution on July 29, 1946 by which its withdrew its former acceptance of the Cabinet Mission Plan. Jinnah was not contented with this negative action. The Muslim League also passed the famous Direct Action resolution by which both the Congress and the British Governments were condemned for their breach of faith with the Muslims. It was declared that the time had come for the

Muslim League to resort to direct action to achieve Pakistan. The resolution authorised the Working Committee of the League to prepare a programme of direct action at once. August 16, 1946 was fixed as the Direct Action Day. On that day Hindu-Muslim riots took place in Calcutta on an unprecedented scale. There was a lot of blood-shed. There was enormous loss of life and property. British Government did nothing to stop this wholesale massacre.

Lord Wavell invited Pandit Jawaharlal Nehru, the President of the Congress, to form the interim Government. The Government formed by Pandit Nehru took office on September 2, 1946. The Muslim League refused to participate in the interim Government. The members of this interim Government were Pandit Nehru, Sardar Patel, Dr. Rajendra Prasad, Mr. Rajagopalachariar, Dr. John Matthai, Sardar Baldev Singh, Sir Shafat Ahmed Khan, Mr. Jagjivan Ram, Syed Ali Zaheer, Mr. Bhabha, Asaf Ali and Sarat Chandra Bose. On October 13, 1946, the Muslim League decided to join the interim Government and on October 15, five members of the Muslim League were included in the interim Government. Some of the above therefore, resigned to make room for the five members of the Muslim League. This Government remained in office till the partition of India in August, 1947.

Constituent Assembly

Elections to the Constituent Assembly took place in July, 1946 and the Constituent Assembly met for the first time in New Delhi on December 9, 1946. The Muslim League refused to participate in its deliberations. Dr. Rajendra Prasad was elected its permanent President on December 11. On December 13, Pandit Jawaharlal Nehru moved the "Objectives Resolution." This resolution was passed on January 22, 1947 and runs:

> "The Constituent Assembly declares its firm and solemn resolve to proclaim India as an independent, sovereign republic and to draw up for her future Government a Constitution : wherein the territories that do not comprise British India, the territories that now form the Indian States and such other parts of India as are outside British India and the States, as well as such other territories, as are willing to be constituted into the independent, sovereign India shall be a Union of them all; and

Wherein the said territories, whether with their present boundaries or with such others as may be determined by the Constituent Assembly and thereafter according to the law of the Constitution shall possess and retain the status of autonomous units, together with residuary powers, and exercise all powers and functions of Government and administration save and except such powers and functions as are vested in or assigned to the Union or as are inherent or implied in the Union or resulting therefrom; and

Wherein all power and authority of the sovereign, independent India, its Constituent parts and organs of Governments are derived from the people; and

"Wherein shall be guaranteed and secured to all the people of India justice, social, economic and political, equality of status, of opportunity, and before the law; freedom of thought, expression, belief, faith, worship, vocation, association and action subject to law and public morality; and

Wherein adequate safeguards shall be provided for minorities, backward and tribal areas, and depressed and other backward classes; and

"Wherein shall be maintained the integrity of the territory of the republic and its sovereign rights on land, sea and air according to justice and the law of civilized nations; and this ancient land attain its rightful and honoured place in the world and make its full and willing contribution to the promotion of the world peace and the welfare of mankind."

Attlee's Statement, February, 1947

In the meanwhile, other important developments took place in the Indian politics. On February 20, 1947, Mr. Attlee, the Prime Minister of England, made his famous declaration. He referred to the differences among the Indian parties which were preventing the Constituent Assembly from functioning as it was intended that it should. It was of the essence of the plan that the Assembly should be fully representative. He said:

"His Majesty's Government desire to hand over their responsibility to authorities established by a constitution approved by all parities in India in accordance with the Cabinet Mission's plan. But unfortunately there is at present no clear prospect that such a constitution and such authorities will emerge. The present state of uncertainty is fraught with danger and cannot be indefinitely prolonged. His Majesty's Government wish to make clear that it is their definite intention to take necessary steps to effect the transference of power to responsible Indian hands by a date not later than June, 1948.

This great sub-continent now containing over four hundred million people has for the last entury enjoyed peace and security as a part of the British Commonwealth and Empire. Continued peace and security are more than ever necessary today if the full possibilities of economic development are to be realised and a higher standard of life attained by the Indian people.

His Majesty's Government are anxious to hand over their responsibilities to a Government which, resting on the sure foundation of the support of the people, is capable of maintaining peace and administering India with justice and efficiency. It is, therefore, essential that all parties should sink their differences in order that they may be ready to shoulder the great responsibilities which will come upon them next year.

After months of hard work by the Cabinet Mission a great measure of agreement was obtained as to the method by which a Constitution should be worked out. This was embodied in their statement of May last. His Majesty's Government there agreed to recommend to Parliament a constitution worked out in accordance with the proposals made therein by a fully representative Constituent Assembly. But if it should appear that such a constitution will not have been worked out by a fully representative Assembly before the time mentioned in paragraph 7, *His Majesty's Government will have to consider to whom the powers of the Central Government in British India should be handed over, on due date, whether as a whole to some form of Central Government for British India, or in some areas to the existing Provincial Governments, or in such other way as may seem most reasonable and in the best interests of the Indian people.*

Although the final transfer of authority may not take place until June, 1948, preparatory measures must be put in hand in advance. It is important that the efficiency of the civil administration should be maintained and that the defence of India should be fully provided for. But inevitably, as the process of transfer proceeds, it will become progressively more difficult to carry out to the letter all the provisions of the Government of India Act, 1935. Legislation will be introduced in due course to give effect to the final transfer of power.

In regard to the Indian States, as was explicitly stated by the Cabinet Mission, His Majesty's Government do not intend to hand over their powers and obligations under Paramountcy to any Government of British India. It is not intended to bring Paramountcy, as a system, to a conclusion earlier than the date of the final transfer of power, but it is contemplated that for the intervening period the relation of the Crown with individual States may be adjusted by agreement.

His Majesty's Government will negotiate agreements in regard to matters arising out of the transfer of power with representatives of those to whom they propose to transfer power.

His Majesty's Government believe that British commercial and industrial interests in India can look forward to a fair field for their enterprise under the new conditions. The commercial connection between India and the United Kingdom has been long and will continue to be to their mutual advantage.

His Majesty's Government cannot conclude this statement without expressing on behalf of the people of this country their goodwill and good wishes towards the people of India as they go forward to this final stage in their achievement of self-government. It will be the wish of everyone in these Islands that, notwithstanding constitutional changes, the association of the British and Indian peoples should not be brought to an end; and they will wish to continue to do all that is in their power to further the well-being of India."

It was also announced that Lord Mountbatten was to succeed Lord Wavell as the Viceroy of India. It was stated that Lord Mountbatten was to be entrusted with the task of transferring to Indian hands the responsibility for the Government of British

India in a manner that would best ensure the future happiness and prosperity of India.

Lord Mountbatten reached New Delhi on March 24, 1947. As soon as he reached India, he declared that he will complete the work of the transfer of power into the Indian hands within the next few months and he held consultations with the Indian leaders for the same purpose. He visited London in May to discuss the matter with the British Government.

The Mountbatten Plan or June 3 Plan

The situation in India was very tense. The Muslim League was carrying on its wear and tear programme for creating chaos in India. At this time, a strong agitation was started for the partition of Bengal and Punjab. It became evident to everybody that the unity of India could not be maintained under any circumstances. Jinnah declar that the "Muslim League will not yield an inch in its demand for Pakistan." It was then that the Mountbatten Plan or June 3 Plan was published. It was stated that

> "it has always been the desire of His Majesty's Government that power should be transferred in accordance with the wishes of the Indian people themselves. This task would have been greatly facilitated if there had been agreement among the Indian political parties. In the absence of such an agreement, the task of devising a method by which the wishes of the Indian people can be ascertained has devolved on His Majesty's Government. After full consultation with political leaders in India, His Majesty's Government have decided to adopt for this purpose the Plan set out below. His Majesty's Government wish to make it clear that they have no intention of attempting to frame any ultimate constitution of India. This is a matter for the Indians themselves. Nor is there anything in this Plan to preclude negotiations between communities for a United India.
>
> It is not the intention of His Majesty's Government to interrupt the work of the existing Constituent Assembly. Now that provision is made for certain provinces specified below, His Majesty's Government trust that, as a consequence of this announcement the Muslim League representatives of those

provinces a majority of whose representatives are already participating in it, will now take their due share in its labours. At the same time, it is clear that any constitution framed by this Assembly cannot apply to those parts of the country which are unwilling to accept it. His Majesty's Government are satisfied that the procedure outlined below embodies the best practical method of ascertaining the wishes of the people of such areas on the issue whether their constitution is to be framed *(a)* in the existing Constituent Assembly; or *(b)* in a new and separate Constituent Assembly consisting of the representatives of those areas which decide not to participate in the existing Constituent Assembly. When this has been done it will be possible to determine the authority or authorities to whom power should be transferred."

In order to ascertain the views of such areas as to whether they wanted a new Constituent Assembly or not, the following procedure was laid down in the June 3, Plan. The Provincial Legislative Assemblies of Bengal and Punjab were to meet in two parts, one representing the Muslim majority districts and the other the rest of the Province. "The members of the two parts of each Legislative Assembly sitting separately will be empowered to vote whether or not the province should be partitioned. If a simple majority of either part decides in favour of partition, partition will take place and arrangements would be made accordingly." The Legislative Assembly of Sind was to take its own decision at special meeting. A decision by referendum was provided for in the case of the North-Western Frontier Province. The Muslim-majority district of Sylhet was to decide by a referendum whether it would join East Bengal or remain in Assam.

It was made clear that the policy of the British Government towards the Indian States remained unchanged. It was the same as was stated on May 12, 1946.

The statement also provided for the creation of a Boundary Commission to settle the details of the boundaries in case partition was decided upon.

The statement concluded thus: "His Majesty's Government propose to introduce legislation during the current session for the transfer of power this year on a Dominion Status basis on one or two successor authorities according to decisions taken as a result of this announcement. This will be without prejudice to the right of the Indian Constituent Assemblies to decide in due course whether or not the part of India in respect of which they have authority will remain within the British Commonwealth."

In his broadcast on June 3, 1947, Lord Mountbatten declared:

"The whole Plan may not be perfect; but like all Plans, its success will depend on the spirit of goodwill with which it is carried out. I have always felt that once it was decided in what way to transfer power the transfer should take place at the earliest possible moment, but the dilemma was that if we waited until a constitutional setup for All India was agreed, we should have to wait a long time, particularly if partition were decided on, whereas if we handed over power before the Constituent Assemblies had finished their work we should leave the country without a constitution. The solution to this dilemma which I put forward, is that His Majesty's Government should transfer power now to one or two Governments of British India each having Dominion Status as soon as the necessary arrangements can be made. This I hope will be within the next few months."

It is to be noted that the Muslim League accepted the June 3 Plan on June 9, 1947 and the All-India Congress Committee on June 15, 1947. It was decided that Bengal and the Punjab were to be partitioned. West Punjab and East Bengal decided to join the new Constituent Assembly. Two Boundary Commissions for the division of Punjab and Bengal were announced. Sind and North-Western Frontier Province decided to join the new Constituent Assembly. Sylhet decided to join Pakistan.

In the meanwhile, the Indian Independence Bill was presented before British Parliament on July 4, 1947 and was passed by Parliament on July 18, 1947.

The Indian Independence Act, 1947

The object of this act was to give effect to the June 3, Plan of Lord Mountbatten. It merely legalized what had already been promised to the people of India.

(1) The Act provided for the partition of India and the establishment of two Dominions of India and Pakistan from the appointed day (15th August, 1947). The Act also

provided for the legislative supremacy of the two Dominions.

(2) The Legislatures of the two Dominions were given full power to make laws having extra-territorial jurisdiction.

(3) The British Government was to have no control over the affairs of the Dominions, Provinces, or any part of the Dominions after 15th August, 1947.

(4) Until a new constitution was framed for each Dominion, the Act made the existing Constituent Assemblies the Dominion Legislatures for the time being. The Assemblies were to exercise all the powers which were formerly exercised by the Central Legislature, in addition to its power regarding the framing of a new constitution.

(5) Pending the framing of a new constitution, each of the Dominions and all the Provinces were to be governed in accordance with the Government of India Act, 1935. Each Dominion was authorised to make modifications in the Government of India Act, 1935 under the Indian Independence Act.

(6) The Governor-General was given the power to modify or adapt the Government of India Act, 1935 as might be considered necessary till 31st March, 1948. After that day it was open to the Constituent Assembly to modify or adapt the same Act.

(7) The right of the King to veto laws or to reserve laws for his pleasure was given up. This right was given to the Governor-General. He was given the full right to assent in the name of His Majesty to any law of the Dominion Legislature made in its ordinary legislative capacity.

(8) The Act provided for the termination of the suzerainty of the Crown over the Indian States. All treaties, agreements and functions exercisable by His Majesty with regard to States and their rulers were to lapse from 15th August, 1947. It was also provided that the existing arrangements between the Government of India and the Indian States were to continue pending the detailed negotiations between the Indian States and the new Dominions.

(9) Agreements with the tribes of the North Western Frontier of India were to be negotiated by the successor Dominion.

(10) The office of the Secretary of State for India was to be abolished and his work was to be taken over by the Secretary of State for Commonwealth Affairs.

(11) The title of "Emperor of India" was to be dropped from the royal style and titles of the King of England.

(12) The Act terminated British authority over India, set up two independent Dominions, each with full authority to make any constitution it pleased. Both the Dominions were given full powers and rights to leave the British Commonwealth of Nations if they so pleased.

The Indian Independence Act of 1947 was a great landmark in the Anglo-Indian relations. It marked the ending of the British rule in India. It was a recognition of the right of the Indians to be free. But unfortunately, it divided India into two parts. Only the future will show as to how far the partition of India was in the true interests of the country. However it was acclaimed as "the noblest and greatest law ever enacted by the British Parliament."

Making of the Constitution.

The Indians had demanded the making of their own Constitution by means of a Constituent Assembly elected by the people of India. The demand was conceded in the Cripps proposals of 1942. A similar provision was made in the Cabinet Mission Scheme of May, 1946 and procedure was also laid down for the summoning of the Constituent Assembly. It was in pursuance of that scheme that the Indian Constituent Assembly met at New Delhi on 9th December, 1946. The Muslim League boycotted the Constituent Assembly and declared that the resolutions passed by that body were "*ultra vires* invalid and illegal." The British bureaucracy in India encouraged the Muslim League in disassociating itself from the deliberations of the Constituent Assembly.

After the passing of the Objectives Resolution, the Constituent Assembly appointed a number of Committees for different purposes. Some of those Committees were the Union Subjects Committee, Provincial Constitution Committee and the Union

Constitution Committee. All these Committees submitted their report in due course.

After the partition of India in August 1947, the Constituent Assembly began to prepare a Constitution only for that part of India which was left after partition. Pakistan was to have its separate Constituent Assembly. On 29th August, 1947, the Constituent Assembly of India set up a Drafting Committee to prepare a Draft Constitution for India. That Committee submitted its report on 21st February, 1948. The Draft Constitution was widely circulated and there was a lot of discussion both through the press and on the platform. The Draft Constitution was introduced in the Constituent Assembly on 5th November, 1948. Seven thousand six hundred and thirty-five amendments were proposed to the Draft Constitution and 2,473 amendments were actually moved. The Constitution was adopted on 26th November, 1949 and came into force on 26th January 1950. In all, there were 11 sessions of the Constituent Assembly. It sat for two years, 11 months and 18 days. The consideration of the Draft Constitution took 114 days. It goes without saying that the Indian Constitution is the outcome of a lot of hard work on the part of the members of the Drafting Committee and the members of the Constituent Assembly.

Index